NOT HAVING BEEN A SOLDIER

NOT HAVING BEEN A SOLDIER

Nigel Austin

'Every man thinks meanly of himself for not having been a soldier, or not having been at sea'
– *Samuel Johnson, in conversation with his biographer James Boswell, 1778*

First published 2020

Copyright © Nigel Austin 2020

Nothaving Books
62 Mellstock Avenue, Dorchester, Dorset DT1 2BQ
www.nigelaustinbooks.com

Nigel Austin has asserted his right to be identified as the author
of this work in accordance with the Copyright, Designs and
Patents Act, 1988

A CIP catalogue record for this title is available from the British
Library.

ISBN 978-1-8380046-1-3

This is for Juliet, Rich and Joggan

Front cover

This shows:

(1) Spitfire squadron, Second World War
(2) Royal Navy Type 23 frigate, with helicopter landing, early 21st century
(3) Italian tanks in the African desert, Second World War.

Author's note

This is a work of non-fiction. Names and locations are undisguised, and the accounts of contemporary events derive from notes made at the time.

Contents

1

Commitment

Tom Brown's Alehouse, Dorchester, Dorset, May 2000

'You've got to commit yourself,' Pete was saying. 'Are you coming?'

'Yo,' I said. 'A definite maybe.' He'd brought some brochures. Duxford Air Show, in September. They showed pictures of a Spitfire and a Hurricane and a Blenheim.

'How long are these planes going to go on for?' I asked. 'They keep crashing. Eventually they're going to run out of them, aren't they?'

'Oh, God no. There are more flying now than there were ten years ago. It's not difficult to fabricate a piece of aluminium section for a wing.'

'There's not a great deal of them that's original,' Mike said.

'They've all got Merlin engines, and you can't fabricate those very easily,' said Pete.

1

'So how many of them are there?' I asked.

'Those engines, they were used in lots of the planes. All right, you can't re-create them. But you can machine new bits for them. And there are quite a lot left, because there were four in a Lancaster, for instance.'

'Is all this information in those aeroplane magazines you get?' someone inquired.

'Yes. The best one at the moment is an encyclopaedia. *Aircraft of the World.* Comes every month. They sent the final one this week. It's got every aeroplane ever built. But the thing is, it hasn't come in chronological order. Each issue is a random selection of pages. And when I checked it all through, I found there was just one page missing. So I wrote off to them, and they sent it to me.'

'Do you suppose everyone had the same page missing?'

'I don't suppose anyone else was sad enough to collect the whole lot.'

'All the pages of this encyclopedia, they come mixed up, and you have to put them in the right place in the folders?'

'Yes.'

'When do you do that?'

'At my surgery.'

'What, you take them to *work*?'

'No, I have them delivered there.'

'So when do you do it? Do you take every Thursday afternoon off, or do you break off in the middle of a filling, and say, 'Oh, I've just got to go and put my aeroplane pages in order'?'

'No, no, you arse. I do it during lunchtime, or when some patient hasn't turned up.'

'And then you take them home?'

'Eventually. But I put them in the waiting room first.'

'*What?* Is anyone interested in them? Apart from you?'

'Probably not, no.'

'So why – '

'They're tax-deductible.'

'Ah.'

'If *Hello* magazine is tax-deductible for a dentist's waiting room, I don't see why *Aeroplane Monthly* shouldn't be. That's another one, by the way. There *are* other magazines there,' he went on. 'Some people bring in their own. I like it when they bring adventurous ones like *Kite Surfing Weekly*, because the other patients might think they're mine. The other thing that happens is that those anti-vivisection people sneak in horrible mags with pictures of dogs being dissected. So we have to check them all through and get rid of those. Not very nice if you're a child aged six and you're about to have your teeth done.'

Then we talked about Stonehenge. There had been a story in the papers about some group of people who had decided to try to reconstruct the journey from where the stones originated in Wales, to their present location on Salisbury Plain. They used the original method of rolling them on logs. They didn't make it. In fact they gave up on the first day.

'Well, of course,' said Pete, 'those lumps of stone, getting all of them together, it was like assembling all the parts of an encyclopaedia. All the other people who were doing that collection, they only bothered to get one or two, and they just left them lying about the countryside in dribs and drabs. You see odd stones all over the place, don't you? – and you don't take a second glance. No-one realises what they were for. But the saddoes who built Stonehenge, they were the only ones who managed to do the whole thing, and build it up into what it was supposed to be.'

'Like you with your aeroplane encyclopaedia.'

'Quite.'

We talked of that Hollywood film *U-571*, which was about the capture of the Enigma code-breaking machine from a German U-boat, but credited it to the Americans whereas of course the ship involved was British. Pete said it's so far removed from the truth of what actually happened that you can treat it as fiction.

'It's all right, it's a good film, and that's all that matters as far as the movie industry's concerned. But *we* know what the truth was. It was in that obituary, of the captain of the ship that captured it in the Atlantic. They hung around until the rest of the convoy had gone, so nobody knew the submarine hadn't been sunk. Nobody knew they boarded it. And they hid the German crew down below so they wouldn't see what they were doing, and they went and got the machine and the code books and took them off the sub. I mean that just doesn't make a good drama. It wouldn't be a decent film.'

We moved on to D-day, and *Saving Private Ryan*, and Nick said, 'It was eighteen, nineteen, twenty-year-olds. They've got no knowledge. That's why they send them to war. You can wind them up to do anything.'

'There were those bomber crews,' said Mike, 'they were only that age too. Like the captain was twenty and the tail gunner was nineteen. They just saw it as a big adventure.'

4

Pete said, 'You wouldn't get 50-year-olds like us in one of those landing craft. You just wouldn't get them to do what 19-year-olds did in the war.'

We talked about the disinformation that was put out for D-day, to make the Germans think the invasion was going to be happening further east up the French coast, and someone mentioned The Man Who Never Was, the dead body shot out from a torpedo tube of a British submarine off Spain, with an attaché case full of fake invasion plans, and the Germans found him – as they were meant to – and took him to Berlin for investigation. Whether it was effective in convincing them that the invasion would take place somewhere else from where it actually did, we didn't know.

'Then there was that stuff they threw out of aeroplanes to fool the German radar,' said Charles. 'To make them think there was a whole load of enemy planes coming. Aluminium foil, wasn't it?'

'Window,' Pete said. 'That was the code name for it. Because they chucked it out the window.'

Here we are, I thought, in the year 2000, a group of forty-to-fifty-year olds discussing the Second World War, which finished before any of us were born. What would our fathers think, our mothers and uncles and aunts and their cousins who were *there*? I could sense them behind us, tapping us on the shoulder, correcting us on points of detail, reminding each other what squadrons of planes were involved in this attack, or what sort of tanks there were in another one, and what ships took part in that engagement in the Atlantic. And yet they would be intrigued at the way their own exploits, those decades ago, have remained in the nation's consciousness, and are ritually brought out when two or three of their sons are gathered together in pubs. The tinge of pride at having been a part of the operation that led the country to salvation would surface again; and they'd be pleased that the younger generation is appreciative. As the young men and women they were, they played their part without hesitation. They saw it as their duty. Mostly, they did not question the actions they were asked to carry out. Now, those actions are being remembered, pored over, analysed, and celebrated by their descendants.

A week before the trip Nick came into the pub with a brochure of another air show, the Farnborough one, held earlier in the year. Reflected in it was the fact that this was partly a business event, with airlines and weapons manufacturers competing. Evidently, one of its main purposes was to sell aeroplanes to commercial customers. There was a photograph of the A340 Airbus.

'They usually put a picture of a bus up against those things,' said Pete, 'and it's just *that* size,' he added, putting his thumb and forefinger an inch apart, 'meaning the plane is absolutely enormous.'

'There was a remark I saw about these modern planes being flown by the automatic pilot,' said Charles. 'It said, there are three items in the cockpit flying the aeroplane. There's a computer, a man and a dog. The computer's job is to fly the plane. The man's job is to feed the dog. And the dog's job is to bite the man if he ever looks like he's going to interfere with the computer.'

* * *

Wittering, Cambridgeshire, March 1941

In war, very occasionally, almost at the moment you kill your enemy, you suffer the same fate yourself.

The Battle of Britain was over. Germany had failed to achieve supremacy in the air, and the threat of invasion from Europe's mainland had receded. 266 Squadron, based at Wittering, was one of scores of RAF fighter units whose job had been to repel the Luftwaffe. But Pilot Officer Peter Ferris, at 27 older than most of his colleagues, had joined the squadron of Spitfires only after those hectic weeks of 1940, and had not had as much opportunity as he might have liked to take part.

Ferris had been brought up with his twin sister and three other siblings near Treloar Hospital in Hampshire, where his father was the engineer looking after the heating plant. On leaving the local grammar school he moved to south London, near other members of his family, and worked at the Air Ministry. Europe's political landscape was already dominated by the dark shadow of Adolf Hitler, and at 24, some eighteen months before war eventually broke out in 1939, he joined the Royal Air Force Volunteer Reserve. There was a fortnight of training, and a further three weeks of it a year later. In such a short time he is unlikely to have flown an aircraft except perhaps for a few moments under close supervision. Instead, there would have been an introduction to flight theory, and to the discipline expected of members of His Majesty's armed forces.

In Germany, war preparations were well advanced. Hitler had introduced compulsory military service four years earlier, negotiated an international agreement permitting him to rebuild the country's navy, and made public the creation of his air force. A few weeks after Ferris joined the Reserve, the German leader annexed Austria. Then came Neville Chamberlain's historic visit to Munich to attempt to stave off the mounting crisis. The triumph of his return to Britain, shown on the newsreels with the Prime Minister standing at the foot of his aircraft steps waving the famous document bearing his and Hitler's signatures, proclaiming 'peace in our time', proved hollow. Six months later Hitler, referring scornfully to that 'scrap of paper', had completed his takeover of Czechoslovakia; and on 1st September he invaded Poland.

The British Cabinet spent the following day locked in discussions on what to do about it. Britain and France had given Poland a guarantee that they would defend her against any aggressor. Consequently, it was not a question of what, but when. By the end of the day a decision had been made. The French government, meanwhile, was moving towards a similar conclusion.

That day, Peter Ferris ceased to be a civilian. He was called up from the Volunteer Reserve, henceforth to be a full-time participant in what was to become the most widespread, expensive and, in terms of lives lost, deadly war of all time. Early on 3rd September Britain's ultimatum was presented, demanding that Germany agree to withdraw their forces; but, inevitably, later that morning Chamberlain's sombre tones echoed from the nation's wireless sets: 'I have to tell you now, that no such undertaking has been received; and that consequently this country is at war with Germany'.

For the first few months much of the population of Britain had little direct experience of war-like activities of any kind. Some could hardly believe the country was in a war at all, and the phrase 'the phoney war' began to be heard. But Ferris, along with thousands of other reservists called up, embarked on a training programme that was all too real. There was nothing phoney about the ease with which, if you were not careful, you could come to grief whilst still a green young pilot in the first few hours of solo flight. There was nothing bogus about the regular disappearance of colleagues you had barely come to know, either through such accidents or by being sacked for not making the grade. The first training aircraft used for potential pilots was a biplane, the Tiger Moth. Success in flying this would lead to other aircraft, all with different handling characteristics. Ferris graduated to a single-wing craft named the Magister, then to another biplane, the Hawker Hart, and finally to the American-built Harvard, a monoplane with chunky looks and a reputation for being unforgiving if not handled with respect. That is to say, even some experienced pilots had lost their lives trying to fly it.

Ferris survived the Harvard. His training was interrupted by something rather more mundane than a crash. In early 1940 he fell ill with tuberculosis, and spent most of the February in an isolation hospital. Fit again, his training resumed, and continued during the Battle of Britain in August and September. It must have been frustrating to have to submit to training exercises rather than take to the skies in a real combat role, especially when many younger men than him were doing just that. By the time he passed his final tests, in October 1940, the most intense period of fighting was over and Hitler's plans to invade Britain had been postponed indefinitely.

But one morning in early March the call came. German bombers had been detected flying in over the North Sea. Ferris and his No. 2, Sergeant Johnny van Schaick, were ordered to investigate. At 10:10 a.m. the two Spitfires roared off from the airfield and headed north-east, towards the Lincolnshire coast.

The incoming raiders were identified as twin-engined bombers, Junkers 88s, one of the most successful and adaptable of the German war planes. Ten thousand were built in all, and British fighter pilots were familiar with huge waves of them droning their way over the Channel and the North Sea to discharge their lethal cargo.

The two Spitfires closed rapidly towards the bombers. Over the radio transmitter van Shaick heard Ferris's voice. 'I've shot down a Junkers! It's on fire and it's going down! Can you follow it down and confirm?' But immediately afterwards came a more urgent message. 'I can't believe it! I'm hit!' Van Schaick heard no more. There was nothing he could do. He turned and flew the fifty miles back to Wittering, and reported what he had seen and heard.

Ferris's service record was duly filled in with the word 'Missing'. In war, nine times out of ten 'missing' turns out to be 'killed'; and when your No. 2 has heard you shout that you are hit, and you do not return to base, and no-one reports you having landed anywhere else, and nothing more is heard from you that day or the next or the next, then the odds against your having survived rise to near-impossible heights; but rules are rules, and Peter Ferris's flying record was not amended with the word

'Killed' until he was washed up, still strapped in his Spitfire seat, from the waters of the North Sea near Skegness a month later. It was confirmed, then, that it had been the man, not the plane, that had received the mortal hit.

Ferris's body was taken to Chawton Cemetery, near Alton in Hampshire, where his parents still lived; and there was erected one of 900,000 headstones of identical form marking the graves of serving men and women of

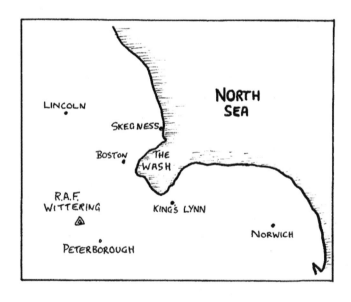

the British forces who died in the wars of 1914-18 and 1939-45. Except for a convex upper edge, these memorials, in graveyards in England, France and elsewhere, consist of a plain rectangle of stone, some thirty inches by eighteen, inscribed in Roman capitals with rank, name, and unit, sometimes with suitable words underneath chosen by the family. Below the Royal Air Force insignia on Ferris's stone, with its motto Ardua ad Astra, is the inscription:

PILOT OFFICER
F. P. FERRIS
ROYAL AIR FORCE
8TH MARCH 1941
AGE 27

A plain cross is below, and, at the base of the stone:

SACRED
TO THE DEAR MEMORY
OF OUR BELOVED SON PETER
FIGHTER PILOT

Later during the war, Ferris's twin sister married; her first-born was a daughter. When her second child arrived, a son, she named him Peter.

* * *

Tom Brown's, September 1998

In Tom Brown's there was talk of dysfunctional families. It started, as no doubt many pub conversations did that week, with the Clinton/Lewinsky story, which – notwithstanding what consenting adults may get up to in private, which is their own business – plumbed new depths of obscenity. Leaving aside the questions of untruthfulness and morality, the airing in public of the entire episode – the salacious questioning, the release of a video of the court case, and the publishing in the newspapers of every word of transcript from both his and her testimony – was deeply unpleasant.

But dysfunctional families are closer to home. 'It seems amazing,' said Jennie to Pete, 'that your mother has had hardly any contact with her siblings for years. Hasn't even spoken to them. Can you imagine that happening to any of our children?'

'Well it can happen, quite easily, actually,' said Pete, 'because somebody's only got to say one thing, there's only got to be one row that's not resolved, and people don't talk to one another. Especially if it's about money. Inheritance.'

'Where there's a will, there's an argument,' someone said.

'How many brothers and sisters has your mother got, that she doesn't talk to?'

'Well, since the war, I mean apart from the one who was killed – '

'Is that the one who was killed in the Spitfire?' I asked.

'Yes. Her twin brother. Apart from him, there are four of them. There had been five including Peter.'

'So you were named after him,' I said, 'which makes two of us, named after relatives who were killed in the war. Except that I got the bum deal as far as the name was concerned.'

'Yes,' said Helen.

'What do you mean, 'yes'?' I said, indignantly.

'Ha, ha!'

'Who else might there be? Come to think of it, it can't be that unusual.' For years it had never occurred to me that I might not be unique in being named after someone killed in the war. Not that I'd given it much thought. Later, Pete spoke to me again.

'I was talking to Gordon the other day.' (A big mate of his. Went to the same boarding school, and used to bunk off to watch his home football team, which happened to be Manchester United.) 'And I mentioned that you and I were both named after who we were named after. And *he* said, he was named after his mother's ex-boyfriend.'

I thought about it for a moment. 'That's *heavy*. Was his father aware of that?'

'Oh, I think so, yes.'

'Well, I'm glad that at least I don't have such complications in who I'm named after.'

Yet perhaps there were many children born in the wake of the war who were deliberately not named after dead relatives. Too painful, no doubt. Years later, Pete himself told me of a conversation with his older sister Susie, who, he said, had been particularly close to their grandmother.

'Our mother's mother, I mean,' he said. 'So the mother of Uncle Peter as well. And she told Susie that when I was born, she'd not wanted me to be called that. She said she'd never wanted to hear the name again.'

* * *

Kulito, Ethiopia, May 1941

Hidden in the bushes, partly shielded from the hot East African sun, the Italian lieutenant-colonel peered out from his tank. For several hours his half-dozen vehicles had lain still, their engines lifeless. Behind a low rise on the far side of the river were enemy mortars, lobbing shells towards his infantry positions. Two companies of British East African troops had already waded across the shallow river towards them. His field-guns were ill-placed and his troops were being bombarded not only by the mortars but also by heavy guns at the rear of the British lines. But the position of his tanks was strong. They were well concealed and he knew he had only to bide his time.

He watched as, bayonets fixed, moving quickly between scattered bushes, the enemy infantry gradually came closer. The mortar fire supporting them had dwindled and, in comparatively open country, they were vulnerable. He would have the advantage of surprise, and with the bridge blown, the enemy had no chance of quickly bringing any armoured fighting vehicles of their own to his side of the river.

He gave the order. Simultaneously, the engines of all half-dozen tanks roared into life. His driver swung the vehicle out from behind the bushes, hurtling towards the opposing forces. Men on foot are no match for a heavily armoured vehicle. The advancing troops scattered, searching for cover amongst the sparse bushes. The tank commander had chosen just the right moment to show his hand. He could have hardly perceived any danger from the single enemy soldier peeling off from the retreating troops and running towards his tank.

*

Born in East Africa and brought up in the scattered communities which farmed the rich but hazardous Kenyan land, Nigel Leakey knew what had to be done not merely to make a living but to stay alive in order to do so. Aided by a British government grant, his mother and father had bought a tract of virgin land north of Nairobi. With his three younger siblings, Nigel watched as they built a house and thorn-tree barricades for the cattle. But the protection was not enough. Close by were lions, which eventually found it easier to kill the cattle instead of zebra. Between them, Nigel's parents found the lions' cave and shot all five.

The family had to be fed, and twice a week his father would ride out into the veldt to shoot a gazelle or bushbuck. But the rains failed, the cattle had to be sold, and Nigel's parents were forced to seek other employment. Soon afterwards, when he was aged 11, crisis struck. Whilst his parents were managing a coffee farm some miles from Nairobi, his mother suffered a burst appendix. The drive over uneven roads from the farm to hospital in the capital cannot have been comfortable, and there she died. His father was unable to look after four children as well as run the farm, and while the two younger boys were placed in a boarding school in Nairobi, Nigel and his sister Agnes were sent to England. An uncle was a housemaster at Bromsgrove School in Worcestershire, and there he stayed during term time. During the holidays he took the train to Surrey, where his mother's brother, a village GP by the name of George Laing, lived in some comfort with his wife and five children.

From the moment he arrived, Nigel hated England. He had been the first intruder into the close-knit family of his cousins. Although Alice, four years older, became fond of him, he was tormented by her tomboyish younger sister Betty, aided by their brother Jim. He wanted only to get back to Kenya. At 16, as soon as he could, he left school and returned to work on his father's coffee and sisal farm. Finally, he bought his own place at Muhoroni, 150 miles north-west of Nairobi; amongst his visitors on one occasion in 1938 was cousin Alice, who had made the long journey by ship to South Africa, thence by rail to Kenya.

During the period he was establishing himself as a farmer in his own right, Italian aggression in Africa culminated in the annexation of Ethiopia, the neighbouring state to the north. Mussolini's dream was to create a new Roman empire to rival that of two thousand years before. When war broke out in Europe in 1939, Italy invaded British Somaliland, and the threat to Britain's sea route to Australasia and the Far East became acute. Along with many of his compatriots Leakey joined the Kenya Regiment, and was posted to the King's African Rifles. Gradually, the British colonial armies drove the Italians back towards the highlands of

Ethiopia, but although Mussolini's forces had given ground, this was a region of high strategic importance they did not intend to relinquish. They had the vehicles, the fire-power and the men to maintain the fight.

*

Nigel Leakey's ammunition had run out. He had been manning one of the mortars behind the advancing troops, lobbing shell after shell over them on to the Italian positions, and when there were none left he ran forward to join his colleagues in the front lines. The resistance was sporadic. Then came the shock. The Italian tanks thundered out from their cover in the bushes, and the British troops ran for cover.

Leakey was probably as surprised as anyone at the sudden emergence of the tanks. Against them, soldiers on foot would be mown down. The aim of capturing the enemy position was in jeopardy. In what can have been little more than an instant, Leakey took in the situation and made a decision which led to a crucial change in the course of the battle.

The contemporary accounts of what took place, as well as the citation accompanying the posthumous award to Leakey of the Victoria Cross, point to the success of his action. The *African Standard* called it 'an act of the greatest gallantry'. The official history refers to 'almost unbelievable heroism'. The award of a V.C., the highest decoration for bravery available to British forces, speaks for itself; the citation tells of 'valour of the highest order' and of Leakey's 'superb courage and magnificent fighting spirit'.

On the fine line between success or failure of such acts hinges the subsequent opinion as to whether it was well-judged or foolish. If the action succeeds then we tend to approve. If it fails we are more likely to think of it as, at best, a brave but ill-judged gesture. But we are just as likely to call it idiocy, behaviour which unnecessarily costs the unit the services of one of their number, reduces its strength and, not least, lowers morale by virtue of its failure. On this occasion, the judgment has been favourable.

Leakey ran towards the leading tank. He had no rifle and no anti-tank gun. His only weapon was his service revolver. But the lieutenant-colonel in the tank had little opportunity to defend himself. Leakey leapt on to the tank, wrenched open the badly-fastened lid of the turret and shot the commander and the gunner. He terrorised the driver and forced him to drive into cover. What his intentions were at this point is unclear, but it seems that he made an attempt to get the tank gun to fire on its own forces. In this he failed. But by this time his job was done. The tank attack had been completely disrupted. The death of the commanding officer at the outset of the assault had deprived the rest of the crews of control and direction. They turned and fled. Inside the leading tank, finding he could not work the cannon, Leakey shot the driver and leapt out. He was heard to shout, 'I'll get them on foot'. He charged across ground which was being swept with machine gun and shell fire from the other tanks. Three of his men succeeded in joining him at this point, and the four of them stalked other enemy tanks. The first two passed. Leakey jumped on the third, opened the turret and killed one of the crew.

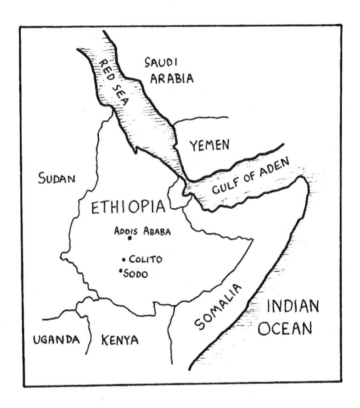

There is some disagreement as to what happened next. One account has a fourth tank opening fire with a machine gun and shooting him to the ground; another has him last seen attempting to open the turret whilst it bore him away into the bush.

The battle continued but the momentum which the British forces had lost was restored. The Italian tank attack had been broken up and, as the V.C. citation continues, 'by [Leakey's] own individual action he saved what would have undoubtedly developed into a most critical situation, for had the Italian tanks succeeded the result would have been the loss of a most valuable bridgehead'.

No trace of Nigel Leakey was seen again. But even though there can be no individual gravestones for service personnel whose bodies are not located, his name too, like Ferris's, is written in stone. One memorial, with a brief description of his actions in battle, was erected in 2019 at a cemetery in Addis Ababa; the second is in his home country, on the East Africa Memorial at Nairobi. The main inscription, in that sombre language reserved for such memorials, a language intended for the comfort of the bereaved, to help persuade them that their loss is civilisation's gain and that the sacrifice was worthwhile, reads:

1939 – 1945

THE COLUMNS IN THIS ENCLOSURE BEAR THE
NAMES OF TWO THOUSAND FOUR HUNDRED MEN
AND WOMEN OF MANY RACES UNITED IN SERVICE
TO THE BRITISH CROWN WHO GAVE THEIR LIVES IN
ITALIAN SOMALILAND, SOUTHERN ETHIOPIA,
KENYA AND MADAGASCAR, BUT TO WHOM THE
FORTUNE OF WAR DENIED A KNOWN AND
HONOURED GRAVE

Following Leakey's action, the British forces pursued the Italians to the nearby town of Sodo. The capture of the town marked the final phase of the victory, and the task of driving out Italian forces from Ethiopia was virtually complete. The Emperor, Haile Selassie, had been restored to the throne, and the threat to British communications with the Far East and the Australias was over. The campaign may nowadays be little remembered, but, as

Len Deighton has pointed out, 'it was the first Allied strategic victory of the war, and came at a time when the Allies desperately needed victory of any sort'[1].

Later during the war, Alice Laing married; and when her own first son was born in 1947, she named him after her cousin.

---

[1] *Blood, Tears and Folly – In the Darkest Hour of the Second World War* (1993).

2

Air Show

The nostalgia is laid on with a trowel.

'Twenty Spitfires in the air at the same time,' intones the commentator on the public-address system. 'Together with three Hurricanes. What a sight, ladies and gentlemen. What a sight ... Watch these three Spitfires approaching now. Here they come ... Here they are ... A number of those brave men who fought in the Battle of Britain are here with us today. This flypast is dedicated to you. We salute you.' Excerpts from Winston Churchill follow. 'Never. Was so much. Owed by so many. To so few ... If the British Empire last a thousand years, men will still say, "This was their finest hour".' The melodrama does its job, creating the obligatory lump in the throat.

It is a hot day. I spend the first hour on my own, having become separated from the others; half the party arrive from Cambridge later, after missing the bus. I wander round the splendid museum of American aircraft, designed by Norman Foster. There is a Flying

Fortress and a Superfortress, and craft from a later generation: a Mustang, and a U2 spy plane, in one of which Gary Powers was shot down by the Russians in 1960. Some of the planes here are out of reach, suspended from the roof, but others are at eye-level, and you can come as close as you like. I have a compulsion to touch them, to run my fingers down the blades of the propellers, feel the almost razor-sharp trailing edges of the wings, place the palm of my hand on the cold metal skin of the fuselage as if to embrace it, to have it as my own, to be a part of the aeroplane's provenance and history: to take part, in a tiny way, in that machine's world. Only once or twice are there notices saying 'Do not touch'. Perhaps the curators of present-day museums recognise the need to make literally tangible the artefacts of the past.

A number of the apparently old aircraft flying here today are replicas. A Sopwith Camel, for example. I find this vaguely unsettling. Others have the label 'restored'. There might be the occasional original rusty old part incorporated, but in essence they are new. And the astonishing thing is that, sixty years after the war in which they became famous, they are still being built. A Bristol Beaufighter, for example, is emerging from the remains of one which crashed somewhere, incorporating a few salvaged pieces. It is a modern version of something that used to fly decades ago. Can it be called a Beaufighter? Is it built to modern safety standards, which presumably are different from those when they first flew? The remains consist of a few bent lengths of aluminium, little else. Volunteers spend hours, weeks, months in loving attention. How would you define a *real* Spitfire?

One which comes off the production line at the same time as the others? Or can it be one merely built to the same design, even though nowadays the construction techniques are unrecognisably different?

*

This is the summer, and we are taking advantage of the new-found need of universities to make money by letting out their rooms when the students are absent. Around the corner from our college accommodation we find the Elm Tree inn. Pete starts to talk but within four words he's being controversial.

'The trouble with me – ' he begins.

'It'll take too long to discuss that,' says Iain.

'We're eating at nine,' adds Graham, 'we haven't got time.'

'We're only here for the weekend.'

'There's far too much material.'

'You expect us to finish that subject within a fortnight?'

Pete giggles helplessly. We never do find out what the trouble with him is. Charles moves on and tells a story about going up in a high-speed lift to the twentieth floor. Just after the nineteenth, it slows down. If you jump in the air just before it starts to decelerate, you hit your head on the ceiling.

'Okay Charles,' says Graham. 'What you have to do is put on your crash helmet. Every time you go up in a lift. But then there'll come the time you forget. You can imagine the casualty officer. "Oh God, it's another of these people who's gone up in a lift to the twentieth floor! Head injury, keep him in overnight for observation"!'

Then there is the discussion about the sound barrier. The sonic boom. What *is* it, exactly? A shock wave, someone says. Yes, but what's a shock wave?

'When Concorde flies over you get a double boom,' says someone else, 'the front of the plane and then the rear.'

'Really? You mean it takes that long, a tenth of a second, to get from here to there, even when it's travelling at over seven hundred miles an hour?'

'Yes.'

'Ah,' says Iain, 'but the shock wave goes with the aircraft. It goes all along behind it, so if you're on the ground, you hear it. It's there all the time.'

'What about a bullet?' asks Charles. 'Does that go faster than the speed of sound?'

'Yes,' says Pete, 'it definitely does.'

'I'm not sure about that,' says Iain. 'Do you hear the sound barrier being broken when a bullet goes past? Like a mini sonic boom?'

'Or is it the sound of the rifle?'

Needless to say there is no conclusion. There is only heat.

We eat at a Turkish restaurant which Charles knows about because his wife has been there, and someone has had the good sense to book. At the next table is a group of a dozen twenty-somethings. It is evidently the birthday of the girl at the head of the table. She eats hardly anything, because she keeps getting up to walk round to check everyone is enjoying themselves, having a chat here and a few words there. She is wearing a very low-cut pink dress, and keeps on having to hitch it up at the sides. Another girl spends half the time with her feet in the lap of the bloke sitting next to her, and he's massaging them. Graham says they must already be an item. 'It would be a bit of a risqué thing to do if they weren't.'

The climax of the evening is Pete kissing the birthday girl. 'Happy Birthday' was played very loud, and we all banged our fists on the table and clapped, and then she stood up to make a speech.

'I don't know all of you,' she says, 'no, I mean of course I know who you all are, and it's very good of you to come, but I don't necessarily know you all that well – '

'What do you mean?' called out Pete from across the room, 'you know us, don't you? We've all been out with you!'

She grinned, and carried on. Afterwards she came over to us. 'Thank you so much for joining in!' she gushed, 'this is the crowning moment, I hope we weren't making too much noise, we were afraid we were disturbing all the other tables – '

'Oh no!' replies Pete. 'We thought you were the entertainment put on for us.'

'It's really good of you,' she says, and Pete puts his arm round her and she bends down and they have a brief kiss. I shift my gaze.

'I saw a look of panic on her face,' I tell him later. 'She was afraid not only was she having to snog *you*, she was going to have to snog the rest of us.'

Back at the college Graham looks at me ominously.

'You on for a run tomorrow morning?' he asks.

'Gorr,' I groan, hanging my head and shaking it.

27

'What time, then? Seven-thirty? What room are you in?'

'The one down the end.'

'Isn't it that one?' he said, pointing to the room Pete is entering, 'that's the room, isn't it?'

'It is NOT that room,' says Pete, confirmed non-runner that he is. 'One thing is certain. That is NOT the room.'

'Oh, I'm sure it is,' says Graham, 'I shall be knocking on that door.'

'Now *look*,' says Pete, wagging his finger, 'the events of this weekend are *sub judice*, right? You're all bound by the Oath of Silence.'

Graham and I duly ran down the river and back, early the following morning. At breakfast in the ancient oak-panelled dining room, with the high table laid at one end, we sat on oak benches and ate from oak tables. Charles looked up at the ceiling. There was a crest carved into the plaster, with the date.

'Oh look. There you are. That's when this place was built. 1807.'

Iain had a look too, at a different part of the ceiling. 'Well, in that case, it took them a long time to get from that bit to that one. Because up there it says 1826.'

'Builders in those days were very thorough.'

'A job like this could keep them in business for centuries.'

'Unlike the jobs I have to do,' Iain replies. 'If you're a builder these days the client wants it done by next week, let alone next century.'

After breakfast Pete handed in the keys and paid the bill.

'Did you ask him where the best place to hire punts is?' I asked.

Iain turned round. 'The river, I should think, is probably the best place.'

'Good hit, Iain,' said Pete.

'Going for a run with Graham this morning has evidently starved the brain of oxygen,' said Nick.

'Well as a matter of fact,' I said, 'when we were out for a run I saw several places on the river where you could hire punts.'

'And the college might have free ones for visitors,' said Charles.

On the way out I asked the porter.

'What's the best place to hire punts?'

'At the river,' he said, with exaggerated patience. 'Just down the bottom of that road. You can either go up the river, or down the river,' he added helpfully.

An hour's punting, then; a walk to Grantchester and a pint or two of Adnams at the Green Man.

'"Stands the church clock at ten to three?"' quoted Pete.

I peered at it round the corner. It was telling the right time, which was ten past twelve.

We talked about the air show. I spoke of my disquiet at the new old planes.

'It's just like the end of a production line,' said Pete. 'Production ceased for a bit, and now it's started up again. It's the same plane.'

'The thing that unsettles me is the purpose. What are they *for*? That's what different. Before, their purpose was to fight, wasn't it. But now, it's something else.'

'Well, the bottom line is, when they produce one of these things, it's worth half a million pounds,' said Pete.

Graham said, 'What are you doing next weekend?'

'Why, what do you have in mind? … Oh, all right. Knock one up. Shouldn't take long. Dig a few old bits up and stick them back together. Easy money.'

*

Some time later I found myself in Lincoln. At the foot of Steep Hill (the clue's in the name) from the cathedral down to the main shopping area was a shop window full of instruments salvaged from military aircraft, along with the requisite large colour photo of a Spitfire in flight, and another of a Dakota showing its D-day invasion stripes. Altimeters, airspeed indicators, oil temperature gauges, vertical speed indicators, fuel indicators, engine speed indicators. Each was labelled with a fluorescent pink or orange card. 'Ex-Jet Provost, £8.00'. 'Ex-Nimrod, £4.00'. 'Ex-Wessex, £5'. 'Ex-Shackleton, £10'. 'Ex-Canberra, £10'. 'Phantom radio control set, £15'. 'Ex-military parachutist altimeter, £25'. 'Ex-Vulcan control unit, £10'. In the pub the following day I showed the pictures I'd taken of them to Pete, thinking he'd be full of admiration at my finding such gems.

'Oh, you can get those anywhere. Two a penny, they are. You can buy a whole instrument panel. Anyway, what would you do with it? – Put it in the loo, and when you sat on the bog, you could pretend you were flying a Spit,' he added, making the engine noises. '*Neeorwargghh!*'

*

At a subsequent Duxford air show, one of the rarer vintage planes crashed. Pete told us about an old patient of his, who'd recently been in his surgery. This was Squadron Leader Beck, who had been in the RAF before the war, and survived it.

'He knows all about that accident the other day, you know, the Fairey Firefly.'

'Can't be many left of them now, can there?' said Nick.

'I don't think there are *any* left now. He ran a squadron after the war, and they still had some Spitfires, but the new pilots coming in had been trained on planes with different engines. Either they were jets, or propeller planes with turbine engines. Not piston engines. The point was that piston engines take longer to respond. And he would never allow the new pilots to fly the Spitfires. He said, if you're only trained to fly the newer planes, you get used to the engine responding instantly. You go into a dive, you pull back the joystick, and if you're in a jet, or a propeller plane with a turbine, you level off. But in something like a Spitfire, you have to be more careful. You go into a dive, and you pull it back, but the plane doesn't respond quite instantly. So if you're a bit close to the ground – '. The two crew had been killed, both experienced flyers.

'I'm not interested in seeing those old planes doing acrobatics at those shows,' Pete went on. 'Why can't they just do a fly-past? Why not take them up and do a low pass? That's all you need to do. There's no need for aerobatics, especially in planes that weren't particularly meant to do them.'

'What else has he told you recently?'

'Ha! I'll tell you one thing he said. He said the best pilots were the ones who flew multi-engined planes. But the fighters were flown by the ones who were gung-ho. They weren't necessarily the best pilots but they had attitude. You needed to be more skilful to fly a multi-engined plane but you needed attitude to be a fighter pilot.'

The conversation put me in mind of another air show, years before, when I'd had the curious sensation of what it is to *know* that something dreadful is about to happen, yet, simultaneously, not *believe* it. It was at the Biggin Hill air show. We were visiting relatives for the weekend and there wasn't time for an all-day outing. Instead of queuing to get in, we sat for a while in a field across a shallow valley from the runway, over which all the aircraft flew immediately after take-off. So we had a good view. Spitfires, a Lancaster, all the usual suspects, zoomed or lumbered their way past us. A WWII American A26 Invader attack plane took off as normal. It made a circuit, ascending slightly, then turned its nose down. But its dive was steeper than those of the previous aircraft, and quite suddenly I knew that it could not pull out of the dive and that it was going to hit the ground. But I did not believe it. The mental state was as contradictory as maintaining black is white. Two seconds later the knowledge was proved correct and the belief was not. The plane met the earth not with a bang but a *whump*, a mass of flame and smoke ensued, and one wheel came bouncing crazily up the hill towards us. We were perhaps two hundred yards away. Within a minute there was little that was recognisably part of an aircraft.

After that I knew that there is such a thing as to be killed instantly. The seven people on the plane would have had, at most, two seconds' awareness that something was happening that was not supposed to, time enough perhaps to be apprehensive, and then all at once would have known no more.

3

Planes and Trains

Pete, Iain and I met at Pete's house to devise the next pub quiz. He'd always wanted to do a round in which competitors are asked to put a name to a number.

'You'll know these,' he said. 'A B-17, for instance.'

'Er ... '

'You know what *that* is, for godsake!'

'Oh, I know. It was one of those, oh, what were they called. Flying Fortress.'

'Right. And what's an F-4?'

'A, um ... I've heard of it, I ought to know – '

'Of course you *ought* to know!' He looked at me accusingly.

'Give me a clue.'

'Oh, for heaven's sake, Austin! An F-4 is a Phantom.'

'Oh yes.'

'And a C-5 is a Galaxy. Transport plane. Come *on*! Those are the easy ones.'

'What do those letters stand for, then?'

'What letters?'

'C. B. F.'

'B is for bomber. C is for cargo. C-47, that was the Dakota. F is Fighter. And A is for Attack, and P is Pursuit.' He had a list of about thirty, and I shook my head.

'No, all right,' he conceded, 'it's unfair, that one.' My resounding failure made him realise his knowledge is rather specialised. On the other hand, we concluded, my idea of asking people to name silhouettes of types of ship, particularly if they are supplied also with a jumbled-up list, was more feasible. Frigate. Destroyer. Battleship. Submarine. Aircraft carrier. With some old sailing vessels, for variation. Schooner. Grecian galley. Brigantine. (But in the event, few teams got more than half-a-dozen right. Ignoramuses!) And we also discussed the idea of giving them the first four lines of a limerick, and awarding points for rhyme, metre and wit in their proposals for a fifth.

We finished off the discussion in the White Hart. At the bar I began telling them about the incident during the Sunday walk when, leading the others, map in hand but deep in conversation, I'd got three-quarters across a field before I noticed the herd of cows in the far corner. In the middle of it were three bulls. Martin had seen them, but, experienced countryman that he is, decided there was no need to say anything. His judgment had been sound, and we had reached the other side with nothing more alarming than the herd succumbing to curiosity and ambling a little closer.

'Martin told us something very interesting,' I said.

'D'you know, I can't imagine *anybody* ever coming back from talking with me and saying *I'd* told them something interesting,' interrupted Pete.

Iain looked philosophical, and turned down the corners of his mouth. 'I'm not sure that I can remember anything you've actually *said*, let alone whether or not it was interesting.'

'Martin said,' I resumed, 'they don't kill people in the classical manner'.

'Oh, I see,' said Pete. 'You mean they do it in a Romantic style. Or maybe Modern.'

'They don't put their heads down and toss you with their horns. What they do is, they knock you over and then they kneel on you. They know they're a lot heavier than you and that you won't be able to get up. And they just crush you. You can't breathe.' Martin himself had nearly been the victim of such an accident on a farm where he'd been working, but fortunately the bull had knocked him down by a wall, and couldn't get close enough to kneel on him properly. The lad with Martin managed to re-insert the stick through the ring on the bull's nose, twist it, and thereby get the animal off. Even so, Martin had been in hospital for a day or two, with a somewhat flattened pelvis and a lot of bruises.

*

A winter walk by the Barle, a tributary of the Exe. Sue and Charles, Jennie and Pete, Helen and me.

'Will we get back in daylight?' asks Sue.

'Oh, yes,' said Pete. 'Well, I bloody well hope we will. We're not going as far as we went last time we were here. It *was* practically dark by the time we finished our walk.'

'That was because you kept getting us lost and going round in circles,' I said, 'and you were looking at the map, and I offered you a compass and you rejected it, and those sheep were looking at us, thinking "What on earth is he using a map for if he hasn't got a compass?", and it slowed us down.'

'No, no, it was a fine walk,' said Charles. 'It wasn't dark. The timing was exactly right. We got back just as it was getting dusk, when the light was nice and gentle, and we were pleasantly tired, not too exhausted, ready to eat and drink, having enjoyed a good day out and with a new-found respect and confidence in our leader.'

'*What*?' I said. 'I was with you until about three-quarters of the way through that. But when you got to the last bit, you lost me. You must have been on a different walk to me.'

We ambled further up the wooded valley. There had been high winds and heavy rain in the previous few days and although the waters had subsided, the banks of the river bore signs that it had overflowed, and the grass looked as if it has been combed. Pete found a sheep's skull, put it on the end of a stick and carried it with him for a bit.

Over a cup of tea at the Tarr Steps Hotel Jennie looked out of the window. 'We haven't got to go up that path there, have we?' she asked, pointing. 'Oh no,' we said. 'Good,' she said. Instead, we went up a path on the other side of the valley. It was at least as steep. There were some cuddly-looking sheep in one field, some with horns.

'Horny,' someone said. 'Grind them up, put them in your cocoa. Do wonders for you at your age.'

Someone else noticed Pete no longer had his sheep's skull.

'Don't you want to bring it home?' Sue asked. 'Do you want to go back and get it?'

'Won't it be all smelly?' I asked.

'No, no, no!' said Pete in an exasperated tone. 'You've got that wrong. We'll have to do that again. Wind back the film. Take two. Okay? Now this time, get the words right, for heaven's sake. What you say is: "But what about the smell?" Go on. Say it! "What about the smell?" Go on.'

'But what about the smell?' I said.

He looked me up and down, sniffing and turning down the corners of his mouth.

'I don't think it'll notice,' he said.

'Ha ha.'

'I keep on telling you! Coaching you! But you never get it right! In spite of my tuition.'

A little further on, well-camouflaged though it was, with its black and yellow striped body hidden in the fallen leaves, Helen found a dead dragon-fly.

Pete held it. 'No, it isn't dead,' he said, 'look. If you hold it there, you can feel it.'

'Give it mouth-to-mouth resuscitation,' I said.

'Eergh,' said Jennie.

'It's all right,' Pete said to Jennie. 'It's done its business. It's bred. So it's all right to be dead.'

'Well, by that token,' she said, 'so have you. *You* ought to be dead.'

'Well, I am nearly,' he said.

Charles came up with Tugby and had a look at the dragonfly, its wings outstretched. Tugby barked at it but the creature did not respond. 'I'd have thought if anyone could get this going, you could,' said Charles to Pete. 'Get an elastic band, and a catapult, fix it to its undercarriage – '

'Oh all right! I can see where this conversation's going. Runeckles the anorak and his model aircraft.'

On a large table in the room in his house reserved for his arty stuff Pete has a diorama of a World War 2 airfield. Model planes, buildings, people. Two Hawker Hurricanes are about to take off, their spinning propellers represented by discs of thin clear plastic. Three more are on the ground, one with the pilot hurrying towards it, one being refuelled, the last with its engine cover removed and being serviced by the little figures of the ground crew. There is a control tower, a fire engine ready for deployment, men running and cycling from one building to another. Above all this, suspended on parallel nylon threads in a separate depiction which you have to regard as unconnected with the airfield below, is the skirmish over the Lincolnshire coast in 1941. On one wire is the Spitfire piloted by his Uncle Peter, and on the other, trailing a cloud of smoke from an engine (cotton wool darkened by an infusion of black) is the Junkers. 'It's as close as I could get it to what I think happened', he says.

*

In Tom's, Nick was showing us a copy of an old Air Ace War Picture Library book he'd bought from the Help the Aged shop. The price was 15p in England, and prices were also printed for Rhodesia, Australia, South Africa and New Zealand. Volunteers from all those countries of the British Empire fought alongside Britons in the Second World War, so their sons would have been as interested in it as us.

'There doesn't seem to be much call for it on mainland Europe,' said Nick. He didn't need to spell out his subtext: the French would be too ashamed because of surrendering to Germany, the Germans too irritated at having eventually lost, the other nations too embarrassed at having been ineffectual. 'You remember I told you I'm continuing this tradition of fathers buying warlike toys for their sons,' he went on. 'That bow and arrow I bought for a pound. I was telling the chaps at work about this, and one of my colleagues pulled out this catalogue, with crossbows – '

'Hold on,' I said. 'This was at work?'

'If you're an anaesthetist,' he informed us, 'the line is, "The job occupies the hours but it may not occupy all the minutes". Anyway. There's a branch of this firm in Portsmouth, and one in Plymouth.'

'All selling crossbows? They're quite lethal.'

Pete said, 'No. Lethal.'

'That's what I said.'

'No you didn't. You said *quite* lethal. Not *quite* lethal. Lethal.'

'They've got a website,' said Nick, called 'Quicks'. But they do this catalogue.'

'And you swop it for your Air Ace,' said Pete. 'You go into work and the nurses say, "Is that an Air Ace in your pocket, or are you just pleased to see me?"'

40

*

A week later, a second visit to the charity shop, and Nick brought in another acquisition. This time it was the War Picture Library, much the same thing as Air Ace but about the infantry – and this was a bumper edition, four comic-strip stories in one volume, usually concerning individuals in personal duels with their counterparts on the German side. They always were good stories, we said to each other.

'There's always a moral to them,' said Pete. 'I used them to write my English essays.'

'What, you wrote essays using the storylines from those comics?'

'Yeah. And I got good marks for them. I used to have to read them out to the class.'

'But didn't all the others know what you'd done?'

'Of course.'

'But the teacher didn't.'

'Of course not. I did one from *Saturday Night and Sunday Morning*[1] once. The teacher wrote on it, "Your spelling and grammar are appalling as usual but you have invented a good original plot".'

'And of course the teacher wouldn't have read it.'

'No. Far too modern. Christ! This *was* a public school, remember.' The kind of school that then, if not now, was renowned for traditional attitudes and the ignoring of any book, or indeed anything, that was not at least thirty years old.

---

[1] Gritty Northern novel by Alan Sillitoe, published in 1958, which anyone of our age in the early 1960s was thought rather daring to have read.

*

On a ski-ing holiday one of the others was Nick's brother Chris, and Chris, it seemed, makes models of Wellington bombers. 'Of course,' he said, 'soon there'll be hardly anyone who knows someone who fought in the war. It'll have gone out of everyone's consciousness. People won't have – ' He broke off, noticing the glances exchanged by Pete and me. 'Sorry. Is this –'

'No; it's all right. It's not your fault. Just a little sub-plot. We have had this conversation before.'

'Oh, sorry – '

'You weren't to know.'

*

For a few weeks my new bicycle light had an additional purpose. I'd collided with a lad crossing the road in the dark some while back, which was my fault because my illumination was almost invisible, and I'd decided – at last, in middle age – to get something decent. I invested in a very bright halogen headlamp powered by a big rechargeable lead-acid battery designed to hang off the crossbar. A lot of bike lights will allow you to be seen but won't enable you to see much of what's ahead. This one was different.

Nick had bought a little powered model aeroplane for his son, but since his son was too young to start the engine or indeed do anything much more than get it out of its box, Nick was forced to do it all for him. There were roundels on the wings, just like an RAF plane. For its maiden flight he took it to a small recreation area in the town known as Salisbury Fields, one of whose features is a row of mature chestnut trees around the perimeter. Afterwards, Nick several times attempted to give a plausible account of how the inevitable happened, whilst trying to deflect attention from the questionable decision to attempt a flight there in the first place. Somehow no-one found it convincing, but that only encouraged him to redouble his efforts. My task, every Tuesday night after leaving the pub, was to shine my light high into the tree in which the flight had terminated, to check if the plane were still there.

'There it is. Look.'

'You can see it glinting. It's the colours on the wings.'

'Trouble is, it's likely to stay there until all the leaves come off the trees,' he said glumly. He showed us a note he'd pinned to the trunk in case it blew down, asking anyone who happened to find it to drop it over the garden wall of someone he knew.

'Can't you climb the tree?' I said.

Nick and Pete both looked at me witheringly.

'It's bloody fifty feet up. Do *you* want to climb it?'

'Not my plane.'

'What, you would if it was yours, would you?'

'Might do.'

'Oh, bollocks you would. You wouldn't get further than where that branch goes off there, look. It's right out in the leaves, on the edge of the tree. The branches would break long before you got there.'

It was far too high for a ladder, and we stopped short of suggesting Nick should call out the fire service.

'If you'd set the rudder a little more to the left, wouldn't you have got it to fly round in more of a curve?'

'The calculation I made was quite a sound one. OK, I would say that, wouldn't I? I made what I thought was due allowance, but the flight characteristics weren't quite what you might have predicted. Well, not what *I* predicted, anyway.'

'And you forgot about the wind.'

Nick looked hurt.

'There are always more variables out there,' he said. 'You'll always have less idea as to their relative importance, on a maiden flight, than after you've done the proper calibrations. Good job I didn't start it off from further back, or it would have gone right over the tree, and come down through someone's window. The angle of the rudder I'd calculated was correct to start with. But it changed course mid-flight. If I'd trimmed the ailerons a bit more on one side, that would have done the trick.'

A couple of months on, when the leaves were beginning to turn brown but hadn't yet begun to fall, I called into Tom's. Amongst the others already there was Nick. After slagging me off for arriving just before he paid for a round of drinks, and therefore just in time to be included in it, he renewed the attack on another front.

'Nice mate you are!' he said. 'Yeah, thanks for being there at exactly the time I needed you to be!'

'What?'

'Where were you on Tuesday night? When there was a howling gale and I was out of the country? When I thought I could rely on having a friend in the right place?'

'*What?*'

44

'It blew a gale, didn't it? And you weren't there! Which way did you go back from the pub, then? Not across Salisbury Fields? Or did you just neglect to look up in the tree for me? You with the powerful light. Didn't think of using it on that occasion, did you?'

'Has it gone, then?'

'Yes it bloody well has! Went and had a look as soon as I got back and the damn thing's not there. Must have got blown down in those strong winds we had on Tuesday. And you didn't look!'

Pete hadn't been at the pub either, and Charles and I had taken the quicker route by road, instead of accompanying him and Nick across Salisbury Fields where the plane had been for at least a couple of months.

'And now it's gone,' said Nick, 'blown out of the tree, and no doubt someone's pinched it.'

'Did you look over the wall into the Sloans' garden?'

'Yes of course I did.'

'Not there?'

'Bloody well wasn't.'

'You should go to the police station,' said Pete. 'You never know, someone might have handed it in.'

Nick looked doubtful, but when we saw him next he'd taken up the suggestion. Without the right result.

*

Model aircraft always come to a sad end. Helen's brother Richard had had a wonderful collection at one time, of balsa-wood replicas he'd built himself from kits. 'They were in the loft in Bristol,' he'd said when we were walking out one evening to the pub, 'and when our dear

Mama was moving house, she persuaded me to throw them out. I decided I really didn't have the space to keep them myself. I was in that flat in Muswell Avenue at the time, and I thought, oh well, I suppose they'll have to go. So I had a ceremonial bonfire. Balsa wood and tissue paper,' he said. 'It went up. Whoosh! Spitfires, Hurricanes, ME109's, Stukas, Lancasters ... You know, there were a lot of planes. I was seriously into it. Okay, they weren't all intact, some of them had crashed, there was a wing hanging off here and there. But they were all painted, and ... I tell you, though I say it myself, they were good models. When I think of that ... Bloody hell.'

We shook our heads ruefully. Model aircraft were a common currency of schoolboys in the Fifties. Even if you didn't build them yourself, you knew someone who did, and you'd see them in a state of half-construction, and you knew all about the way the tissue paper would stretch rigid after coating it with dope, and how long you had to leave it before painting it; and you particularly knew how frail these models were, and that major repairs were invariably needed after just a few flights if not the first.

But it wasn't only model aircraft that were stuck together with glue. At Tom's on a later occasion there were comments on the badminton, which we play in the winter. Unlike Tuesday tennis, we rotate partners. Sometimes there are four people present, sometimes five; it would be perfectly OK with six.

'No doubt who was the best player. Whoever was playing with Graham won,' said Charles.

'Oh, what a coincidence!' exclaimed Pete. 'That is just a coincidence. It's what a coincidence is, when a lot of things happen and you think there's a cause for them all occurring, some common factor, and there isn't. You think it's something to do with Graham, but it isn't! It's just a coincidence. That's what a coincidence is!'

'Yes but it happened the week before as well,' said Charles.

'It happened the week before as well? That just goes to prove my point! It's even more of a coincidence! An even better example of a coincidence!'

He changed the subject. 'Did you see that good obit the other day, about this bloke who dropped the four thousand pound bomb from a Mosquito into a railway tunnel and got it right in there? Bloody good marksmanship, eh?'

'Course, a Mosquito could carry a lot of bombs,' said Nick.

'Yeah, the payload for bombs in a Mosquito was almost as much as a Flying Fortress, because a Flying Fortress had a lot of armament, which made it a lot heavier.'

'Built of plywood and glue the Mosquitoes were,' said Nick.

'Araldite,' said Pete.

'Not Araldite,' I said. 'That was similar, an offshoot of it, but they didn't develop that till later. Aerolite it was called.'

'Right,' said Pete.

'Did your dad have some?'

'Yeah.'

'Mine did. It was powder and some liquid in a bottle that you brushed on. I remember him telling me it was what they made wooden aeroplanes with in the war. That's why it's called Aerolite.'

'The Germans made one,' said Pete, 'and they called *theirs* a Mosquito.'

'What, you mean they found out what our plans were? Or one crashed, and they copied it?'

'No, no, they were just on the same design trail. They made something similar, out of the same kind of materials, and they happened to call it the same name. It's in my *Aircraft of the World*. But we bombed the factory where they made the glue, and they had to use some other stuff.'

'Flour and water paste,' said Nick.

'And it didn't work so well, and the wings fell off.'

'Did we know they were producing this stuff at the factory, and was that why we bombed it? Or was it just luck?'

'Don't push me too far,' said Pete.

'The knowledge is only a veneer,' said Charles.

'It's a micron thin,' said Pete.

'If you scratch it,' said Nick, 'the whole edifice falls apart.'

'Like the German glue,' said Charles. (He didn't, but he should have done.)

So our knowledge is not complete. It is backed up by magazines, part-works that reveal something new every week, and you have to wait to find out what's in the next instalment.

*

The past, the past. In a second-hand bookshop I found a copy of *Eagle Annual Number 4*. I bought it, for £7.

'If only I hadn't sold my copy of this to Jones minor when I was eleven,' I said, 'for two and six.'

The proprietor indulged me with a smile. 'Yes, well, we all do things like that. If only we knew.'

Actually, I hadn't sold it to Jones minor for two-and-six. That was just a way of putting it. I'd bought it off Aldridge major for one and six, a whole week's pocket money. It was him who'd be regretting selling it to me. But what happened to it after that, after I'd read it twenty times over the years, I don't know. I suppose it was one of those books I gave away in one of my mother's periodic purges. These took the form of suggestions that I might have grown out of them, and wouldn't it be a nice thought if I gave them away so that they went to a children's home. She was scrupulous in giving me the decision on what I wanted rid of and what I didn't, but there was a fairly clear moral imperative that I should give *some* of them away. But I'd bet I was a great deal fonder of *Eagle Annual Number 4* than its subsequent owner, whoever that might have been.

The shop also had *Eagle Annual Number 3*, but when I looked at it (it had the same formula mixture of adventure strips, stories, factual articles, cut-away drawings, cartoons and jokes), I realised I wasn't interested in collecting books from the past, only in collecting books from *my* past. And when I'd acquired that *Eagle Annual Number 4*, the notion of reclaiming little bits from my childhood began to take hold; and for three long years an image from another book floated before me, the reproduction of a photo showing the damage caused by one particular German bomb.

*

When I was about eight, I was given a book about trains. Like most books of its type, it consisted of text and photographs, but the main interest lay in the latter, and I read little of the text save the captions. In it was a chapter about the railways in Britain during the Second World War. One of the photographs showed a wrecked railway station which had been bombed by the Luftwaffe. The caption read: 'As one railwayman was heard to say, tongue in cheek, "Looks a sight worse than Bank 'Oliday!" ' I had not heard the phrase 'tongue in cheek', and did not at first understand it, but I worked out that it couldn't be meant literally, because I tried sticking my tongue in my cheek, and speaking at the same time, and found it almost impossible. In the same chapter was a double-page picture of a shattered locomotive lying on its side with its name, over the main driving wheels, in the foreground of the picture: 'Sir Josiah Wedgwood'. I thought it odd that trains should have names. Ships, yes; but a train called after a man seemed strange.

I kept that book on the bottom shelf of my bookcase and looked at it every now and then. I went away to boarding school; later, my parents moved house. And at some point during this time the book went the same route as *Eagle Annual Number 4*.

I thought no more of it. But decades later I remembered that picture and its caption, and I wanted to see it again. I wanted to see not only the picture, but the rest of the book too. This was years before the internet made it possible to locate just about any book you wanted within five minutes, and I began to scour second-hand bookshops. The obsession grew. Several times I went to a shop in Bournemouth entirely devoted to books on transport, with a large second-hand section. And every time I saw a second-hand bookshop elsewhere, I went in and searched. One of my problems was that although I could remember the name of the author, Paul Townend, I could not remember the title[1]. I did recall the outside of the book: it bore a predominantly dark brown painting of a massive locomotive, seen at an angle from the front, and a diminutive figure or two in the foreground.

Then it occurred to me that my best chance of finding it would be to visit Hay-on-Wye. That small town was reputed not only to have a much larger number of second-hand bookshops than so small a place ought, but to have the biggest collection of them of any town or city in the country. My job took me one day to Oswestry, in Shropshire, and a day or two before the trip I made up my mind to start a little earlier in order to take a detour.

The January day was wet and very windy. I queued for three-quarters of an hour to cross the Severn Bridge while the police removed a high-sided vehicle that had blown over. But eventually I reached Hay-on-Wye, and found it indeed stuffed with the most astonishing collection of second-hand bookshops one could ever imagine, twenty or thirty of them, from middle-sized to huge; and when, a couple of hours later, I left, in a paper

---

[1] *The Modern World Book of Railways*, by Paul Townend, published by Sampson Low, Marston & Co. (publication date not stated).

bag beside me on the front seat of the car was the object of those years of searching.

Or a copy of it, at any rate. As I told the shop assistant, after regaling him with the story of the 'sight worse than Bank 'Oliday', and showing him the illustration, 'There's only one thing wrong with it.'

He raised his eyebrows.

'It's not mine,' I said.

'Yours would have had your name in it, would it?'

'It would.'

The only inscription in this copy, in pencil, was '£3'. But I would have given him £23. Or £33. Or £103. Well, maybe not.

Yet memory is not always reliable. A visualisation of something you have seen, which you would expect to be something like a photographic record, proves to be a construction built up of only half-remembered images, with gaps artificially filled in. The smashed-up engine was not Sir Josiah Wedgwood but Sir Ralph Wedgwood. The bank holiday picture turned out not to occupy the top of a right-hand page, with the caption underneath it, as I had remembered it, but the bottom of a left-hand one, with the caption above. And the phrase used was not what I have quoted, but 'said, with his tongue in his cheek'; and it wasn't 'Bank 'Oliday' but 'Bank Holiday'. Small details, but fortunately my memory was not being tested in a murder case.

I told the chap on the desk that I'd lived in Hereford for a while, and Hay-on-Wye hadn't been renowned for second-hand bookshops then. 'Quite a recent thing, isn't it?' I asked. 'Within the last twenty years?'

'1969,' he said. 'That was when David Booth started up. He's got this one' (an enormous collection of books straggled through several buildings comprising the Castle), 'and another one down the road.' He showed me on the map. 'Place like Hay, people said it would never work. Now, everyone who worked for him in the first place left and opened their own bookshop. But his is the biggest. The main rival is the old Cinema Bookshop. Owned by a bloke from London. He just came in with lots of money, bought a huge amount of books. But he's not doing so well now.'

'Where do the customers come from?'

'All over. This is the biggest collection of second-hand bookshops in the world. Every nationality you get here. You name it. Americans, Japanese – '

'Japanese! Why do *they* buy English books?'

He shrugged. 'Collect them. Mostly the more expensive ones. Leather-bound.'

'Can they read them?'

He laughed, and shrugged again.

*

Tennis. Pete and I were faring badly. Charles was getting every ball back and making hardly any mistakes, and so of course was Graham.

'What are we going to do now?' he said in desperation.

'Change partners,' I said.

'I'm not sure that would make any difference, but I will give Jennie a ring on my mobile just to see what her reaction is.'

In the pub afterwards we talked about old Dinky toys. 'One of the best ones I've got is a Vauxhall Cresta,' said Pete. 'A two-tone one, red and white. I'm proud of that. It's immaculate.' This was ironic, because the real Vauxhall Crestas, in the 1950s, began to rust away almost as soon as you took delivery.

'I've got all those old Army vehicles as well,' he said.

'Centurion tank,' I said.

'Personnel carrier,' said Nick.

'Tank transporter,' continued Pete. 'But they're not in such good condition. They all got shot with an air gun. I blew them up loads of times, down on my father's old vegetable patch. I should think if anybody's got their vegetables planted there now, their whole family will get lead poisoning.'

4

The Dam Busters ... and the Mudguard

Tom's.

'It's a politically incorrect pub, this,' Pete said. 'Full of smoke. No carpet on the floor.'

'Uncomfortable chairs.'

'Hardly any women.'

'But very good beer.'

'Which is why we're here.'

We argued about the respective merits of the *Telegraph* and the *Times*, Max Hastings and Conrad Black (editor and proprietor, respectively, of the *Telegraph*) versus their counterparts at the *Times*, Peter Stothard and Rupert Murdoch. Pete claimed to dislike Murdoch and his right-wing empire-building; I maintained that wasn't a good enough reason for not reading a particular paper – what about the quality of the writing, for example? And, I said, how can you, an unreconstructed child of the Sixties, read a paper that's so unashamedly Tory as the *Telegraph*? At that time Pete hadn't yet been able to bring himself to buy it regularly himself, but he did read the copy brought daily to his dental surgery by one of his employees; and the one regular feature to which he always referred admiringly was the crop of obituaries of Second World War veterans.

'They're all in their seventies and eighties now,' he said, 'and of course they're all dying. So you've got a little history, practically every day, of what they did, and what happened, in the desert or after D-Day or in India or wherever it was.'

'The golden age of obituaries,' said Nick. 'It's a bit sad. We're all living in the past.'

'Does it only happen here?' I asked. 'Are we the only country to have those obituaries? What about America? They probably don't in Germany or France because they're too ashamed. In ten years' time there won't be any of this. There'll be nobody reading those things. They'll all be dead.'

We'd all read the one about a James Leathart, who

was awarded an immediate DSO for pulling off a remarkable rescue while covering the Dunkirk evacuation in May 1940. Leathart was leading No. 54, a Spitfire squadron, when he saw another Spitfire going down at Marck airfield, on the edge of Calais. On returning to base he learned that Squadron Leader Drogo White, the commander of No. 74 squadron, was missing. Leathart at once set off back to Calais in search of him, flying an unarmed Miles Master two-seat trainer, and escorted by his flight commanders, the New Zealander Al Deere and Johnny Allen. After landing, Leathart could see no sign of White, and so took off to rejoin his escort. He had reached 1,000 feet when Deere yelled 'Messerschmitts!' Leathart headed for the safety of the ground, and, as soon as he had landed, jumped into a ditch. To his astonishment he almost fell on top of the missing White, who was hiding from some German tanks. The Luftwaffe somehow failed to spot the bright orange Master trainer, and after cranking the engine manually, the pair headed home at 6 ft. above the Channel[1].

'Fell in the ditch!' exclaimed Pete. 'Right on top of him! – "What are *you* doing here?!" – "How very good to see you!"'

'No self-starters on those planes. You had to go – ' and Nick demonstrated pulling on the propeller to start the plane. 'But in those Commando comics, you get a completely biased view. It wasn't all like that. You were a real exception if you shot several planes down.'

'Or if you sank one submarine,' said Pete. 'For a lot of people, there was very little going on. Every one of those blokes you see the obituaries about, there must have been ten who did absolutely nothing. It was just a question of opportunity, if you were there at the time, when you *were* able to do something like that. And there was one bloke I read about, who took his squadron *away* from the action. And they complained about him, that they never even saw any enemy.'

'What?' I asked, 'they complained because not enough of them were getting shot down?'

---

[1] *Daily Telegraph*, 4th December 1998.

'Yes. Exactly. And it probably wasn't that uncommon. But when you look at us – I mean, think what I've done. You know. 'Got up. Went to school. Became a dentist. Died.' That's my obituary. But those deeds lasted what, a few minutes, a few hours, a very small proportion of their lives, and that's what they're remembered for ever since. For a lot of them, afterwards, their lives really weren't very successful at all.' We'd also seen another obituary about a bloke who'd carried out heroic deeds during the war but who, later, when serving in the Army in Germany, had been caught consorting with young men at a club, and – sexual mores being completely different then – had had to resign in disgrace.

And of course we agreed that we regretted not having the opportunity to do this sort of thing ourselves. But would we have done so? Would *we* have been heroic – we, who have led such soft lives? Maybe, we thought, given the same circumstances we might have done, or some of us; and so might our own sons.

*

The Bermuda Triangle in Poole. You could probably be forgiven for remaining in it for very long periods. People would understand if you didn't come out. The pub you can disappear in with no questions asked. It's what's expected, after all. It opened at five-thirty and ten minutes after opening time several men were already there, all regulars by the sound of their easy familiarity with the barman. This was expressed in words ('Evening, Bill. Pint of this one? You're a creature of habit' ... 'Sold three of these already this evening'), and by body language (approaching with a swagger; slapping a couple of pound coins down; leaning on an elbow on the bar). 'Beer range varies', said the *Good Beer Guide*. I drank a beer I didn't recognise.

'Where's that one from?'

He looked up to the ceiling, thinking. 'Pontefract.'

'Sell much of this?' I asked, indicating the Goldfinch Midnight Blinder pumpclip.

'Sells quite steady, yeah.'

'It's at my local. He makes it himself, out the back.'

'Dorchester?'

'Yeah. Tom Brown's. It's just a boozer, nothing fancy like this,' I said, looking around. 'Just boards on the floor. Best beer in Dorchester.'

This place had clearly been recently done up, and on the wall was a description of the patch of the Atlantic Ocean from which it had taken its title: 'The Bermuda Triangle lies between Florida, Bermuda and the Sargasso Sea, in which there have been numerous inexplicable disappearances of ships and aircraft'. Elsewhere was a list of them all, dating back to the 19th century. Its reputation intensified in the years following the Second World War, notably in 1945 after five U.S Navy Avengers, torpedo bombers, vanished. They had been flying in the opposite direction to what they'd thought, and it was concluded that they might have ditched in the sea because they ran out of fuel – but, the account said, there was still no explanation as to why they were flying the wrong way. Rescue planes and boats set off, and a Martin Mariner, which was a larger plane, also disappeared with its thirteen crew. They were found eventually, during a search for wreckage of the Challenger space shuttle in 1986.

Then there were facsimile newspaper cuttings, including the famous front page of the New York Times reporting the loss of the *Titanic*. Suspended from the ceiling were the ailerons of a small plane. Off the main bar was a snug which had been floored, walled and ceilinged in wood, with portholes, evidently intended to resemble the interior of a ship. But I decided to forgive them all this because the beer was so good.

A few days later Nick brought a newspaper article to Tom's. (He always claims not to buy newspapers himself. This appears to be because he does not wish to be identified with any political stance – wishy-washy pinko Liberal as represented by the *Guardian*, blimpish reactionary Conservative by the *Telegraph*, or aggressive Thatcherite capitalism by the *Times*. 'It's an article my spies searched out for me,' he'll say, or 'My press cuttings officer found this one.') On this occasion the piece was from the *Times*. It seemed 'Britain's own Bermuda triangle', somewhere in the North Sea off Scotland, had been identified as an area in which a vent in the sea bed, 500 feet below the surface, every now and then produces a large gob of methane gas. When this rises, it reduces the density of the water, so that any ship which happens to be immediately above the vent sinks like a stone. Even sailors wearing lifejackets who manage to jump into the sea will sink. Something similar to this, it is thought, explains the sudden mysterious disappearance of apparently seaworthy ships in the original Bermuda triangle in the Caribbean. It also explains the disappearance of aircraft in the same area: a cloud of methane rising from the sea will starve aero engines of oxygen, thus causing them to fail, and when the methane is of sufficient concentration, the sparks from the engine can cause it to explode.

Years later I caught up with Graeme, a college friend who turned out to have exercised a key role (more accurately: was involuntarily assigned an off-stage bit part) in the saga of the Bermuda Triangle. One that for him, nonetheless, was highly significant. 'Bermuda Triangle – My Part in the Mystery' you might call his story.

His part took place early in the life of the legend, as well as early in his – he was fifteen months old at the time. In January 1948 an Avro Tudor, a passenger-carrying offshoot of the Lancaster bomber, was flying a contingent of high-ranking British military staff from the Azores, bound for Bermuda. Also aboard was Graeme's father, a surgeon who was back in civvies after Royal Navy service and had arranged to look into a possible job at the new University of the West Indies in Jamaica. Nearing Bermuda, the aeroplane, named the *Star Tiger*, vanished. No distress message was received. Extensive searches were mounted, but nothing of the plane itself, or the 31 people on it, was ever found.

The conclusion to the official report on the incident, published by the Ministry of Civil Aviation later that year, states:

> In closing this Report it may truly be said that no more baffling problem has ever been presented for investigation. In the complete absence of any reliable evidence as to either the nature or the

cause of the disaster to "Star Tiger" the Court has not been able to do more than suggest possibilities, none of which reaches the level even of probability. Into all activities which involve the co-operation of man and machine two elements enter of very diverse character. There is the incalculable element of the human equation dependent upon imperfectly known factors: and there is the mechanical element subject to quite different laws. A breakdown may occur in either separately or in both in conjunction. Or some external cause may overwhelm both man and machine. What happened in this case will never be known and the fate of "Star Tiger" must remain an unsolved mystery.

In what was otherwise a sober piece of officialese, it was of course the sentence 'Or some external cause may overwhelm both man and machine' that prompted the decades of intrigue, and even hints of the paranormal. Subsequent conjecture has suggested that *Star Tiger* simply ran out of fuel. But fuel for the legend kept being replenished, particularly when, almost exactly a year later, an identical aircraft, the *Star Ariel*, flying over the same part of the Atlantic Ocean, disappeared also without trace and with no distress call being received.

*

My job took me once more to Poole and this time I looked out the Blue Boar. 'Former merchant's house in the old town, sympathetically converted: a comfortable lounge on the ground floor and an extensive cellar bar', according to the *Good Beer Guide*. On a wall in the cellar bar was a copy of the Royal Air Force orders for the Dam Busters raid:

Top Secret. Code name: This operation will be known by a code name which will be issued separately. Date for attack: The operation is to take place on the first suitable date after 15th May 1943 ... Outline plan: The twenty special Lancasters from 617 Squadron are to fly from base to target area and return in moonlight at low level by the routes given in Appendix A. The squadron is to be divided into three main waves ... The first wave is to consist of three sections spaced at ten minute intervals, each section consisting of three aircraft. They are to take the southern route to the target area and attack Target X. The attack is to be continued until the Dam has been clearly breached. It is estimated that this might require three effective attacks. When this has been achieved, the leader is to divert the remainder of this wave to Target Y, where similar tactics are to be followed ...

That phrase. 'The Dam Busters'. When I first heard it, as a child, I had no idea what was being talked about. The words held a whiff of danger. I almost looked round to see if an adult had overheard, and was going to tear us off a strip for using both foul language and slang in one sentence.

Poole is also a town with naval connections. The Special Boat Squadron, naval equivalent of the SAS, is based there. Framed on the wall were photographs of the Navy between the wars. There was HMS *Revenge* leading the *Royal Sovereign* and *Ramillies* home after exercises in the English Channel, and there was HMS *Hood*.

On the hearth of one of the coal-effect gas fires was a curious item looking like a smooth elongated stone. Pinned to it was a label in a little frame. 'This is a lead ingot from a support ship for the Spanish Armada, found on the Bartholomew Ledges in the Scillies.' Roughly triangular in section, tapering at both ends, it was about two and a half feet long, six inches wide in the middle and three or four inches thick – and so heavy I could hardly lift even one end of it. By the other fire was another one, but bigger. This pub had more interesting things than most, and the difference between them and a lot of others was that these were originals.

*

Sunday morning, and a country walk. By the time we rendezvoused at the car park it was drizzling steadily. Someone suggested we might just as well all go back home to bed, but everyone else thought we'd never live it down. On the way through Cerne Abbas we commented on the Giant, the massive chalk figure cut into the hillside. In one hand he is waving a club, but that isn't his most celebrated feature. We talked about the woman who'd been trying to get pregnant for years and succeeded only after mating one night on his cock.

'A steep slope like that,' said Neal, 'you'd think they'd slide down.'

'Need an ice axe to hold you there,' said Brian. 'Crampons.'

Pete – who fancies himself as an artist – told us of his visit to Lymington the previous day to have lunch with his parents at the yacht club. There he bumped into an old friend. This was only the second time he'd seen him in thirty years.

'It's so refreshing to meet a friend of yours who doesn't say, "Oh, how are you, good to see you, do tell me what you're doing now". What this bloke said, straight out, was "For God's sake, Runeckles, when's that picture of yours going to make me some money? When am I going to get a profit out of it instead of using it in the attic roof to keep the rain out?".'

The path took us up a short steep hill, leaving the valley behind. The sun was out, coats came off and there was puffing and panting.

'The view's behind us,' I said. 'If we'd been doing this walk the other way round, we'd have a nice view right now.'

'You're pretty good at talking out of your arse,' Pete retorted, 'I should have thought you could see out of it as well.' With the toe of his boot he made a breach in the thin wall of mud holding a puddle on the farm track. The water started to run away into the ditch and he hummed the Dam Busters film theme. He walked on and I shouted after him.

'Aren't you going to come and look at the valley? The devastated villages?' But he had departed the scene of destruction and was away looking at another puddle, where there were tracks of some small creature. Between the imprint of its feet was a steady line, as if something has been dragged.

'Its tail,' someone suggested. 'A newt.'

'Could be its willy.'

'Nah,' said Pete. 'Water's cold.'

A little later there was a sudden stench.

'What's that smell?' asked someone.

'That pile of manure,' said Brian. 'One of the worst things I did this winter,' he went on, 'was to dig up some artichokes and instead of getting rid of them straight away I left them in a bucket. And it rained, and the smell was unbelievable. There was this froth on top.'

'You could have made it into a stew,' said Neal, 'and sold it.'

'Or got drunk on it,' said Iain.

'And thrown up, immediately afterwards.'

'There was this programme,' said Brian, 'did any one see it? – it was about Sarawak, or somewhere, some stuff they have to drink, and the TV companies come to record it, they brew it up, make some horrible mixture and start rolling around dead drunk, and honk it up again.'

'Yeah,' said Pete, 'and when the film crew's gone, they all put their normal clothes back on and watch *Neighbours*.'

*

Framed on the wall of one of the large rooms at the White Horse in Milford-on-Sea is a map of Britain surrounded by silhouettes and drawings of war-planes. On one side are the attacking German planes – Dorniers, Heinkels, Messerschmitts and Junkers, and, lined up against them on the other, the defending British ones – Hurricanes, Defiants and of course Spitfires, the most glamorous of the lot. The map is marked with all the RAF bases, and the insignia of the various squadrons.

This room is evidently the meeting-place of the local Royal Air Force Association. The man behind the bar, indeed, looks an ex-RAF type, although at roughly sixty he is too young to have fought in the war. Nonetheless, he exhibits the regulation handlebar moustache and brisk manner. I wonder what happens in this room. Probably, a regular meeting of a dozen or so ex-servicemen, death reducing their number year by year: they gather because they have this in common, that they took part in the same conflict. Perhaps younger people are also present; others, retired from the Air Force, who did not fight in the war but regard themselves in the same tradition. How long will this last? How long will the map remain on the wall? You do not see similar rooms devoted to the men and machines of the First World War. In thirty or forty years' time, or possibly fifty or sixty, this room will have changed, the pictures will be stored in someone's loft or thrown in a skip for landfill, and, along with the meetings and the men themselves, forgotten. The events they commemorate will no longer be celebrated in anyone's memory since there will be no-one alive with the memory to celebrate them. Only in books, perhaps, condensed and summarised, might these events have a shadowy, twilight existence.

What would my father have said? He would have been quite happy to pop in there for a drink, and re-live some past events; but he would have come out saying to me, that's all very well, but you can't keep looking backwards – it's over, okay we did it, we went through all that, but there's a life to be led in the here and now.

I swallowed the rest of the beer and drove to my mother's house. I'd go there periodically on weekdays when my work took me in that direction, keep her company for the evening, and return to work the following day. I mowed the lawn and did one of my periodic inspections of the shed, gradually deteriorating at the end of the garden. And it was then that I realised the bicycle mudguard was missing.

The bike itself had gone after my father's death but the mudguard had been there for years, hanging on a nail in the shed. My mother had been clearing out; as she approached the end of her life, she gradually divested herself of its trappings, getting rid of items she perceived as redundant to her.

My father himself had put it there. I had been slightly disappointed when he had removed it from the bicycle, together with its companion the front mudguard, and replaced them with new ones; but they had certainly been getting a bit rusty, dating as they did from 1932. But, no doubt for the same sentimental reasons as I would have done, the rear one he kept.

After the war he had rarely ridden his bike and when I went to boarding school he allowed me to take it with me, leaving it there during the holidays and riding my own when I was at home. The conversations with other boys at school went like this.

'See this?' I'd say, pointing to a jagged hole about an inch in diameter near the top of the rear mudguard. 'Guess how it got there.'

'Someone hit it with a hammer.'

'You couldn't do that with a hammer,' I'd reply. 'Wouldn't go through steel.'

'A chisel, then. A screwdriver.'

'No. Anyway, what would they do that for?'

'I know! Something fell on it. Something sharp.'

'Better. But still not right.'

'Well, someone was mending the bike, and they'd taken off the mudguard and they damaged it somehow.'

'Nope. The mudguard was on the bike when the hole was made.'

'What? Couldn't have been.'

'It was.'

'Come on, then. What?'

'Look at the hole. Why couldn't it have been caused by something falling on the mudguard?'

No response.

'Look at the edges of the hole.' The edges were sharp, as if indeed something had gone through with some force; but those jagged edges were bent outwards all around the hole, indicating that whatever made it had come from the inside of the mudguard.

'The hole was made from *that* way through, not the other way. You can see that.'

'What? – It couldn't have done. Don't believe you.'

'It's true.'

'What was it, then, clever dick? Come on.'

'Air raid. During the war. Bomb went off nearby, piece of shrapnel bounced off the ground and went up through it, that way, made the hole with the edges pointing outwards.'

'Bollocks! Couldn't have done, it would have ruined the tyre!'

'It did ruin the tyre. Course it did. You don't think this is the same one, do you? He put a new one on.'

Pause.

'Blimey.'

It had happened one day when my father was on leave; he'd left his bike standing against a wall, outside a shop, perhaps, or a pub, in Bristol where he'd been born and brought up. For at least thirty years after, and possibly forty, that mudguard stayed in place on the bike, a perpetual token of the relationship of my father with his bicycle and the war. When I saw it first on the wall of the shed, I thought: Good; I'm sorry he's felt he had to replace the mudguards with new ones, but I'm glad he wants to preserve that little bit of the past. I don't have to worry. *He's* taken care of it. But now the bare wall of the shed stared at me blankly. That black-rusted semi-circle shouted its irredeemable absence.

Well. What would I have done with it?

I'd have kept it.

And put it? – put it where?

Oh ... at home somewhere. In the loft. In the garage.

What for? Who would have seen it? Would I have framed it? Painted it?

No ... none of those things. Probably hardly anyone would have seen it, except me. Certainly no-one would have remarked upon it unless I'd pointed it out to them.

So. What would have been the value of keeping it?

I would have kept it because ... it reminded me of my father. It defined for me a period in his life, and hence in mine. It was an icon, but more than an icon, because it had a history of its own, and a scar to bear witness. It fixed the past. I could look at it and say, This object attests to the reality of those events. Normally, time smooths out the bumps, irons away the evidence of upheaval; the processes of inevitable, if gradual, change wear away the effects of sudden cataclysm. But every now and then, something remains of the cataclysm, unaffected by time. That mudguard with its jagged hole was one such item. *Was*.

5

Those who talk and those who don't

Not everyone wants to reminisce about the war.

We'd been to Normandy to look at the D-day landing beaches. On the drive back home from the Portsmouth ferry I asked Jennie about her father. He'd been in the merchant navy during the first part of the war and was later commissioned into the Royal Navy.

'He never spoke about it. I know nothing except that he was torpedoed in the North Sea and spent three days in an open boat before being rescued. He lost a lot of friends on the ship. I don't even know if that was before he was commissioned in the Royal Navy or afterwards. I do know he named my brother Ross after his best mate, who was one of the ones who was lost. But he never kept in touch with any of those people he was with. Never spoke to them again, after the war.'

Later at a dinner party I spoke with Sally. She'd just been to her father's funeral.

'He was a Japanese prisoner of war for three and a half years. He'd been a sub-lieutenant in HMS *Exeter*. Sunk off

Java in 1942. He was on the building of the Burma railway. Seventy-five per cent of them didn't survive. He weighed 4½ stone when he came back. The British authorities after the war wouldn't release them straight away – they made sure they recovered properly and got up to at least 7 stone before they went back home ... I learned more about him after his funeral than I'd ever known before. His prisoner of war colleagues were our godparents. They'd nearly all been tortured. Perhaps it helped him survive that he'd been born in India and was there for the first six years of his life, before being sent to boarding school in England. That sort of climate, culture perhaps. The ones who had the worst experiences there are the ones who didn't talk about it afterwards.'

*

Early during the beginnings of my awareness of The War, my sister did an exchange with a French girl. When she was in France, our parents were invited to stay for a couple of days with the family, near Paris. My father tried to engage them in discussion about the war. He spoke enough French to do so, and mentioned that he had been in France during 1944. But he got nowhere. The subject was changed. He tried again the following day, taking a different tack. It was clear that Monsieur whatever-his-name-was was not interested. Clearly, the subject was not a comfortable one, and my father found out nothing. He told me this on his return. I thought: 'Oh. Not everyone likes to talk about it, then'.

Whatever side you were on, then, depending partly on where you happened to be, you might well have had a bad time of it. The fortunes of war might deny to some the honour of a known grave. But to some of those who survive it denies rather more. Bearable memories, in some cases. Dignity, in others. A subsequent life without anguish. Freedom from guilt, even if one believed in the justness of one's cause: the guilt of the survivor ('why me?'). Sufficient faith in human nature to keep one from killing oneself. Look at Primo Levi, the Italian concentration camp survivor and author of *If This is a Man*, who in the end, having done the major work of his lifetime by telling his story, jumped to his death in the stairwell of the block of flats in which he lived. (That book, and similar ones such as *Auschwitz: A Doctor's Eyewitness Account* by Miklós Nyiszli, I find almost too painful to read because they are so simply and directly written. Speaking so unemotionally of the unspeakable, the descriptions they contain of what took place have the paradoxical power to create extreme emotion in the reader.) Is the silence of such people maintained as self-protection, to prevent those perpetually painful memories nudging them towards the only way to free themselves from them, by ending their own lives?

*

In Tom Brown's I spoke with Tony.

'I'm not saying Alan hasn't done this pub up quite nicely,' he was saying, 'but it's still quite a traditional kind of place, like pubs used to be, isn't it? – I mean, years ago, you'd never see women in pubs. They just weren't there. Weren't welcome. And of course women do come in here, but it's still – ' and he glanced round.

'I think you get a lot more of that tradition in the North,' I said, and told him about one of the pubs Helen and I had visited in the centre of Leeds, which was quite obviously a male preserve, and although they weren't unfriendly, we'd felt uncomfortable when we went in together.

'My father would never think of taking a woman into a pub,' he said. 'He's a Scot, and all right, it's different up there again, but as far as he's concerned, you just don't do that kind of thing, it's not right. It's like when my wife started earning more than I did, he was astonished. I said, "Look, there have been times when I've earned more than her, but now, yes, she earns more than me, that's how it is". He just couldn't understand it. He's an intelligent man, but that's been the tradition in his life.'

'What did he do for a living?'

'He was in the Navy. He had an apprenticeship in engineering to start with, but he didn't like that, so he joined up. When he was sixteen. Before the war.'

'What kind of ships was he in?'

'Ended up as a captain of a destroyer. I don't really know much about it. He never talks about it.'

'That's a great shame.'

'Oh, he won't say anything. Changes the subject if I try to ask him. Maybe it was his experiences, I don't know. His ship was sunk, in the North Sea.'

'What, the one he was captain of?'

'Yes. Torpedoed.'

'And he survived.'

'Yeah. Not many did, I think.'

'That must be the worst thing that can happen to you, if you're the captain. Having your ship sunk underneath you. Maybe worse than for anyone else on board.' And to survive when many of your men, for whom you are responsible, didn't. 'He won't talk about it?'

'No. I think my mother might know more about it. But she wouldn't tell me. And I can't ask her, not really. It would be going behind his back. If I was to go behind his back, and try to find out things he doesn't want to talk about, he'd be mortally offended. I couldn't do that.'

'Pity … Old photographs, anything like that? Documents, records?'

'Very little. I've looked for them. But as far as I know, they're just not there. Maybe when he's dead, I might be able to find out more. But not while he's alive.'

'Did he stay in the Navy, after the war?'

'No. Left at the end of it.'

'Had enough, probably.'

'He's very against war. Vehemently against it.'

'Maybe if your experiences really are bad, then you want to put it behind you.'

'That's it, I think. He just wants to blank it out.'

'There are some things you could find out. There will be records of the movements of the ship, and all that. If she was sunk, there'll be official histories.'

'If I find out anything, I'll let you know,' he promised.

A few months later I asked him if he'd made any progress.

'Well as a matter of fact,' he said, 'he's died.'

I mouthed some condolences.

'And so has my mother. Just before Christmas. Died within eight days of one another. Emphysema he had. Mother had asthma. Both were heavy smokers. We were told she was in intensive care, so we flew up there, my brother and me, and discovered both of them were in intensive care. We flew back, she died, flew back up again, buried her, flew back again and then he died. Just gave up. He said, yeah, well, she's gone, that's it. He would have been no good without her. Used to rely on her ... I did try to find out some more about his war record. He probably told Mother at some time, but not me. It was his sister who told me. She's in America. No, she didn't come over for the funeral ... Lieutenant-Commander he was, in the marine commandos. Later he took part in the first wave of the D-day landings and lost most of his men in the assault. Never talked about that either. Apparently he was involved in a lot of hush-hush work. I didn't even know he was in the Marine Commando. No, I still don't know the name of the ship that was sunk under him. He left very little. A bit of paperwork. His medals. Nothing else.'

Thus there are those who suffered terribly, or, which may be worse, saw others suffer, and are left with a legacy of anxieties, night terrors, post-traumatic stress, mental breakdowns; an anguish that may be superficially healed but is never forgotten, and which, if the wrong questions are asked, or the wrong television programme seen, or for no identifiable reason, wells up unbidden and engulfs the consciousness in an uncontrollable flood.

*

Dinner at Mike and Carole's. Before the meal, whilst both the hosts were out of the room, I got up from a stool to pass round some nibbles. When I sat down the two rear legs gave way and I collapsed backwards against the radiator, though I did manage not to spill my gin. Everyone guffawed.

'There is a God!' spluttered Pete.

But before order could be restored, there was a rending sound, Pete yelped, and leaped out of his chair, leaving a ragged hole in the seat. The laughter was redoubled, and Mike and Carole returned to confront the wreckage of their sitting room.

Mike told us he was born in Australia. His father's parents had emigrated there, but his father felt it his duty to volunteer for the British forces during the war, and he came to England where he joined the RAF. He returned Down Under after the war with a Scots wife, but she didn't settle, and when Mike was six they all moved to England. And – joy upon joy! – his flying logbooks have now found their way into Mike's possession. He brought them out. They were immaculately hand-written, recording his father's training flights in 1941 in Tiger Moths, from which he progressed to Harvards and Oxfords. 'A bit heavy on the controls' was one supervisor's comment, but when he moved to Blenheims in 1942 his bombing skills were judged 'exceptional' and his photography 'above average'. He was finally assessed overall as 'above average', and from December 1943 to March 1945, with his five fellow crew – radio operator, navigator/bomb aimer, observer/nose gunner, tail gunner and waist gunner – he piloted a Wellington[1].

---

[1] De Havilland Tiger Moth: 1930s biplane. Harvard: American-built trainer (known in the USA as the North American T-6 Texan). Airspeed Oxford: twin-engined trainer. Bristol Blenheim: twin-engined light bomber. Vickers Wellington: twin-engined long-range medium bomber.

Pete, of course, was ecstatic, and at the end of the evening we left him there poring over them.

*

At tennis, Pete and I discussed which sides of the court we should take.

'I think we're best like this,' he said, resolutely striding to the left-hand side.

'It could relate to the position you sleep in,' I mused. 'Right, left ... Which side of the bed do you sleep on?'

'On top.'

'You traditionalist.'

'Except when I'm really lucky,' he said.

Later, in the pub, we talked about anger.

'Where anger is denied in a family,' Charles said loftily, 'you cannot have effective separation of children from their parents. Anorexics,' he went on, 'always come from families where the emotions are kept on a tight rein and no-one's allowed to get angry with anyone else, and arguments are banned. Love is made conditional. "If you disagree with me, or if you get angry, then I won't love you." And although the parents may get angry inside with their children, they don't ever allow themselves to show it, and in those families it is therefore not all right for anger to be expressed by anyone.'

We had a discussion about this, and because Charles put one point of view, I put the other: that yes, you need to be able to disagree, but this does not necessarily mean overt arguments, or acting out one's anger. You can disagree quietly. You can be sullen and uncommunicative, rather than loudly argumentative.

'Yes,' he said, 'but a lot of my patients are hung-up people who haven't separated from their parents because they haven't dared disagree with them. Disagreements aren't permitted. It's all too controlled.'

'Yeah, but you don't have to have a stand-up fight,' I protested.

'You can have a situation where people don't speak to each other for years,' said Pete. 'My mother's siblings, for example. Talk about not getting on! And if her twin brother had been around, there would have been even more of them to quarrel.'

'Twin brother?' queried Nick.

'The one I was named after.'

'Oh yeah. Remind me. What did he do?'

'He was a Spitfire pilot. Shot down in the war. I went to the Public Record Office, you know, the one at Kew. I managed to find it, all the stuff about his unit. The squadron records. What you've got is a complete history, every day, what they did. Each incident of the day was recorded by the duty officer. And most of the entries, they just show how random and haphazard it all was. And how little happened. For most of the time, nothing.'

'So what would be in the book?'

'"0945 hrs, enemy bombers reported 12 miles south-west of Dungeness, course north-north-west. Squadron-Leader X and Flight Officer Y sent to intercept, reported back 1030, nothing found". There's a lot of that. "Three planes sent to investigate, nothing further to report". The interesting thing,' he went on, 'really poignant, was on the day he was shot down there was a record of him taking off, he was sent to investigate a sighting or something, and then, instead of saying when he came back, what time he landed, like in previous entries, there was just – a dot.' He punctuated the air with his finger.

Nick said, 'This is great, Pete. Having an uncle who flew a Spitfire in the war, and was shot down! We'd all like to have that in his family history. So you go for it. Find out all you can. We're all with you. You're not just doing it for yourself, you're doing it for us.'

'It does gets obsessional,' Pete said. 'I don't know why. These things in the past. My mother, yes, she is quite interested, but I think she's a bit surprised at *me* being interested. I think what she feels is, at the time it happened, it was just an ordinary event, the sort of thing that happened to a lot of people, and you kind of expected it. You didn't take any particular note of all the surrounding detail.'

*

At a drinks party I spoke with Cathy, a few years older than me.

'I found the telegram on top of the kitchen cupboard,' she said. 'When it came, and my mother opened it, I knew something had happened. But she didn't tell me. She hid it. But I looked for it, and there it was. I was only five. I must have stood on a chair or something. There were some long words in it, and I didn't understand all of them, but I must have got the gist of it.'

Her father had been reported missing. He had been in a Lancaster bomber shot down over Alsace. It was known that some of the crew had baled out. But for two years there was no news of him.

'So you were three when you last saw him? Do you remember him?' I asked.

'Yes! – oh, yes … When it happened, my mother dreamt about it. She had a dream about his plane being shot down. And her sister, my aunt, who lived just along the road, she had a dream too, and it was exactly the same, and they compared notes, and they'd had the dream at the same time of night. Then when they checked with the authorities who told them the time the plane had gone down, my mother said, oh no, it was just a coincidence, because the time of the dreams wasn't the same as the time of the crash. But then of course they realised there was the hour's difference between the local time in France and the time here … You see, at the time, my mother never spoke of it. It wasn't talked about. Those two years, she had to hang on without knowing, and somehow she coped. Somehow. Because you had to. There were lots of families who lost someone. It happened to everyone. You didn't complain about it. People just got on with their lives. It didn't do to make any kind of a fuss … Isn't it interesting that I became a bereavement counsellor? And my mother never went to see his grave. His parents never did, either. But Phil and I went, a couple of years ago. It was there; there were three graves, and there were flowers on them. We did it all through the War Graves Commission, and I must say they were extremely helpful. A tiny village it was, with this minute church, and just these three headstones, together.'

'Did you speak to anyone?' I asked, a scenario going through my mind involving poignant conversations with locals ('last saw my father when I was three, missing for two years, mother never visited, yes this is the first time, what a peaceful place, I'm so glad to have come'), all conducted in broken French with sympathetic and considerate villagers. But no.

'We did go into the church, and there were some people there, some very ancient village folk, but you see, all over that area, there are hundreds of these graves, and as far as they're concerned, this is always happening, people coming over from England and America. One visitor is the same as any other, and they see them every week ... My father was the navigator. He was much older than the others, he was 32, and he was the only one who had a wife and child. The others were all aged twenty. Twenty! It doesn't bear thinking about, what they did at that age. The pilot survived, along with the tail-gunner. He was sort of sucked out of the aeroplane, but my father, and the others, they remained inside, and went down with it ... I think he somehow felt responsible for me. He came to see us after the war. You see we hadn't known exactly what had happened. We had the telegram, in 1944, that said he was missing, but we didn't know for two years whether he was dead, or alive in some prisoner-of-war camp or perhaps hidden in a friendly French village.'

'Two years?' I asked. 'He was shot down in 1944? The war ended in 1945.'

'Ah, yes,' she explained, 'but the arrangements for releasing prisoners of war from the camps didn't all get sorted out until 1946, and the pilot had been captured, he'd spent the rest of the war as a prisoner. Anyway, he came to see us then. His family were very protective of him, because there he was, a twenty-one-year-old, and my mother, single with me, in her thirties, and they thought she might try to trap him. Because with a child to support, of course she could have done with a husband. And that was the last time I saw him – until the other day, when he got in contact again. To start with, he advertised for me, but he got no joy. But he managed to track me down. My maiden name, my father's name, was Tillotson, but his middle name was Lever, because there was a connection with Lever Brothers, you know? – the soap people. And he – the pilot – guessed it might have had something to do with them, so he wrote to them, and because there *was* a connection, he managed to trace me.' Her voice almost broke. 'He was so pleased to see me. He hugged me. He's a gorgeous old chap of 76. Doesn't look it. I think he still felt some sort of responsibility, even though my mother married again.'

'Are you writing this down, making a record of this so your children have it?' I asked, 'so it's passed down? Otherwise it'll be lost.'

'I think that's why he came to see me,' she said. 'To establish some sort of continuity. This is the important thing, the continuity, the connections.'

*

A little later at Cathy and Phil's house I met him, Douglas Bridges, the pilot of the Lancaster. He turned out nearly as loquacious as the Ancient Mariner, but, unlike the wedding-guest detained by Coleridge's greybeard, I was delighted to be regaled with his tale.

Cathy's father had been with the crew for only two sorties. The previous navigator had been transferred to other duties out of the squadron, because on two successive occasions he had refused to fly on when the plane, fully loaded with fuel and bombs, reached the assembly point in the air before continuing to Germany. He'd apparently met a girl, and decided to shirk it. With a non-co-operative navigator, the pilot had had no option but to abort the mission and return to the airfield.

Douglas told me he'd thought a good deal about the question why he had survived and others didn't. He had spent some years tracing the families of the others in the plane at the time.

'Some of them are interested and some aren't. The brother of one of them, for instance, he said, "Well, it's history, and I'm not interested". And you have to respect that.'

He also made clear his feeling of responsibility. He had been the pilot. If they could, pilots would often continue to fly their planes until everyone else had had a chance to get out, before attempting to escape themselves.

'The plane that shot us down was a Messerschmitt 110, and he'd done the right thing and shot the fuel tank rather than the engine, because then there'd be a fire you wouldn't be able to put out. What a fighter pilot would do, he'd come up alongside to take our number, otherwise he couldn't be credited with the shooting-down when he landed. That's what he did, and I saw him looking at us, and then of course he was off. We were on autopilot at the time, and my co-pilot shut the engine down, feathered the blades perhaps just a bit too soon. He thought it was the engine that was on fire, but whereas if we'd realised it was the fuel tank, then we

85

could have kept on flying for a little bit more on full power, all four engines, and possibly people could have baled out. But with only three engines, we were probably losing speed, and suddenly it was too much for the autopilot and the plane just flipped over, went into a spin, and I don't know why, I just found myself floating free in the sky. Parachute opened. I was so lucky. I could see the trees below, and the parachute got caught in them, and I didn't hit the ground, I was left dangling. I hadn't been strapped in, you see. I'd changed to a different sort of parachute two days previously, to a type where you didn't have to be strapped into the aircraft, and you'd just fall free without having to unstrap yourself. Two days! You look back at that, and think, well, why? That piece of luck ... Then of course the place to try to get to was Switzerland, neutral country. I was on my way down the road and I spotted this other chap in the bushes, and I said to him, "You're not very well hidden!" He was a survivor from one of the other planes that had been shot down.'

So they set off, but were captured, and sent to Stalag Luft III (from which the Great Escape[1] had taken place). He remained there until February 1945, when he was transferred to another camp, at Bremen.

'It was run by the Luftwaffe, and of course there was great respect between them and us, and we were very well treated.' In later years he met the pilots of some of the Messerschmitts that had been around on the day he was shot down.

---

[1] A mass escape via tunnels of 76 Allied prisoners of war, in March 1943. Most were caught and shot.

'We've had reunions. Of course, in bombers you were that much further from the action. You didn't see the sort of things that soldiers saw, because you flew to your target, you dropped your bombs and didn't see the effect they had.'

He still has that guilt at surviving, the same syndrome as Primo Levi, whose suicide took place at 76, the same age Douglas was when I met him. For his part, Douglas was working through the obsession by travelling up and down to Kew to look at the war service records. 'Of course, I couldn't do earlier because of records being kept secret for thirty years. It's only been in the last ten or fifteen years I've been able to do this.'

'I think memories get clearer at that age,' said Cathy to me afterwards.

*

'How's your father?' I asked Dikko, old flatmate of mine from student days, Welsh as the valleys.

'I pick him up from his residential home at ten. Drive him down to Wetherspoons. We have a tea and a coffee. I don't have any alcohol because there are things I need to do later in the day. But he does. Rosé, Nige, it's fashionable just at the moment. Everyone loves him.'

'How old is he?'

'Ninety-one. Women, they're all over him. Young ones, they say, "Hello Glyn, how are you?", and the thirty-year olds, them as well, all the way up to those who are his age. He's got a swagger about him, a bit of presence. He still tells good stories. But not so many about the war. Must be one of the few remaining ex-Japanese POWs. He was in Singapore. When they found out the Japs were on the way he was playing hockey. Most of the others in the team were the enlisted men – Indians, you know, wizard with the stickwork but a touch temperamental. His superior officer came up to him at half-time and said, "I think it'll be best if you don't play the second half." So he had to come off and help plan for the invasion. When was it the Japs got to Singapore? – '42[1], I think it might have been. Spent the rest of the time as a prisoner. At one time he was in the *Bridge on the River Kwai* camp.'

'What! – with Alec Guinness[2]?'

'Ha! – yes. The only other story he told was about the flag on top of the British Embassy. The official line is that it was saved and brought back to this country. He knew for a fact that wasn't true. You know, everyone was alarmed at the prospect of the Japs arriving, because they knew how brutal they were to the enemies they had defeated. But there was one subaltern in particular who Glyn says, his nerves were shot to pieces. And to give this man something to do, so as to take his mind off it all, he said, "Come on, we're going to go up on the roof and rescue the flag". So they climbed up the stairs to take it down, and this young chap suddenly turned round and threw himself off the parapet. My Dad took the flag down, and buried him in it in the grounds of the embassy. Of course, there may have been more than one flag. But that's what happened to the one that was flying.'

---

[1] February 1942.

[2] Alec Guinness played the British commanding officer in the semi-fictional film *The Bridge on the River Kwai* (1957).

*

Hanging in a little triangular corner cupboard on the landing of Helen's friends Mary and Pope's isolated house in Welsh border country I noticed a Military Cross. Pope's father had apparently been awarded it during WWII, but had never mentioned it. Pope had found out what he'd done by investigating the internet records a few years back. It was all there, the history of some battle in the Burma campaign during which he'd stuck to his machine gun post in the face of concerted enemy fire. When he died, Pope's mother had given his medals to his sister, Pope's aunt. Years later, after the aunt had also died, her son had written to him to say he now had them but didn't know why, and thought they should be Pope's.

So there was his father's MC, in its little wooden cabinet; and at some time in the future, perhaps, it will appear in some auctioneer's saleroom; and unless someone has taken the trouble to attach its provenance, the story will die.

6

... and over here

'Almost all the young men had gone. There were only old men and the heads of families left. Five years without a man is a long time. Of course the women slept with Germans.'

The words are those of an inhabitant of Villeret in north-west France, speaking of events during the First World War. They are recorded by Ben Macintyre in *A Foreign Field*. If the women of a village will sleep with the invading forces, how much more likely is it that they will do so with men from other countries on their own side? In Macintyre's book the central event is the birth of a daughter to one of the local girls and a British soldier being sheltered by the village.

But stronger still is the likelihood that young women will consort with members of allied forces with whom they already share a language. The phrase 'overpaid, overfed, oversexed and over here' is associated with the comedian Tommy Trinder, but it had wider and more seriously-taken currency than most catchphrases. It reflected a certain degree of truth, together with jealousy on the part of the men of the country whose womenfolk's hearts they stole. It was what was said of the American servicemen who arrived in Britain after the USA had entered the war in late 1941; and one statistic I've seen is that 9,000 babies were born out of wedlock as a result of their liaisons. How many were left here, when the Yanks returned home? Most of them, I'd guess.

Where do people with only half a family history get their identity? There are enough of them, Lord knows; it's hardly unusual for a woman to bring up a child on her own. 'Who is my Daddy?' If you're unlucky, the subject might immediately be changed, and you'd learn not to ask. But otherwise you might get: 'His name's George.' (Or: 'His name *was* George'.) 'Where is my Daddy?' 'He had to go back to America.' You get half the history from one of your parents and the other half is mostly missing. You see films about America. You read the papers. You construct the story for yourself. But one day you might want to test it. To know for sure. You do some digging, and maybe you find out.

And if you can't find out, you are left with the story you made up, because that is all you have. That is what you tell to *your* children. I read once that our greatest need after a nuclear holocaust would be not for doctors and builders, who would put back together our bodies and houses, but for storytellers, people who would give us that sense of history and destiny which marks us out as human. At the time, I thought it was poppycock, but perhaps the writer merely overstated the case; there might have been a modicum of truth in it. But the storytellers would need to be practised. They would have to tell the tales with no hindrances to the flow, no ums or ers or I-can't-remembers or what-was-his-name-nows. The combination of content on the one hand, and style of delivery on the other, would have to be forceful enough to take us out of ourselves and into other worlds. And it is not only the long tales, the sagas that would be needed. You would want the little ones, the ones that gave a flavour of a life in which, however long ago it was lived, the protagonists were not mythical heroes from a perfect age, but fallible. Human, and brief enough not to be lost in a succession of Chinese whispers down the decades. Like the one my father used to tell about his older brother Harry. One day when Harry was about five, the local vicar came to the house to pay his respects.

'And is Harry a good little boy then, hmm?' asked the vicar, patting Harry on the head.

'Oh, I think so, aren't you, Harry dear?' beamed their mother.

'Yes,' Harry agreed, thoughtfully. 'But I says "bugger" sometimes.'

*

That would have been shortly before the First World War, not the Second. But wherever they are set, such stories are not only *about* the past. For the people who hear them, they *become* the past. That is what the past is. It is the words spoken by our fathers and mothers; and when the storytellers after Armageddon manage to find themselves the means of setting it all down in books, that history will be fixed a little better for our children's children.

Except that books get thrown away.

I went to Iain's house to borrow a router, to make a decorative edging on the wooden shelves I'd decided to put up above the computer.

'It's the only place in the entire house where there's any wall space left,' I said.

'What are they for?'

'Oh ... Books. They're just lying about on tables. Piled up. I've got some in the loft in boxes, already. Books from college those are, mainly. The other stuff – you know, novels, encyclopaedias, books about the war – they're all downstairs.'

'So you'll put them on the shelves. What'll happen to them?'

'Well, they'll just ... stay there.'

He looked at me. 'Yeah. They'll stay there. And then when you move house, you'll wonder what on earth to do with them, why you kept them. Or when you peg it, your kids'll say, "What the hell's this lot?" And they'll bin them.'

He's probably right, I thought. Then I thought: Maybe the novels, or most of them. But surely not the books about the war. Those are *important*. Part of my history. Not only my history but that of my parents *and* my children. And won't they recognise that? I shall need to put a note on the cover of the ones I think they ought to keep. 'Do not throw away. This is part of your heritage. This is what made you.' Will they take notice?

*

Resentment of the extravagance and amorous tendencies of the American troops was countered by tales of their alleged military incompetence. According to my father there was the remark by a German airman, taken prisoner by the British after being shot down, who told his captors, 'Ven ze Luftwaffe fly over, ze Allies duck. Ven ze RAF fly over, ze Chermans duck. Ven ze Americans fly over, everybody ducks!'

Of course, as my father said, we could not have done without the Americans. In 1966 France, which for decades after the war had an uneasy relationship with the USA, no doubt tied up with their mixed feelings about having needed to be rescued by them, announced that they would withdraw their forces from the integrated NATO command and develop their independent defence capability. The French President, Charles de Gaulle, who had been the leader of the Free French forces – the Resistance – but of necessity spent most of the war exiled in London, demanded that all US servicemen be removed from its soil. Lyndon Johnson, the US president, was outraged. Referring to the thousands of Americans buried in France, from both world wars, Johnson (who himself had been a combatant in WWII, if very briefly) is reputed to have said, 'Does that include the dead ones?'[1]

*

---

[1] This sounds apocryphal but internet research confirms that in essence the story is true. France rejoined NATO in 2009, under President Nicolas Sarkozy.

Even though my parents were from the same country, they too were from entirely different backgrounds, and would never have married had it not been for the war. The classes in Britain in the first half of the 20th century were more clearly defined than today. There was the upper class – the aristocracy, the landed gentry, the titled, the inheritors of great wealth. There was the upper middle class, the professions such as law and medicine and the directors of large businesses, possessors of more moderate but still comfortable monetary means, many of whom would have had investments as well as earned income to support them. Next there was the lower middle class, consisting of shopkeepers, traders, small businessmen, and perhaps less-well-paid professionals such as teachers, nurses and clerks. And finally there was the working class, including labourers, factory hands, shop assistants and railway workers.

My father's father was a bricklayer, a man who, though respectably brought up and married, was destined – because of his own origins as the son of farming folk in Somerset – to learn a trade and eke out his living in employment which would never allow him or his family to live by means other than extremely modest. He became a site foreman, presiding over the building of the great red brick Wills tobacco factory in Bristol. When I was about eleven I was taken, with my sister, on a tour of the premises with its intricate, oily, clacking machinery producing the endless cigarette which, a little further down the production line, was cut into three-inch lengths to be packed together in tens and twenties. The building, alas, was pulled down during the 1970s to be replaced in its function by a spanking new steel and glass edifice on the outskirts of the city, later itself to be made redundant as the tobacco industry continued its decline. The old building survives only as a portion of its façade, hiding a shopping mall.

My mother, by contrast, was the daughter of a village doctor in Surrey, and the family lived, if not richly, at any rate comfortably. Her father married into a family which could trace its ancestry back to Louis XIV of France, via a mistress of his who later married a doctor and emigrated to England. (If this is interesting, it is so only because someone, or several people over a number of years, took the trouble to keep or rediscover records and make a note of them. Take back almost any family tree a few generations and you will uncover links to someone in the history books.) The family was well respected in the community; they lived in a large house in the village, and prospered. There were servants: a couple of maids, a cook, and a general factotum who looked after the horses and the motor-cars. Upper middle class would have been an apt designation.

The marriage, then, between my mother and my father was an unlikely one. That it happened at all was due to the great leveller, the Second World War. Whilst the conflagration by no means eliminated class distinctions in Britain, it did cause members of the various classes to mix more freely than before, and paved the way for a greater lowering of those barriers in the second half of the twentieth century. They met when both were working in a reception centre for the wounded at New Malden on the southern outskirts of London. My mother had trained as a dispenser (of medicines, a job usually associated with chemist's shops), and had worked before the war for her father, whose surgery, and dispensary, were at the family home. My father was then a sergeant in the Royal Army Medical Corps. They married in early 1944, and their first child, a girl, was born in December of that year; I was born two years later, and our brother five years after that.

Because of these two distinct strands of my family's history, from time to time I was aware of a certain tension. This hardly ever manifested itself overtly between my father and mother, who temperamentally speaking appeared to me to complement one another. Perhaps more to the point, they came from backgrounds which, although very different in material wealth, had a shared understanding of manners, morals, social expectations and respect. But on occasions when there was contact with either his family or hers, then, just discernible to my sister and me as children, there were undertones of disdain on the one side and bruised pride on the other. These were expressed by nothing more tangible than tone of voice, or pursing of lips; hardly ever did insinuation spill over into statement. My sister and I were aware of the undercurrents, and felt sorry for our relatives on our father's side. But we did not feel ashamed of them; and perhaps that was because, in spite of our father's success in elevating himself, we did feel they had an adequate self-respect of their own.

After both my parents had died I was at liberty to ask my mother's sister Betty, who lived to a great age, to tell me of those early days. She acknowledged the class divide: 'In our father's eyes – your grandfather of course – your father was saved by being good at athletics. But ... of course, now I wouldn't say he was ignorant, but he wasn't as well educated as we were. So he did have a lot to learn. Stoking boilers, yes: you can't get much lower than that … Do you remember Arthur's wife, Mary? – When she met Victor, he had a habit of having his hands behind his back, and of course speaking in his Somerset accent. She said, "Dreadful common man! Wiped his hand behind him, and then stuck it out to me and said 'Pleased to meet yer'!"'

I thought: perhaps at the time it was polite behaviour amongst manual workers, in the absence of running water and clean towel, to do just that. But who knows? Tiny social habits, amongst other manifestations of the age into which one is born, change over the years, and are forgotten.

*

It wasn't just the Americans who came over here to help us out. On the outskirts of Lymington, on the way to see my mother, I stopped at the Tollhouse Inn, previously the Monkey House, previously the Crown. Three or four men, mostly the same age as me, were moderately chatty in a lightly-oiled early-eveningish sort of way. An elderly man came in, with thick glasses.

'Hello, Charlie,' said the landlord, and another bloke at the bar, simultaneously.

'I've only come in for some fags,' said Charlie. 'Just been to Safeway. Done some shopping. And I got home, and I looked in me fag packet, and I only had five left. And *they* won't do me, tonight and tomorrow morning. Oh, bugger, I thought, I should have looked before I went to the supermarket, then I could have got 'em there; better go out to the pub and get some.'

'So you haven't come in for a drink, then?' said the landlord, pleasantly.

'Well, now I'm here,' said Charlie. 'Heh, heh!'

'You've done this before, haven't you, Charlie?' said the other man at the bar, smoothing his red jumper down over his paunch.

Charlie looked at him. 'Yes,' he said.

'More than once.'

'Yes,' Charlie acknowledged, agreeably.

'How is it?' asks the landlord, turning to me.

'Mmm. Not bad at all,' I said.

'A nice mouthful,' he agreed. 'Malty. You get a good flavour round the back of your palate. – Here's a question for you,' he said to Redjumper, and anyone else listening. 'Who was Captain Charles Upham? What's significant about him? He died just recently.'

'He was ... let's see. He was the last surviving man to win two V.C.s,' said Redjumper.

'Right. There weren't very many. And he was the only one left. And his obituary was in the *Telegraph* the other day. Very good. New Zealander, he was. Pilot.'

'You just read the obituaries, do you?' asked another.

'Oh, they're quite interesting.'

'Yes,' I interrupted, repeating Pete's remarks of a few weeks previously. 'They're all dying, aren't they? All those veterans of the Second World War, they're in their seventies and eighties now. You get one or two good obituaries every day. You can get a comprehensive history of the war, reading those.'

At the other end of the bar another man was poring over the *Telegraph* crossword. He'd done most of it, but there were a few clues he couldn't get. The barman gave him some hints. It turned out he'd already completed his copy of it that morning. I tried to help as well, but on a Biblical reference got mixed up between Noah's sons and Adam's.

When I left, the pint of beer sat pleasantly in the bottom of my stomach and there was no vague uneasy feeling. But there should have been. In the Air Force there is no such rank as Captain. Group Captain, yes, but not plain Captain, as in the Army and Navy. 'Captain Charles Upham', the landlord had said. 'Pilot.' Later I looked up the information. He wasn't a pilot at all. He'd been an infantry officer, earning his first V.C. in Crete in 1941 and the second in the Western Desert the following year.

Upham was, by all accounts, diffident about his achievements, maintaining – along with a great many soldiers who survive a war, whether or not they were decorated – that 'anyone would have done it'. If that is so, then surely it is presupposed that the 'anyone' of the phrase is a person who has already accepted his possible fate. John Keegan[1] was discussing it one day when I turned the radio to *Desert Island Discs*.

'Soldiers are not driven by money,' he said. 'That is not what they are motivated by. They are a race apart. They are different from other people, because they have mortgaged their future. They have settled up ahead of

---

[1] Military historian; author of, amongst other books, *The Face of Battle*.

time, as the Americans would put it. They don't like war, but when one comes round then they do what they have to do. They know what the limitations of violence are, what violence can and can't settle, and they know it can't settle much. They are quite realistic about that. A very senior general said to me recently, "Violence almost never decides anything".' (I thought: what about the threat of violence, then?) 'I only learned by accident that in order to understand what happened in a battle, it is essential to go to the battlefield. You can't understand Little Bighorn[1] unless you go there. It looks so peculiar on the map. They were all killed – the whole of Custer's party, seventh cavalry, about two hundred men. There *was* a last stand, on a little mound. And when you stand on it, you see stretching out, in a line, leading away to where the charge started, little white dots in the scrub. And these are the headstones of the soldiers, and they are buried where they fell; and in one glance I understood what had happened in the battle, which I had not been able to make out at all, either from the descriptions or from the maps. With a single sweep of vision, there it all was. That's unusual, you don't usually get that on a battlefield, but nevertheless you always discover something.'

'The point that's often made about war through the ages,' remarked Sue Lawley, the interviewer, 'is that it's moved across from hand-to-hand combat in the Middle Ages to this sort of long-distance, long range deadly stuff – you know, you could be killed by a cruise missile which

---

[1] Site in Montana of Custer's 'Last Stand', 1876, in the war against the American Sioux Indians led by Sitting Bull.

you didn't even know was coming. It makes the warrior through the ages a very different creature, doesn't it, because now the warrior can kill a hundred men at a stroke, but he probably couldn't kill one hand to hand – '

'Well, I wouldn't bet on it,' interrupted Keegan. 'He doesn't often get to that sort of close quarters, nowadays. At Agincourt, in the fifteenth century, it was the only sort of war there was. Medieval man was altogether more bloodthirsty and realistic about life and death, the taking of life, than anybody in the Western world today. War represents one aspect of civilisation; it is completely uncivilised in one way, but a dutiful and well-trained moral army is an instrument of civilisation. Look what goes on in Bosnia: what stands between innocent people and bestiality are precisely these highly motivated, civilised soldiers from the Western armies.'

7

We Did It at School

Of all my father's tales, my favourite was the one about the stick of bombs.

He was a sergeant at the time, resident in south London at the receiving-station for injured soldiers where he met my mother. Bombs were dropped in clusters, and because the aircraft releasing them was moving, they would land one after the other in a straight line, the second falling perhaps fifty yards from the first, the third another fifty yards further on, and so on. Woken early one morning by the sound of enemy aircraft overhead, my father heard the noise of a bomb exploding uncomfortably close, a field or two behind the house in which he was billeted. A moment later there was another explosion, this time closer. A third followed, and he realised the bombs were heading directly for the house. He leapt out of bed and dived underneath it, for a hit on the building or very close to it would likely bring the ceiling down, or worse, and the bed would provide some, if frail, protection. There was a further huge explosion at the end of the back garden, and he shut his eyes waiting for his end to come. Fortunately, the next bomb fell not on the house, but harmlessly on the other side of the road, its explosion rocking the building and rattling the windows.

My father scrambled out from his temporary refuge and climbed back into bed. A second later there was a banging of doors and a clattering of feet on the stairs. His corporal burst into the room.

'Sarge! D'you hear that bomb?'

My father looked at him poker-faced.

'Bomb? What bomb?'

The corporal stared at him open-mouthed.

'Bleedin' 'ell!' he exclaimed. 'Bastard's bleedin' deaf,' and he turned and ambled from the room.

I heard my father tell that story at least three times; and each time I joined in his roar of laughter as he finished. 'Bomb? What bomb? Hahahaha!' And after he'd told it, especially as I grew older, I used to think: Nothing like this has happened to me so far, and I don't see any prospect of anything as interesting ever happening in the future; so what on earth am I going to do when my children expect me to tell them what I did when I was younger?

Not that my father enthralled all of us. My sister was frequently impatient with his repetitions, my brother rarely interested at all. I was the only one who not only enjoyed listening, but did not mind stories being told again and again. I'd say, 'What about the time when – ', and he'd reply, 'I've told you that before, haven't I? You don't want to hear that again,' and my sister would say,

'Not particularly', but I'd say, 'Well, yes, but I can't quite remember what happened,' even though I knew it word for word. And he'd tell the whole thing again. It wasn't just the war. He'd tell stories about his running (athletics meetings on summer Saturdays, in those days as popular as football in the winter), or his early experiences with motor cars (very unreliable, and inclined to catch fire at any time), or the one about the time he was born. This, he told us, was the exact moment when the local football team Bristol City scored the goal which clinched promotion to the First Division. 'My Pa was at the game,' he said, 'and there was a huge roar from the crowd, and my Ma got such a shock she gave one last heave! – and out I popped.'

It wasn't until after he died, which meant that unfortunately I was unable to discuss it with him, that I discovered he could not have been right. I'd given a book on the Football League to one of my sons for his birthday, and it contained every final league table from every year of its history, and I looked up the year in question, which was 1910, and found that Bristol City weren't promoted at all. But I was only slightly disappointed, because, from the position of the team in the league at the end of the season, namely third from bottom, it was clear that if any goal had been scored at that crucial moment, then, although it couldn't have been the one that clinched promotion, it might very well have been the one that saved them from relegation.

I said to him once: 'It seems to me that you either had a good time in the war or a terrible time. Nothing in between. If you didn't get killed or seriously injured, then you had a good time; but if you did, then obviously you didn't.'

'Yes. Generally speaking, yes.'

Reading what some people have written, and listening to what others say, it wasn't as simple as that. But there was a kernel of truth in that summary. The war did give large numbers of people something else to do from their pre-war lives (and unemployment had been high in the 1930s), and something to look back on in later life if they were so inclined.

In much the same way, if you were at boarding school after the war then joining the cadet force provided some distraction from the academic grind. Some days it involved cleaning rifles and oiling them and marching up and down with them, but only rarely did it come anywhere near using them. There was a Friday afternoon parade and there were annual camps. And then there was the occasional day trip.

*

It takes me about twenty minutes to walk to Tom Brown's. If I go alone then I often find myself whistling. I make no particular effort to choose a tune; it wells up from somewhere within. Sometimes there are a few bars from a sixties pop song, like *I Want To Stay Here* by Eydie Gormé and Steve Lawrence, or *It Doesn't Matter Any More* by Buddy Holly. Sometimes there is a hymn tune, reinforced by countless church services during my early years, and in the cathedral of the town where I was at boarding school. There might be a nursery rhyme I used to sing with my children, one with a strong rhythm like

Bobby Shafto. And then there is another tune, a stirring marching song which most people know as 'British Grenadiers'.

But dotted about the country are perhaps a dozen members of an exclusive band, erstwhile members of the Hereford Cathedral School Combined Cadet Force who took part in a trip to Salisbury Plain in 1963, who know it by another name. 'British Grenadiers' it may be to others, but to these Corps veterans it will never be called by anything else but the curious name of 'Hot Lumpy'.

The words of this song were invented by Jeremy, the then Company Sergeant-Major, following the inspiration of one of our number with a droll sense of humour whose name was Roger, and were the glorious pinnacle of three hours of aching laughter at the back of a school bus.

The day was grey, the journey to the Army encampment at Larkhill tedious, and the events dull. The Army authorities treated us to a variety of delights of the general flavour and bathos which are best recalled by Spike Milligan in *Adolf Hitler: My Part in his Downfall*. In the middle of it, we were ordered back on to the bus to have lunch. This consisted of mugs of a strikingly nondescript soup – or 'soup', as I think it would be more accurate, typographically speaking, to represent it. We looked at it suspiciously.

'What *is* it?' someone asked.

There was a low sound of voices, as we searched for words which would describe it; after much struggling, one of our number observed that it was hot. Roger, with his fixed smile, and high-pitched Harry Secombe Goon-like voice, made a natural cheerleader.

'Hot!' he cried, standing in the aisle of the bus holding his mug aloft; 'yes, it's . . . ' (pause) 'hot. Let's call it . . . (pause again) "Hot".' Murmurings of assent: hot it was, agreed the rest of us; this proposition was passed *nem. con.*, and 'Hot' was what we decided to name it. It was a satisfactorily economical little word for something that was, after all, pretty economical on flavour, and attractiveness, and indeed everything else.

'Are you enjoying your Hot?' we said to each other. 'Hmm! I see you've managed to get yourself a bigger helping of Hot than me.' 'Be careful with that Hot! You'll burn your tongue if you swig it too quickly.' There was a slurping sound from the length of the bus; conversation fell away for a minute or two, as we racked our collective brain for other words of description. At last, someone else noticed that there was, after all, another property possessed by this substance. It appeared to have lumps in it. No-one could venture a guess as to what those lumps might consist of; even their colour was somehow impossible to label. We supposed, then, that it might be described as 'lumpy'.

A moment later, in that inspired way in which natural leaders command the loyalty of their followers, Roger gave expression to the thought that was half-forming somewhere in the minds of the rest of us. He drew himself up, spread his hands, and announced, triumphantly: 'It's ... hot?' (and here he looked around the throng, inviting our agreement; as one man, we nodded, and waited for the next part of the speech), 'and it's ... lumpy.' He had us in the palm of his hand. 'It must be called ... "Hot" ... ' (a long pause here) ... '"Lumpy".' '"Hot Lumpy"!'

'Hot Lumpy!' we yelled, in unison; yes, it was hot, and, most certainly, it was lumpy. 'Hot Lumpy'. What else could it possibly be named? What was in it, no-one had the faintest idea; what it tasted of, we could not be sure; what anonymous W. D.[1] chef had invented the recipe, no-one wished to know: but what was absolutely certain was that it had two characteristics only, and by them it was to be known. Hot Lumpy.

After that, the rest of the day, peppered as it was by foolish activities such as running to a tank by numbers[2] and climbing on it by numbers and looking around it by numbers and getting off it by numbers, firing a 25-pounder gun by numbers, and, I don't doubt, finally getting on the coach for the return trip by numbers, was punctuated by gales of laughter as one person after another gave voice to ever-more bizarre or revolting things that might be done to, with, or in that 'soup'.

And when the bus finally departed there was still no let-up. An hour went by; the jokes became more and more outrageous and the laughter was continuous. Everyone was too full of glee to notice Jeremy, sitting quietly by the window, looking pre-occupied, joining in only fitfully. But suddenly he jumped up out of his seat.

'Wait!' he shouted. 'Everyone listen! I've got it! Okay now,' and, to the rousing tune of British Grenadiers, he sang:

---

[1] War Department.

[2] 'By numbers': in the military this refers to performing a sequence of actions step by step, each move being made on the call of a number: 'On the count of 1, you are to run to the tank! On the count of 2, climb on the tank! Squaaad ... WAIT FOR IT! ... *One*!' (etc.).

Some talk of Yorkshire pudding
And some of Cheshire cheese.
Some think of raspberry jelly
And such great names as these.
But of all the world's great fancy foods
There's none will make you grumpy
Like the slip-slop-slip-slop-slip-slop-slip
Of W. D. Hot Lumpy[1].

How we cheered! How we roared! How we shouted, and stamped our feet, and clapped the author on the back! If some of us had never cried with laughter before, we certainly did then. And the journey back to Hereford, those hundred miles, flew by like no other coach trip before or since.

The following year Jeremy went part-way towards the destiny presaged by this achievement, and into the Army. Sadly, though, he failed to follow what would clearly have been the most appropriate route, namely into the Catering Corps.

*

In a second-hand bookshop in Bournemouth I find a volume named *Rovering to Success*, by Lord Baden-Powell. It is manual for young men, full of advice, and anecdotes to back it up. 'You Young Fellows!' it says on

[1] The first verse of the original runs: Some talk of Alexander / And some of Hercules / Of Hector and Lysander / And such great names as these / But of all the world's great heroes / There's none that can compare / With a tow, row row row, row row row / To the British Grenadiers.

the back of the dust-jacket. 'A book intended to help young men of all classes to get on the right track and make the best of their lives.' The frontispiece, a line drawing by the author showing a canoeist making his way between several large rocks each topped by an unlikely figure, is explained: 'This picture-chart of your voyage to success shows some of the bigger rocks that you have to look out for. There is a bright side to the darkest rock … you gain "character" as you round each rock and you gain your goal of Happiness in the end … ' Rock Number One is Horses: 'The dark side of this Rock is the loafing and betting at races and football, and prize-fighting. The bright side the active enjoyment of true sport and hobbies, and earning your own living.' Number Two is Wine, Number Three is Women, Number Four is Cuckoos and Humbugs and Number Five is Irreligion.

Written in an upbeat, jolly manner (and the word 'jolly' occurs quite a bit, as in jolly good, jolly fine, and jolly well done) there are homilies on how to be a sport, and what temptations there are on the way to finding a woman who will make you a jolly good wife, and how atheists have a jolly miserable time of it because they don't appreciate what jolly good things there are in the world if you appreciate nature and the wonderful things God has put in it. Although some of the remarks are hopelessly dated, simply because they are rooted in a society which was different from today's, such as his strictures against the development of professional sport (sport being a jolly good thing to improve the mind and the body and develop pluck and breathe fresh air and foster team spirit instead of individual glory), some of the advice, were it expressed in up-to-date language, could today be regarded as perfectly sensible, if a trifle right-wing and stilted. But the curious thing was that as I read bits of the book, all the attitudes seemed 'standard'. That is, they were the ones I grew up with and unconsciously absorbed when I was a boy, and which, looking back, seemed to underpin everything that was done and said by the grown-ups at home and in church and on the radio and at the kind of schools that Paul and Pete and Nick and Charles and I went to – lower-division boarding schools in some cases including mine, upper in others, including Pete's.

The more famous book by Baden-Powell is *Scouting for Boys*, written during the period in which the author founded the Boy Scouts, now the Scout Association. In small towns and allied with a few churches it is still with us. The book is no longer in print, but in the mid-fifties, if you joined the Scouts then you had to buy a copy. But even then, with its stories of tracking and subterfuge in Africa in the early years of the 20th century, not a lot of it seemed relevant to me – except the gung-ho style in which it was written.

And some of its advice I did not even understand, at any rate until someone told me years later. 'There is one temptation that is pretty sure to come to you at one time or another, and I want just to warn you against it. It is called in our schools 'beastliness', and that is about the best name for it … Men have nothing but contempt for a fellow who gives way to it.' (Yes. They call them 'tossers'.) 'Sometimes the desire is brought on by indigestion, or from eating too rich food, or from constipation. It can therefore be cured by correcting these, and by bathing at once in cold water, or by exercising the upper part of the body by arm exercises, boxing, etc.' To say nothing of hand exercises.

Both these books saw their greatest sales between the wars, a whole generation before my schooldays began, but the attitudes expressed in them persisted virtually unchanged from late Victorian times until the 1950s. A certain smugness pervades them, as if there is no room for questioning what one ought to do in any of life's trials. Baden-Powell does refer to difficulties and doubt, but invariably he then says that if only one takes a little trouble to reflect on it *this* way, one will immediately see that the difficulty can be overcome – with, that is, a little pluck and manliness.

*

Pete told us about the CCF camp he went on at school.

'It was run by the Scots Guards. We had a special train.'

'What, you were the only people on it?'

'On this particular coach, yes. And it was shunted into a siding at Pirbright, for us to get sorted out. I tell you, being shunted into a siding might not seem much to you, but it was *just us*, no-one else. Have *you* been shunted into a siding? Just you and your mates? No, well then. And these Scots Guards came to get us off the train, yeah? – and they had these hats with cheesecutter peaks – you know, with the peak almost vertical, practically down over the eyes, and they looked at you like this,' he said, holding his head up high and tipping it back, which of course they had to do in order to see anything at all.

'Tough, were they?' I asked.

'Tough! Worrgh!'

'Spot of discipline?'

'Christ! Wow, yeah.'

'Bit hard for you, was it?'

'Well, no, it was all right.'

'You liked it, then.'

He shrugged.

'Jennie's back home, is she, getting her uniform on? But in your case it isn't what most people think, is it? Most people, when they go for a discipline session, then it's Nazi uniforms. But no, Pete's not into that, it's Scots Guards. All ready for you is she, with her cheesecutter brim?'

'Ye feckin' radge!' he shouts, pushing his face close to mine, *Trainspotting*-style. 'Ah'll *see yew! Jummy!*'

'A spot of discipline'. The original 'spot of discipline' was of course what all we schoolboys in the sixties were said by our elders-and-betters to be in need of. Nowadays you hardly hear the phrase. Teachers still use the word but the military references have dimmed. 'Discipline' was associated with a clipped style of speaking echoed in countless WWII films and then, parodied so successfully by *The Goon Show* and *Beyond the Fringe* and, later, *Monty Python*, that one could hardly hear a military man speak in that manner without wondering how he could keep a straight face. Yet the essence of that staccato style was clarity. The fewer the number of words, then (ran the assumption) the smaller the opportunity for misinterpretation, and the briefer the time needed in which to transmit the message, whether by live speech or by field-telephone or in code across the airwaves. In schools during the 1960s the notion of making vague suggestions to pupils, without explicitly instructing them or being clear about what was required, quickly proved its limitations as a guiding principle for teaching. Discovery learning has its place and there are certain educational objectives to which it is suited, but when you have too much of it then direct instruction is a welcome relief. Its most obvious application is in the initial stages of learning a skill, where brevity and clarity need to be maximised and discussion minimised.

*

One evening I attended a coaching session at the local tennis club. Taking it was Rod, who, tall and solidly-built as he was, might equally have passed as a flanker on the rugby pitch as a tennis coach, and whose day job was as a helicopter pilot in the Royal Navy. The instructions were firm. And he made it clear by his manner that he expected you to do as he said. There were no jokes if you didn't, merely an ironic smile that did little to diminish his disapproval. There was a brief introduction to what he wanted us to practise, 'Any questions?' and we'd start.

'We were supposed to be doing backhand crosscourt after the serve, Nigel. Why did you run round your backhand?'

'I –'

'Do a backhand next time, please ... Now then. Paul. What did I say about interception at the net?'

'Don't leave your partner exposed?'

'Your partner was exposed and you lost the point.'

Point made, then.

115

*

Helen and I drove to Llanberis for a walking weekend. In the Lake Padarn Hotel I was confronted with the worst piece of cod I'd ever had. Nor was there real beer: it was either nitrofizz or lager. But as Fred said, 'Yep. The food's crap. There's no beer. Surroundings are terrible. But we have a great time.' He wouldn't be the multinational telecommunications executive that he is, without that optimism. Other things help, of course, like understanding the market and knowing your technical stuff and always answering your mail, but to get a long way in a commercial organisation you need to be positive.

The first time I had seen the mountains of North Wales was on a school Army cadet expedition. When we had set off from the campsite at the southern end of Llyn Ogwen there was sunshine, and on the ridge joining Carnedd Dafydd and Carnedd Llewellyn, quite suddenly I realised that what I was seeing was what people called *beautiful scenery*. I had never walked in such places before, and although of course I'd seen pictures of hills – my mother's photographs of the Lake District, amongst others, from a cycling holiday in 1936, when she was aged 27 – I had not previously associated them with the notion of *beauty*; and no-one had suggested that the principal reason for walking in such parts might be the enjoyment of the surroundings. After all, these annual trips were billed as Arduous Training Camps, and the emphasis was on the arduousness.

What did I think, as I looked at those hills and valleys? 'If this is beauty, then I like it', perhaps; or, simply, 'I like this'. It was a day or two after we had been driven from Llanberis up to Pen-y-Pass in an Army truck, from the back of which I could see those astonishingly steep boulder-strewn hillsides rising from the mountain road – so far above you that, peering out from the truck, you couldn't see the sky without tipping your head right backwards. You could almost stretch out your arms and touch both sides of the valley. This was my introduction to mountain country. I had seen nothing like it, and although I was familiar with the Avon Gorge in Bristol, that consisted of vertical rock, and was therefore inaccessible. You could look at it, but unless you were a rock climber, and I decidedly wasn't, it was impossible to go up it. You had no opportunity to feel its hardness, and its yieldingness, under your feet; you could not have intimate knowledge of it. It was the view from the Carnedds[1] which triggered in me the impulse to return again and again to rocks, and slopes, and angles of landscape.

*

When I returned home after that first trip I said nothing about the beauty. But I did tell my mother and father where we'd been.

'Ogwen,' my father repeated. 'I was there during the war. When I was on OCTU.' (Officer Cadet Training Unit.) 'The sergeant major there. I remember him all

---

[1] Properly, Carneddau, the plural in Welsh.

right. He was a swine. He'd inspect our kit every morning. And if you'd got so much as a scuff on your boots, or you were holding your rifle a bit crooked, he'd thrust his face up close and he'd say, "Wanna buy a Bren gun?" I can hear him now. "Wanna buy a Bren gun? Wanna buy a Bren gun?"'

Why did he say that? I wanted to know. Because, I learned, stripping down a Bren gun (probably the best-known light machine gun of the period and for decades afterwards), cleaning it and oiling it and then, if you could remember the procedure in reverse, putting it back together, was a routine punishment, beloved of sergeant-majors.

'There was another one. Little round bloke he was. We'd be doing a route march, up these flaming mountains in full battle kit. You could hear him puffing and panting behind you. "Got to beat the Hun! Got to beat the bloody Hun! Get a move on, Austin, got to beat the Hun!"'

The water we drank when walking in these parts was always from the mountain streams, which was at least as wholesome as anything from a tap. And of course we used it for cooking when we'd stopped and pitched our tents for the night. But we did not stop off every few minutes to drink water from a plastic bottle, and to put on or take off clothes, depending on the weather and the steepness of the terrain. It seemed surprising that now, during this weekend at Llanberis, we should be doing that in these days of technologically-advanced equipment which is waterproof but breathable, and allegedly keeps you at the right temperature. After all, we had all followed the advertising recommendations that tell us that there's no such thing as bad weather, only inappropriate clothing, and we'd all spent a fortune on Gore-Tex and Sprayway and Rohan and Berghaus and Lowe Alpine. But then we were a mixed party, few of whose members' mountain-walking habits had been drilled into them by an offshoot of the Armed Forces with its emphasis on making do with little, ignoring hardship, and getting the miles covered.

Behind us was the sheer triangle of Tryfan, as pointed as an Egyptian pyramid. Most people probably walk the route around the Carnedds from that direction, and therefore only when they turn around to look back down the hill will they see the pinnacle rising straight out of the southern end of the lake. Magnificently vertical it stood, with a background of shoulders and ridges; I could understand how any mountain walker looking at this view might burn with the desire to meet its challenge and climb it.

The path was rough and slow. The route seemed longer every time we look at the map. Ann gave Fred a hard time.

'How much further have we got?'

'We're there,' he said, pointing at the map, 'and we've got to go to … there. We're about a third of the way round.'

'A *third of the way round*! We started at ten. It's three o'clock now. And you say we're a *third* of the way round?'

Fred pored over the map. I said, 'It was a difficult path to start with, with all those boulders by the side of the lake. But we've done most of the climbing.'

'I thought we were just going to go across to that lake and back down there,' said Ann.

'No,' said Fred. 'Down this way, and by *that* lake there.'

He relented in the end, and we took a short cut. From the ascending ridge of Y Gribin was the view across the valley to Twll Du, the Devil's Kitchen, the deep dark cleft slashed vertically in rock strata bent in a perfect shallow U. Wisps of low cloud hung above the valley just below the mountain tops. As we left the summit of Glyder Fawr, the cloud descended again. We were just off the edge of the visible portion of my map. Fred assumed his most conciliatory management-speak, so subtle that at first I did not notice the stiletto concealed within his words.

'When it comes to the post-mortem about the trip,' he said quietly, 'and you're giving an account of what happened in your expedition over the mountains, and the investigating officer asks you to give your version of the sequence of events, and where it all started going wrong, and you say, "Well, I couldn't be bothered to get me map out of the map-case and turn it over", then – '

But he was watching for the glint of comprehension in my eyes, and before I could react, he took two steps backwards, out of range, taking shelter behind Helen.

'You *bastard*,' I said.

'Hahaha!'

Back in Llanberis, after the evening meal Helen and I turned down the idea of a pub crawl – and missed out on the male voice choir.

'It was in the pub up the road,' Fred told us the next day. 'We heard them, and so we went in.' He patted his chest. 'It got you just *there*. Weren't very many of them.

Five, ten. Old bloke on the piano. Oh, it was wonderful. We sat in that alcove we were in last year, remember? Our usual spot. We pulled out our chairs and joined in. Ooh, they liked that. And they kept on, and we were chatting to them at the end, they wanted us to stay on tonight – there's a concert at Betwys-y-Coed or somewhere. Welsh national anthem at the end, and they all stood. Of course we stood as well. They were teaching us the chorus.'

I'm learning them again, I thought, those old mountain names. Pen-yr-ole-wen. Craig Llugwy. I learned them before, nearly forty years ago. When you're about to climb them again, you think: I've done it before, should be easy. Or at least familiar. And therefore there'll be no trouble, it won't be difficult. But it's never like that. The assumption that it will be easier works against you. If anything, it's harder. And on the far side of Ogwen there was Glyder Fach and Glyder Fawr. It was between Fach and Fawr those thirty-nine years ago that I gazed on the mass of abandoned, broken stones littering the mountaintop and thought: Who put these here? Why? How did they get here? Surely no-one just plonked them down. There's no quarrying up here, no roads. It was only with a sense of wonder that I came to realise that the only way they could have arrived was by some other means, infinitely slower, over geological time. Humankind could not have been involved. Erosion of rocks so hard may take a long time; but it is thorough, and remorseless. And now that incomprehension at those millions of years it must all have taken was with me again; and thus were uncovered, piece by piece, the memory traces from my youth whose continuity with my present life seemed so tenuous. I was like an archaeologist, squatting by an ancient floor mosaic, scraping at the debris of earth and stones more recently deposited.

*

Back home and in Tom Brown's we talked about a recent TV programme about the RAF in the war. 'They weren't all these upper-class public school types,' said Pete, 'it wasn't all handlebar moustaches and "Jolly good, Carruthers!" and talk about getting into scrapes and having prangs. A lot of them came from different social backgrounds, and there was quite a lot of discord between the upper-class ones and the working-class. For a start, the ones from the lower social groups, usually they became the sergeant pilots, whereas the public school people became officers.'

I told them about my father, and his experience in trying to become an officer in the Army. I had been talking about it with my aunt Betty, my mother's younger sister, a week or two previously, when we were discussing his marriage to my mother; both of them had died by then, and I was free to ask her questions. Acceptance into my mother's family, difficult enough as it was from his humble origins, would have been still more awkward had he not managed to pass the training course. What made matters worse was that he had already been married, albeit briefly, and therefore the wedding could not be in a church.

'But then straight afterwards,' Betty said, 'we had a blessing, in Limpsfield church. When they'd met, he was just a sergeant, in the RAMC[1]. But if you were in the RAMC and you weren't a doctor, then you couldn't become an officer. So he had to leave that regiment, in order to become an officer. But then of course, at first, he failed.'

I explained then why he had failed, a story he had told me years previously. He did well enough in all the necessary preliminaries – written exams and practical exercises of various sorts – before the final interview in front of a panel. The interview went satisfactorily, so he thought, until this question.

'Now then, Sergeant Austin. Tell us, what public school was it you went to?'

To which, of course, he could only reply:

'I didn't go to a public school, sir.'

'Ah.'

And quite suddenly the attitude of the selection board morphed from neutral to frosty; at which point my father knew he would not be regarded as officer material.

'Yes,' said Betty. 'I can believe it.'

Later, when – of necessity – the selection methods had changed, and the identity of the school you had attended no longer mattered, he was accepted. He joined the RASC (Royal Army Service Corps), the regiment which serviced the rest of the army – organising the supplies of ammunition, food and other supplies.

'But the important thing,' said Betty, 'was that at his wedding, he was able to wear the uniform of an officer.'

---

[1]Royal Army Medical Corps.

*

'When those French boys came over to England, they wanted to learn English because it was the only way they could play computer games,' said Pete, talking about the exchanges our children did with the French a few years ago. 'Before that, they were hostile.' The subject was cultural imperialism, the globe of today being overrun by American concepts and American brands, if not, these days, American troops.

'Okay, some of them aren't actually essential,' I said. 'The world could function without Coca-Cola or Nike – '

'But people want them,' said Pete.

'Yeah, I know they want them, but they're not essential. What is essential, is Boeing and Microsoft.'

'Well, Microsoft I think, yeah okay.'

Then we talked about Napoleon and *his* imperialist tendencies. There had been a recent television programme about him, with computer-generated maps and old paintings, and silent acting to accompany the commentary. The actor in the title role was an astonishingly good likeness of the pictures of Napoleon and his death-mask.

'What I can't understand is why Napoleon got to be so important,' I said. 'How did he manage to impose his will? How did he manage to come back after his exile? Half the French seemed to fall for him and the other half were against him, but Wellington – '

'And Sir John Moore at Corunna,' said Nick. '"Not a drum was heard" – '

'"Not a funeral note",' joined in Pete. '"As his corse to the rampart we hurried – "'

'"Not a soldier discharged his farewell shot/O'er the grave where our hero we buried",' they recited in unison, whilst I shifted my gaze from one to the other. Evidently they had learned this poem, whatever it was[1], by rote at school.

'I'm afraid I only went to a second-rate public school,' I said.

'You could see the way my thoughts were going!' said Pete. 'Now,' he went on, 'I know you think Runeckles' Theories are complete crap, but I've got another. My theory is, why did Napoleon go into Russia? Eh? And Hitler as well. What were they going to *do* when they got there? Tie up a whole lot of troops in subjugating the Russians? I mean, what did they think was actually going to happen, after they'd beaten the Russian army and occupied Moscow?'

'*I* don't know.'

'Nor do I. Nor did they, probably. The point is, they thought they could easily get there. But of course they never got that far, and my theory is, in all the atlases, all countries are shown the same size. On one page you've got one country, filling the whole page. And the next page is filled up with another. But they're on a completely different scale. You've got a map of England, or France. And on the next, there's one of Russia. They're made to fit the page. But if they had the map of Russia on the same scale as the others, there'd be pages and pages of it. A whole chapter. And of course you do realise it, you know it intellectually. But somehow, when it comes to it, you just forget.'

---

[1] *The Burial of Sir John Moore*, by Charles Wolfe.

'So Napoleon allowed himself to think it wasn't any further to nip across to Moscow than it was to catch the ferry from Cherbourg to Portsmouth.'

'Exactly.'

*

A weekend walk in the New Forest. We stayed in a mobile home at Sandy Balls camping-n-caravanning park. This was somewhat naff, but unlike at a youth hostel, you didn't get told off by a warden for coming in late and/or drunk.

The colours were autumnal, predominantly the bronze of fallen beech leaves, the yellowish gravel of the laid paths, mud ranging from almost white to dark brown, and the grey of smooth beech-tree trunks. Sharp, clear light, but the path was indistinct.

'I've just heard three worrying things,' said Rob. '"I think it's that way", "The map doesn't seem to show this path" and "It's not as far as it looks".'

The forest floor was covered with oak and beech leaves, spongy underfoot, and every now and then the hazard of ankle-deep mud. 'Careful now, old fella,' said Pete, as I slipped and dropped my walking-stick.

'Are these the normal sorts of insult you get?' asked Bob, a relative newcomer to the walks.

'Nah. This is Third Division stuff. You should hear them when they're on form.'

Paul peed against a tree and developed a new theory about why the moss is greener on that side of the trunk. 'All that uric acid. Those nutrients. Allows the moss to grow.'

'Normally people pee on the other side of the trunk,' said Mike, 'and the moss is washed off. High-powered steam cleaning.'

I poked my stick right through the trunk of a rotten tree. 'Perfectly all right, this tree was,' said Graham, 'until people started peeing on it.'

We settled by a fine wood fire at the Cartwheel at Whitsbury, and afterwards climbed the hill to the little parish church, built of brick and flint, with views across rolling fields. There was no noise except the wind in the trees and the grass. The route took us along a road for a short distance and then we struck out across fields.

'Ridge at three miles,' said Charles.

'That far, you reckon it is?'

'Yes,' he said. 'Take account of the dead ground, relative size of features.'

'Learned that in the CCF at Sedbergh, did you? You were in it, I take it?'

'I spent as little time in it as I could. I went off and joined the Signals and Music section. I've no wish to be reminded of four unhappy years. I've no wish to go back there, or talk to any of those people.'

'You haven't been to any school reunions, then, Charles?'

'No I bloody haven't. I did tentatively cycle round there when I went to Ribble Head, though.'

'Your school got you where you wanted to get,' I said. 'I'm just surprised at the vehemence in your comments. Does that happen every time you leave a place? Will that happen when – if – you leave Dorchester? You'll put it all in the past, you'll never have anything to do with any of us lot, never want to see us again, you'll say, "Those buggers? No, I'm not interested"?'

'No,' said Charles, generously, 'because *you're* not a load of tossers.'

'I don't go back to these things either, particularly. When did you guys go back to one?' I asked anyone who was listening.

'I went to one,' said Bob.

'Yeah, but did you go to the next one?' said Pete. 'You meet someone you don't particularly like, and the last time you saw them was thirty years ago, and it takes you about five seconds to remember why you didn't like them then either.'

I said, 'I find myself thinking about those times. I don't mean wishing for them, but every so often they just cross my mind. The school, and the classrooms, and the dormitories, and the people there. There just seems a mismatch between the thoughts, and the fact that I never see those people.' And in fact, I thought, there *were* certain aspects of the CCF I did actually enjoy.

Between Breamore and Wood Green was a brick-built mill house, with two side-streams of the River Avon flowing underneath it.

'Did you see on that corner?' Pete said. 'There's a pill box. And look, on this outbuilding. See? They've cut gun-slits.' In the middle of the red brick was a small square hole, topped by a concrete lintel. There was another on an adjacent side of the building.

'The Avon was a line of defence, when we nearly got invaded, you know, in about 1940. The tanks the Germans had then wouldn't have got across the river.' At this point the Avon is about forty yards wide. 'The ones they had later, the Tiger, they could have driven them straight across. The earlier tanks were really very small. They didn't even have those snorkel things, to take the exhaust pipe above the water.'

*

Helen came with me to the pub. Pete was there. We discussed ski-ing.

'I'm going this winter,' said Pete. 'I don't know about Graham. He's very skilful,' he added. 'He's got good balance, a low centre of gravity. Uses his arms well, keeps his feet together. Good co-ordination. Strong legs. And he's brave. He's the best person I've been with.'

'Sickening,' I said.

'Well,' said Helen, trying to think of something nice to say about me, 'you're good.'

'Yes!' said Pete. 'And without any of those advantages!'

Then he spoke about the difference in outlook between people of our age and those a bit older.

'My sister was born four years earlier than me, and it wasn't the same generation. So she's different somehow. There's none of that let-it-all-hang-out stuff.'

'Beatles,' said Helen.

'And those fashion designers.'

'She's more … staid?' I asked.

'Maybe … Sloaney. Just didn't have quite the attitude. She went to a boarding school too. But she didn't get up to the same kind of thing as me.'

'Like?'

'Ha! There was this tunnel on the train journey back to London from Rugby. And at the end of one term, one of the chaps had a rocket with him, you know, left over from Bonfire Night. It was a long tunnel, and he held it in his hand out of the window, and we were at the end of the train, the last coach, and as we went into the tunnel he lit it, and it went *whoosh!* right up the front, and of course it exploded, up by the engine, and it produced all these stars, like rockets do, going *pop! poof! bang!* It was wonderful, in that darkness, in the middle of the tunnel. And the next station, the police were waiting for us, and they came round, and wanted to know what had happened, who'd done it. Well, we just shrugged. "Didn't see a thing. Dunno anything about it. Nothing to do with us." And the other thing you could do, on those corridor trains, you'd open a compartment full of boys from school and you'd roll a banger in on the floor and shut the door, and it would produce complete chaos and panic. But the thing is, they didn't need to panic. All they had to do was wait for it to go off. But they didn't. You know, people would jump up on the seats, and in the luggage rack ... And when we went back to school, we used to meet up in London, at a strip club. We'd leave home early to rendezvous, tell our parents we'd got to go up on the earlier train to get back to school to get a few things done. Anyway, this strip club, it was in Soho, Greek Street. We'd meet in there, it was this tiny room like half the size of this, and there was this stripper, and a few of us'd be there and then someone else would come in, and we'd say, "Ah! How did you get on in the holidays then, Bloggs minor?" and no-one was interested in this poor girl, who was, you know, just trying to take the next item of her kit off. And we'd all be talking to each other and she'd get cross, and then she'd take something off and go *whack*, hit somebody over the head with it in the front row – '

'"Be quiet over there!"'

'"Pay attention to the lesson!"'

'"Stop mucking about while I'm trying to teach you!"'

'Haha! Oh, God!'

*

Late September, and the last Tuesday evening tennis game. By seven o'clock it was becoming so murky you could hardly see the ball, particularly if it was one of the dirty old balls marked A for Austin instead a spanking new bright yellow ball of Paul's. As usual, Paul graciously declined the standing invitation for a drink, but this time because he'd promised his elder daughter a driving lesson. The rest of us cycled down to Tom's and discussed Pete's chairmanship of the Film Society.

'Oh dear,' he said. 'It feels very strange being involved with the running of something.'

'I understand,' I said consolingly. 'It's your alter ego, isn't it? Which you've now discovered is still there, after you'd thought you'd rebelled sufficiently when you were at public school to extinguish it. That part of yourself which they fostered,' (Pete was nodding all the time), 'that bit of responsibility. Leadership. Respectability. The very thing the school always set itself to instil in its pupils, which you put two fingers up to, it's there after all, isn't it? They got you in the end! Your public school education succeeded. Your dad didn't waste all his money after all. It's a bit late, but at last it's coming out!'

Pete admitted to being surprised that all of this had actually happened to him. It was out of kilter with the image of himself he developed during his later years at school and as a post-school adolescent. He'd cherished that persona all those years, resisting – as he thought – the blandishments of mid-life and all it traditionally brings, but found, in the end, that he couldn't maintain it. He'd thought – nay, hoped, even assumed – it would never alter, never renege on him, that he'd always stay a Peter Pan creature, and never become a boring old adult like his parents. And now he was finding differently. He laughed ruefully.

8

The Ladder-catchers and the Frozen

Near the end of one of the classic escape books of the war, *The Colditz Story*, Patrick Reid makes an observation about reactions to a crisis. He and his companion are about to cross from Germany into neutral Switzerland after their escape from the notorious castle fortress[1]:

> Why had we run instead of creeping forward warily? The answer is that instinct dictated it and, I think in this case, instinct was right. Escapers' experience has borne out that the psychological

---

[1] Colditz was a supposedly escape-proof castle in eastern Germany used for persistent escapees from other camps as well as other prisoners the Germans regarded as difficult, but from which a few successful escapes did take place. The German prisoner-of-war establishments were of course a completely different proposition from the concentration camps, and their inmates – if hardly comfortable – were kept in much more humane conditions, with the protocols of the Geneva convention on the treatment of prisoners of war being largely observed.

reaction of a fleeing man to a shouted command, such as 'Halt', varies. If a man is walking or creeping the reaction is to stop. If he is running the reaction is to run faster. It is in the split seconds of such instinctive decisions that success or failure may be determined.

Whilst I am sure this is generally sound, what Reid leaves out is the psychological make-up of the individual concerned. Some people, the cautious ones intent on life-preservation above all else, might be constitutionally more likely to stop whether they were running or walking. Others, the men of action, might go faster, taking the attitude – in the heat of the moment, without stopping to think – *To hell with this, I'm going for it.* War, no doubt, needs both types of Service personnel; and indeed needs all of them to act cautiously in some circumstances, boldly in others. Without good judgment, the loss of a man's life or a tank or an aircraft or a battle is more probable. Most of us, I would guess, are stoppers rather than runners. But for an army to succeed, it must contain at least some of the latter. In any armed conflict involving men rather than merely machines, they will inspire the former as well as achieve highly themselves.

One morning in the high-ceilinged changing room at my school a long, heavy wooden ladder standing up against the wall began to fall. Someone had probably knocked into it whilst passing. Several of us – all aged about twelve – saw it. I understood immediately what was going to happen. It would hit the edge of a central clothes-rail, then bounce crazily to the floor, perhaps being deflected against the legs of a couple of boys close by. I did not move. I sat on the bench, frozen. Others stopped in mid-sentence and stood motionless. But one, by the name of Bruce, moved quickly towards the ladder, positioned himself in front of it with his hands extended upwards, and caught it before it had had a chance to fall more than thirty degrees from the vertical.

Several of us had been in a position to do that. Only one moved. Why?

Bruce did not, either before that or afterwards, strike me as endowed with particularly unusual qualities. He was neither a gang-leader nor a camp-follower. He was not conspicuously looked up to, nor down upon. He fitted into the group in an average kind of way. He was a very good hockey player, that I do remember. But I doubt if that predisposed him to be a good ladder-catcher. Would he have shown similar behaviour in all emergencies when quick, almost unthinking, action needs to be taken to avert a catastrophe? I would think: Not necessarily. Would all of the rest of us have failed to? Again, not necessarily. The fall of a ladder would hardly have deserved such an epithet anyway. But I think the incident was instructive. Under unexpected pressure, the behaviour of individuals differs. It also differs at various times in the same individual. Even the most timid of us could not categorically be predicted to act timidly under all circumstances. I would say only that, if presented with a dozen emergencies, some people would act heroically in more of them than would others.

*

The ladder-catcher *par excellence* of my life was Nigel Leakey's younger brother Rea[1]. A year after Nigel and sister Agnes had been sent to England from Kenya when their mother died, Rea and his brother Robert followed. They too were taken in by the family of his uncle in Surrey, whose eldest child was my mother. Younger than Nigel, and perhaps benefiting from his having paved the way, Rea and Robert settled better. They spent the term-times at Weymouth College, a small boarding school on the south coast, returning, like Nigel, to Surrey during the summer holidays.

Rea joined the Army and became exceptionally successful as a soldier. After the war, when they met, he and my father struck up a good friendship. I did not see him often, but various visits did take place, and our two families holidayed together a couple of times. Both my parents would refer to him often, my mother in affectionate terms and my father in ones of admiration. When his obituary appeared in *The Times* in 1999 the description accorded exactly with everything I had seen and heard of him over the years. Its opening lines used some of the biggest guns available to the writers of obituaries of military men:

> One of the very few brave men who deserve the accolade of 'the bravest of the brave' for outstanding courage sustained over a long period – indeed, for the whole of the Second World War – Rea Leakey was a born soldier, who ... excelled in battle. His two MCs (it was widely rumoured that

---

[1] Pronounced Ray, the name is from a Kikuyu word meaning 'sun'.

the second had been a recommendation for the VC), his Czech MC and his DSO symbolise his bravery, which was legendary ...

In his autobiography, published a few months before his death, is a description of an incident in which, separated from his unit in a solitary Jeep in the North African desert, he encountered Field-Marshal Rommel himself, in characteristically chivalrous mode:

> To this day I still recall the sound of guns being cocked and Rommel's voice shouting at his men ... clearly he was saying, 'No, no, hold your fire, give the poor bastard a chance'. Then a hail of bullets whistled round my head, and once again my guardian angel looked after me.

On another occasion he narrowly avoided losing some thirty men and their vehicles to starvation when he attempted – with typical enthusiasm, probably allied to a lack of caution – to find a rumoured pass out of the Qattara Depression in the Egyptian desert. He tells of clearing minefields by crawling across the ground in darkness and carefully picking at the surface to expose the antennae of the buried mines. He describes a tank battle against superior forces in which – after almost every other British vehicle had been incapacitated following an error of judgment on the part of the commanding officer – he surprised the enemy by opening fire when everyone else had thought the action was finished, and climbing out of the tank three seconds before it exploded. The most hair-raising incident took place when, with two Australians, he occupied a makeshift forward observation post a quarter of a mile from the opposing lines. Via a field telephone they were able to direct their own artillery as to the most effective points to attack. Eventually they were discovered, and 'at least fifty' of the enemy emerged to attack them. At this point both the Bren and Thompson sub-machine guns, idle all day and jammed up with sand, refused to work. Whilst the Australians lobbed grenades down at the attackers, Rea worked feverishly to free the guns, doing so just in time to shoot an attacker between the eyes as he appeared immediately in front of him with bayonet fixed and aimed at Rea's stomach: 'It was the best shot of my life'. They escaped from their position only by staggering slowly past the enemy positions disguised with German helmets from the dead of the force that had attacked them. By the time the ruse was discovered they were far enough away, and sufficiently lucky, to dodge the bullets and shells that rained down, and ran as hard as they could the four miles back to their own base at Tobruk.

Was this really bravery, or was it foolhardiness? Selflessness or stupidity? Sometimes it was his own daring, and his persistence in pursuing the enemy long after most people would have taken a cautious way back to safety, that would get Rea into an almost impossible situation, following which he would then need to get himself out of it. But he rarely returned without valuable reconnaissance information or taking out some of the enemy. He hated inactivity and volunteered for every piece of action he could.

Most of us do not get the chance to display such behaviour. It is probably just as well, because most of us would be found wanting. In such circumstances we would have been too frightened. We would have sat on the bench, our instinct for self-preservation expressed by inaction, leaving the Bruces and the Leakeys of this world to do the necessary. Their own instincts for self-preservation are expressed by the opposite, by grasping the situation by the throat and forcing it into the shape on which they have decided. The kind of activities Rea undertook sounded very much like what his brother was doing when he was killed. Did Nigel's death affect the way Rea behaved? Did it make him more prudent or less? In the book he does not dwell on it. I doubt if it made any difference; and in fact he did not know about it until at least half-way through the war. He was just *like* that.

To someone brought up in Britain in the decades after the Second World War, during which (leaving aside certain terrorist incidents) in most of Europe there has been continuous peace, deeds of this nature are almost unbelievable and almost incomprehensible. Their audacity is astonishing. And Leakey, and men like him, did not do such things just once. Some of them went on and on doing them. Anyone who does them, of course, runs colossal risks, even if, like Rea, they have their wits about them. He knew instinctively, in every situation, when to make a move and how far to go. He was also lucky. Lucky not to get killed, lucky not even to get wounded apart from a couple of shell-splinters in his backside. If a bullet has your name on it, they used to say, then there is nothing you can do about it. None of the bullets fired in Rea's direction did. The closest was from an anti-tank gun in the weeks following D-Day in 1944:

I was standing with my legs apart looking through my binoculars when the Germans fired at me. I would like to have met that German gunner and congratulated him on his marksmanship. He had evidently been taught [correctly] to shoot at the bottom of the [bullseye], and as a result the shot passed between my legs, and all it did was to burn two holes in my trousers and singe my crutch. An inch higher and he would have claimed the family jewels.

He called his book *Leakey's Luck*[1], and there seems no doubt, from his account, that he was indeed fortunate. But he must also have had good judgment: without it, good fortune will run out sooner rather than later. From his account, it sometimes seems that the longer he went on, the more that fortune smiled on him. Perhaps the famous remark usually attributed to the golfer Gary Player is apposite. Accused by an onlooker of playing a lucky shot, he did not demur, but replied 'The more I practise, the luckier I get'.

Rea's luck, or rather the practice that led to it, was no doubt one of the consequences of the experiences of his early childhood on the small family farm in Kenya. In his own account, he devotes a few pages only to these years; but they do contain one or two clues, such as that tale of his parents shooting a pride of lions which was threatening the cattle – his mother got two, his father three. The suggestion is that you did not think long before

---

[1] Leakey, Rea with Forty, George. *Leakey's Luck: A Tank Commander with Nine Lives.* Sutton Publishing, 1999.

carrying out such deeds. You rapidly assessed the situation, and acted. You had to survive, and to carry out what was necessary in order to do so. And in the war, bored by inaction, whenever there was a difficult or dangerous task to be done he would offer his services. As a result he probably became better at them than most other people. In particular, he probably came to know how to handle fear and prevent it from distorting sound judgment.

On nearly every page, like servicemen everywhere he understates the dangers, using words such as 'excitement' instead of 'deadly fighting', 'faintly surprised' in place of 'astonished', 'a slight mistake' when he means 'complete cock-up which could have led to dozens of people being killed'. And the word he employs in his description of a stretch of no-man's-land which 'had been sown with every known type of mine and booby-trap' is merely 'unhealthy'.

But Rea did recognise that more than one sort of soldier can be successful, and respected. Describing one of his commanding officers as 'a strange man', he adds

I suppose the experience of being captured bred in him the fear of the same thing happening again … I was told that he was held in very high regard by all ranks. On joining them he addressed the Regiment with roughly these words: 'I will not lead you from the front into battle because I have not the nerve. But I assure you that never will you be sent into battle unless I am quite convinced that you will have the support of the artillery and other arms.' He was as good as his word.

My father described Rea Leakey, approvingly, as 'a man's man'. What *is* a 'man's man'? What's to be approved? How can it be explained to someone not familiar with army life, or with 1940s and 1950s parlance, from which the phrase comes? Our post-feminist age does not have the same nuances of the differences between male and female as did the first half of the twentieth century, during which a paternalistic culture prevailed, emphasising the view of women as the weaker sex, to be looked after and to be gallant towards. I suppose one way of putting it is to say a man's man is a man whom other men would like to be like, though that hardly answers the question.

But I did notice that whether you were a woman or a man – or a child, then adolescent and young man, as I became – Rea made you feel good merely by the enthusiasm with which he greeted you. He was socially adept, making his presence felt effortlessly; he smiled a good deal when he talked, and was able to be bold or self-deprecatory, with a chuckle and yet with an ability to be serious; he was not tall, but was physically fit, muscular and strong; direct, but not threatening; intimidated by no-one; not afraid to speak forthrightly, but – when the mood took him, which, admittedly, it did not always – with sensitivity and respect. And always ready to see the lighter side and indeed to make light of difficulties; to judge a situation well enough to act in a way he had estimated was both desirable and possible. His willingness to take on any task himself did not, as it does in the case of people who are loners, put off others from joining in: on the contrary, he would initiate activity in a spirit of co-operation, treating others as equals in what had to be done. Thus his actions both encouraged others to take part and also inspired liking and loyalty. He would say, simply and directly, I consider we should do this or that or stand up for so-and-so or for what we believe needs to be done, and we shall pursue that as far as we can: he would say it firmly, without having to shout, in a manner that would convince people that he was right – or at any rate that he would brook little argument. In his person and in his style, in the way he carried himself and the way he communicated – giving his own views yet respecting those of other people – he was the embodiment of what many self-respecting males would like to have been.

Yet what have we, most of those of my generation, in these years since the war, done which remotely compares? We may have joined the cadet force at school and fired a few .303 calibre rounds from a rifle on an Army firing range. Spent a few weeks under canvas getting wet. Struggled up the mountains of Scotland and Wales carrying what we needed for a few days' camping, which conspicuously did not include the heavier supplies such as anti-tank guns and rifles and ammunition. And we have sat in cinemas and watched *The Longest Day* and *The Cruel Sea* and *Reach for the Sky* and *I Was Monty's Double*, consolidating the evidence from the history books and the mouths of our elders that these events actually did happen, and are not just inventions for the screen.

Here was a man who took part in them; and, in spite of the inactivity of most of us, there are still people like him. Every now and then there is someone who does not think 'meanly of himself for not having been a soldier', because he *is* one, or has been one. Where does the force of that remark originate? Deep in the male psyche is the notion that only in war can a man prove himself. Only in war can the true test of manhood be encountered. Only in combat, where death is one of the faces of the dice to be thrown, can one's ability to defy it, and earn the right to live, be tested. Life may be given by God, or Fate. But that is the trouble: it is given, not earned. To deserve it, you must wrest it from the jaws of death. And you can only truly put yourself to the test in a situation where you have to act courageously in order to survive. Some people do this by pitting themselves against the elements. But I am not sure that climbing unconquered peaks in the Andes or trekking to the North Pole or sailing single-handedly around Cape Horn, arduous and dangerous though they certainly are, constitute true tests. Those activities require prudence, and the calculation of risk, and of course endurance and resourcefulness. If the calculation is wrong, or you are not careful enough, or (as, indeed, in many other human activities) you are unlucky, then, yes, you die. But the forces ranged against you are impersonal. In war, by contrast, someone is actively trying to kill you. When you have fought for your own life, and won, against a foe who is consciously and intelligently trying to take it from you, only then will you deserve to have it.

And even though luck plays a part, it does not affect any judgment on your manliness. Manliness is independent of luck. Whether or not you have been brave, whether or not you have proved yourself a man, you may be lucky, and survive: or you may be unlucky, and die[1].

Perhaps the most fortunate are those who were brave, either by inclination or because, somehow, they learned to be, then were lucky enough not to get killed, and thereafter continued to demonstrate their bravery. Probably rightly, they are the ones who receive the most honour from their comrades and from history. Because they survived, they will have been the ones most likely to attain high rank later in their careers. Rea Leakey finished his as a general, the last commander of the British troops in Malta and Libya.

*

In my head is a script. It is public property, for it underlies vast numbers of books, newspaper articles, films and television documentaries. But for many people it is also personal, because it has been lent that aspect by one or more of our relatives. That is why the obsession with the war on the part of people of my generation is so enduring:

---

[1] I should acknowledge that the notion of 'manliness', as discussed here, derives from conceptualisations belonging more to the first half of the 20th century, rather than the first quarter of the 21st, by which time it had long since appeared outdated and blimpish – and inappropriate in an age when stereotypes of male and female characteristics have, to say the least, changed. The notion of 'being a man' owes much to the last line of Rudyard Kipling's poem *If*, whatever the author's ironic intentions. (Beginning "If you can keep your head when all about you are losing theirs …", and continuing through "If you can meet with Triumph and Disaster and treat those two impostors just the same", etc., it ends "you'll be a Man, my son!")

its primary force is the second-hand knowledge we have received from people close to us. I use 'second-hand' here as distinct from 'third-hand' or 'academic'. If you have second-hand knowledge of the war then there are people in your family who lived through it, fought in it, and who tell you about it – who tell you about it, moreover, in a way which contains a package of moral imperatives regarding your own life. It emphasises the perception that we – the Allies – were pursuing a Cause, and one of unimpeachable moral status. 'Third-hand' means told to you by someone else, one who did not have a personal stake in it, or who had been told about it themselves; whilst 'academic' refers to knowledge picked up from books or magazines or broadcasts.

The script has not been placed in our heads deliberately. It is a synthesis of our own making, from all three types of sources: a part of our heritage. Cliché-ridden, and probably with some hyperbole, mine runs like this.

> *'You owe everything to your elders and their part in that great conflict. Many of them were killed: and it is right that you should pay proper respect to their memory, for they gave their lives for you. They served bravely, doing so in the knowledge they might die or be maimed. Though most were conscripted and not volunteers[1], and*

---

[1] As Max Hastings, in one of his series of magisterial books about the War, puts it – of combatants on both sides: 'It should never be forgotten … that few of those wearing uniforms thought of themselves as soldiers. The tide of history had merely swept them into an unwelcome season's masquerade as warriors' (*Armageddon: The battle for Germany 1944-45* (2004)).

though they perhaps fought for each other rather than the country, they did it in order that Right should prevail over Evil. The fact that your country is not under the heel of the jackboot, governed by a hateful regime, is down to them. You should salute those who died and you should look with humility and respect upon the ones fortunate enough to survive. Those who lived through one battle carried the flag to the next; if they survived that, then they stepped forward to serve again. Many performed heroic deeds. Many of your own forebears, men and women, took their part, did what they were asked and more, standing alongside thousands of others.

'And you must remember that it was not just those who fought that you must thank. For – "They also serve who only stand who only stand and wait". They also served who manned the factories, the railways, the telephone lines, who cheerfully cleared up after the enemy bombs had done their damage. The whole country, inspired by the resilience and courage of one of the greatest wartime leaders, stood alone in 1940. The Poles, the Czechs, the Belgians, the Dutch had been trampled on. France had surrendered. Alone against the evil of Nazism in Germany and Fascism in Italy, Britain, under-equipped and on the brink of starvation, fought on: and through the will of its people and its leader, fought on to win. There was never any question of surrender; and because of that spirit, the forces of darkness were finally defeated.

'You therefore have much to be grateful for. Be thankful, for those lives were given for you. Your life is rooted in their death. Always remember that, and

recognise that this places upon you the obligation to make good use of the life bestowed upon you. Go forth and do justice to that generation. Make full use of whatever talents have been given you. Justify the sacrifice others made, and contribute something worthwhile!'

But I suspect there are few of us with that substrate to their self-awareness who feel they have been able, in the decades since those heroic years, to make good the debt, to absolve themselves of what they owe. No job, no activity, no achievement is good enough. Whatever we do, however successful we may be in life, in however worthy an occupation, we still retain a sense of obligation.

The reality is, of course, that repayment of that debt is not possible. It is not possible because gifts of this nature – of the time, the health, the lives of one generation, given to the next – are not returnable. It is wrong-headed to think they are, just as it is wrong-headed to think children 'owe' something to their parents. Even if they do, then it is not owed in the way a debt of money is owed. The love which parents have for their children is not transitive. It is not to be repaid by the younger generation to the older. Instead it is passed down by the children to their own children. Parents do not have a right to expect their children to be grateful for what they did for them. If the parents are lucky then the children may be suitably respectful, but the resources of the children need to be reserved for their own offspring; and what they need to do for their own children is likely to be different from what their parents did for them, because the world they inhabit will have changed from the one that went before.

*

But that script has not been the only one permeating my life. The cultural mix in this country is wide, and there exists a variety of opinions, stereotypes and role models from which, wittingly or unwittingly, everyone draws to a greater or lesser extent in the living of their lives. Throughout the latter half of the twentieth century and the beginning of the twenty-first there has existed a Left-leaning orthodoxy which might not ostensibly seek to belittle the efforts of those who fought on the winning side in The War but which nonetheless has had that effect. I know this because, since my teens and the counter-culture of the Sixties, I have always found elements of it in myself.

This set of attitudes is rooted in rebellion against the Establishment of the time, of which perhaps the most prominent aspect related to the Vietnam war ('Ho! Ho! Ho Chi Minh!' ran the demonstrators' marching song). As a part of its anti-authority stance, it has incorporated a more or less wilful ignorance of things military, which can sometimes amount to naiveté.

It encompasses little sympathy with the armed forces, or knowledge of what it is to serve in them. It avoids recognition of the qualities that were necessary for the establishment of the post-war world with the freedoms from which we all benefit. Even if the holders of such views have mingled with the people who showed those qualities (and the person of my age who has had no relatives in the Forces would be rare), they have rejected them. This is ironic, because if those holding these views had been adults in 1939 then, probably, as many of them would have shown those qualities as did people at the time. But the spirit of the later age which shaped them has been reflective, analytic, sceptical, and, at times, cynical and anti-heroic. The armed forces have occupied a smaller part of the national budget and of our consciousness, and there have been many fewer families with a son, a brother – or, these days, a daughter or sister – who are soldiers, sailors or aircrew. The Forces merely represent another career. That is reflected in the advertisements for them. They do not occupy a central position in our scheme of things, as they did in the decade or so after the Second World War. The customs, concepts and parlance of the military are no longer central to our consciousness.

But, I reflected at Rea Leakey's death, this attitude represents a wilful misunderstanding, even a derision, of the qualities which drove him and his companions. Bravery? It would mock the notion. Fighting? It would ridicule the suggestion that a civilised person should have anything to do with it. Leadership, setting an example on the battlefield? Jingoistic concepts from a warmongering era. And indeed, these days, the directness with which Rea expressed his views would probably be an anachronism, and there would be complaints of political incorrectness. His kind of leadership would not have passed muster now. But then nor did Churchill's in late 1945, when his style was rightly perceived as unlikely to lend itself to peacetime conditions, whereas during the circumstances of war he had been exactly the right person. Cometh the hour, cometh the man.

What was done by Leakey and his ilk, some of whom survived whilst others did not, is what has enabled us all to meet in the pub at the beginning of the twenty-first century. And if we look down our noses at the armed forces, do we not seem a little too much like the spiritual descendants of the pacifists of the Thirties who would have built no warships, no fighter planes, no tanks? Maybe even after the war there were some of them who went to their deathbeds still believing right was on their side, and that peace should have been made with Germany, if not before 1939 then certainly in 1940; but if their view had prevailed, then at the cessation of hostilities the British government, whether led by Attlee or someone else, would have been a puppet organisation in thrall to Hitler.

*

There was one Saturday when our family visited the Leakeys for lunch. The war in Vietnam was grinding its interminable way through the decade and the anti-militaristic feeling among students, of whom I was one, was mounting. There were difficult economic conditions and Harold Wilson's Labour government had announced a series of massive spending cuts, especially to the military. Over a gin before lunch there was brief discussion of it. At one point Rea said something like, 'All this cash they're putting into these do-gooders. Keeping those civil servants in clover. Pen-pushers. Useless.

Cutting the Forces budget. They should be increasing it, not reducing it.'

'I don't agree,' I said. 'To buy what?'

'Keep the Army up to strength,' he said. 'The Navy, the Air Force. Guns. Atom bombs.'

'Atom bombs? Who wants *them*?' I said, as scornfully as I dared.

'Only way to keep the country strong,' said Rea. 'Everybody with any sense thinks so. Who are these people, anyway, arguing against it?'

At that point I was rash enough to mention the name of the philosopher Bertrand Russell, who was one of the leading lights in the Campaign for Nuclear Disarmament and had once been briefly imprisoned for a breach of the peace during a demo in Trafalgar Square.

'Aagh! That – ' (and here he evidently thought better of using the word that had first occurred to him – there were ladies present, after all) ' – man!'

It is at least arguable that CND, whose aims enjoyed wide support, did have some effect in the process which eventually brought about strategic arms limitation and nuclear non-proliferation treaties, if not much actual disarmament. But what Rea could have gone on to say was that without retaining a strong defence capability, we might very well lose the luxury of liberal and pacifist attitudes, finding, instead, our actions and publicly-expressed opinions severely constrained by the oppressive regime that would overrun the country while left-leaners like me were denouncing the very armed forces that might have saved us. However, this was a family occasion, and the subject was changed.

*

At his funeral I asked myself: Why should this death mean so much to me, a mere cousin once removed, with whom I have had but sporadic contact over the years?

His death represents an end; that, perhaps, was the answer. An end of an age; an end of a certain kind of consciousness, or view of the world: a heroic age, even, which has yielded to a hegemony of anti-heroism, a mean-spiritedness that does not recognise the necessity of people like him. However incautiously outspoken he may frequently have been, there was something noble about Rea Leakey. Like Churchill, his qualities were nourished by the times in which he lived, and particularly by the Second World War; it was the six years of that all-enveloping conflict that provided the conditions for him, and others like him, to thrive.

At his memorial service in the chapel at Sandhurst, one of the addresses was given by an ex-colleague from the Army. He finished quite splendidly.

'I don't know everything that Rea will be doing up there,' he barked, pointing heavenwards, 'but I imagine there will be conversations about military tactics with Napoleon and Alexander the Great. And I'm sure of one thing. When Rea arrived there at the gates, he'll have thrust his grinning face up to St. Peter, grabbed him by the hand, punched him in the stomach with the other fist, and said, "How are you, you old bugger!"'

9

Memorials and Museums

On a television talk show the interviewee was Julian Barnes, author of various novels and non-fiction books. He stood by a painting he reproduces in *A History of the World in 10½ Chapters*. It is a 19th century depiction of desperate men and women clinging to a raft, apparently a rendition of a true-life shipwreck[1]. Describing it, Barnes said, uncontroversially enough, that one of the functions of art is to record the depths of human affairs. But he went further. He said what seemed to amount to the reciprocal of this, to the effect that tragedies occur in order to be commemorated in art. That is their purpose.

Melvyn Bragg, the interviewer, struggled with this for a bit, trying to get Barnes to explain just in what sense he meant it. How could this be? In what sense of the use of the words he was employing was this proposition true? Julian Barnes struggled too, and in the end was driven to say, with a smile, 'Well, it is difficult to explain ... and

---

[1] *The Raft of the Medusa*, by Théodore Géricoult.

perhaps in a sense I'm just trying it on a little bit.' Flying a kite, trying to get people to accept what he had just articulated only poorly himself and which he was not sure he believed either.

But that is, is it not, one of the characteristics of words: that it is not always possible to use them precisely, that one does not always know what one means, but that a phenomenon or point of view or interpretation that is hard to explain may nonetheless deserve to have the attempt made? 'Perhaps I was trying it on a little', far from meaning we should disregard what he says, asks us to redouble our attempts at comprehending. Words alone are not always enough to bring about understanding, and concepts such as causality and intention and purpose cannot always be described by them. If one uses only words to bring about the understanding of the notion that human tragedies occur in order to be celebrated in art, then one runs into the brick wall of apparent paradox. But if one looks at examples, and approaches the problem through senses other than the logical or rational one which is mediated by words, then a cognition of sorts is possible. If Julian Barnes' concept were to be examined in a court of law, then no doubt it would be found wanting. The opposition barrister would make mincemeat of the notion. But the case *for* the proposition, in the hands of perhaps a more skilled barrister aiming to counter the first, might be argued, if not sufficiently clearly to persuade the jury he was right, then at any rate well enough to make them feel he had a point worth making. For art is supposed to engage the emotions; and nothing engages the emotions more than tragedies; and the biggest tragedies, in which the largest number of people get killed, the most families are bereaved and the greatest destruction is caused, are wars: of which the largest, on any reckoning, was World War Two.

So perhaps what Barnes was getting at was that tragedies (or some of them) and art (or some of it) both have particular effects, namely the prompting of emotion – which tragedies accomplish inadvertently, whilst art does so intentionally. Can the site of a tragedy, left as it was at the time, count as art? Certainly it evokes emotion, and sometimes an unwilling confrontation with it. A postcard arrives from Pete.

'"In the morning the soldiers came": I expect you remember the opening and the final episode of "The World at War",' he wrote. 'This is the village still left as it was with rusted cars and bedsteads and sewing machines in the houses ... No jokes from here, just another in my series of sites of infamy from WWII. You can start a collection.'

This was Oradour-sur-Glane in southern France, in which the occupation forces took reprisals against the whole village because of the alleged capture of a German officer by the Resistance. The men were forced into barns and machine-gunned. The women and children were herded into the village church and also shot. The doors were locked, the building set on fire and those still alive were burned to death. Ten people survived out of a population of 652.

The gutted church stands out against the peaceful countryside as a reminder of the sunny June day, just before the harvest, when the village and its inhabitants suddenly ceased to exist. Where once a window stood is a little sign: 'Madame Rouffance, the only survivor from the church, escaped through this window'.[1]

A *little* whimsy at the end of Pete's postcard, which you would expect from him after all; but no more than this, because when you are in a place like that you are hardly able to have any feelings save those of the most sombre kind, let alone words to express them; and perhaps we are the last generation who will feel about that war in the acute way that we do. It is not as if we were there, but that feeling is demonstrable because we don't feel quite the same about the first world war, terrible though that was too. World War One was fought by our grandparents' generation, and therefore is an emotional distance away from us that World War Two is not. By the same token, our children will never feel about the war as we do, because it was *our* parents' generation that was involved, not theirs; so however much they may know about it (and certainly they know less than we do, in spite of the flood of information, which is greater than it has ever been), it will never hold for them that strange mixture of nostalgia, guilt, thankfulness, and awe as it does for us. We will be the last generation to visit a place connected with it, or a museum, or to read a book about it, and think: *My father was here* (or *uncle, cousin, one of their friends*). *And I owe my freedom to what they did.* We may not have had the privileged horror of taking part in such an event, but our immediate forebears did, and they told us about it. The further back you go in history, to the first world war and beyond, to battles and wars of the past,

---

[1] *The Rise and Fall of the Third Reich*, by William Shirer, 1959.

the harder it is to put that kind of construction on it, and to have those feelings.

Oradour-sur-Glane is a representative of the places where the war actually happened. Whether the remains of the village could by any conceptual stretch be called art may be trivial, or perhaps insultingly frivolous. Perhaps in the same category are the sites of concentration camps. Some time after Pete's postcard Helen and I took a detour with my brother and his wife in Northern Germany to Bergen-Belsen. I felt uncomfortable and didn't particularly enjoy the visit. Do I need this? I asked myself. To which the rejoinder was: *About as much as reading Primo Levi, I suppose, which you have already done, and found absolutely necessary.* There was a film to be seen before we started. I didn't want to see it, but the others did, so we stayed. I didn't want to walk all the way round, but the others did, and so we all did. The previous day we had visited Berlin and rejoiced in its new-found confidence following the fall of the Wall, and after that, this was hardly a bundle of fun. 'Human kind cannot bear very much reality', said T. S. Eliot[1]. I thought: well, I can't, anyway.

Little remains except large burial mounds, longitudinal in section, and paths round the site. But there are the foundations of two huts, numbered 9 and 10, each of which, apparently, at the end of the war contained 1,600 Hungarian Jews. I paced them out. They measured about ninety metres by eighteen. Clearly, the conditions inside were appalling. But they were not quite unimaginable, which made it worse.

---

[1] In *Burnt Norton* (1935).

During the visit I learned that, unlike Auschwitz or Dachau, Belsen was not an extermination camp designed specifically for killing people. In effect it might have been not far short of that, certainly, but its original notoriety derived largely from the fact that it was the first such camp entered by the Allied forces after the end of the war (the British in this case), and therefore the first to be reported to the world. It was originally two separate camps – a prisoner of war camp and a concentration camp for undesirables. Late in the war, when it was obvious to everyone except Hitler that Germany was losing, thousands were moved to it from elsewhere. Many came, in fact, from the extermination camps, because the Germans did not want the Allies to find out what had happened in them. Unlike at the extermination camps, systematic killings did not take place at Belsen, and the reason for the huge number of deaths, which nearly all occurred in the closing months of the conflict, was simply that there was not enough food. All right, we can accept that the incarceration of 'undesirables' – Jews, Communists, homosexuals, the mentally deficient – was criminal. But, whatever the reason for their being there, the simple problem was that the place was grossly overcrowded. That was the consequence of war. In the circumstances the Germans found themselves, their actions – or inaction – may not be excusable, but it is understandable: more understandable, at any rate, than deliberate extermination. Any country, any people with those problems on its hands, whether self-inflicted or not, might also end up simply allowing the inmates to die. They were hardly high on the Germans' list of priorities. The rationale must have been something like 'Why are we keeping these people alive? They are our enemies. We are wasting food on them. We need it for ourselves, for our soldiers, our own people. These people are not our priority. They have had a lot more life than they might have had. Every day is a bonus for them. They should be grateful.' I don't say that reasoning is right. But it is comprehensible, in its context. It would be interesting to know if it *were* the rationale, but the trouble is, we haven't heard about it from the people who did it, because they were executed, or they escaped and wouldn't say anything about it; and they're probably dead now anyway, most of them. Their testimony would have been just as useful as that of the survivors, because only in it could there be any clue as to how to avoid it in the future. But in the exhibition hall there was nothing of that nature.

*

I spent a weekend moving my daughter's belongings out of her flat in London, where she had spent her final university year, and back home. When I was at college I could get most of my stuff in a trunk, though later on I needed my Mini. But for this lot I needed a Transit. On the Monday I drove it back to the depot where the hire company kept its vehicles. This was in a location known as 'up at the Barracks' or 'behind the Barracks'.

There is an article, or maybe a book, to be written about the demilitarisation of British culture. 'The Barracks' is where the Dorset Regiment was based. Aside from what was known as the Keep, a castle-like stone structure with battlements which is now the Military Museum, there is a smaller stone edifice consisting of two wings and, between them, a grand central entrance. There is a larger brick building which contained the Sergeants' Mess, and no doubt served a number of other functions. Other buildings, of varying ages, are spread haphazardly over what is now a parking area. The military function of all these buildings has long since gone. The car park was, of course, originally a parade ground, a square laid out for the principal purpose of square-bashing.

Aside from the ever-dwindling number of people in the forces, and their close relatives or friends, it is unlikely that many people below the age of forty know what that phrase means, because it is only older people who will have had relatives who talked to them about their military experiences. It merely means practising marching, in big black Army boots with shiny toe-caps, on the area of tarmac or concrete that served as the drill-ground. (Atten ... SHUN! By the left, quee-ick ... MARCH! Left, right, left, right! Riiight ... WHEEL! Squaaad ... HALT! Aybout ... TURN! Squaaad ... Stannaaat ... HEASE!)

For some, those military experiences were in the war. For those born a little too late to take part, they took place during their National Service. This was a two-year compulsory stint in the Army, Navy or Air Force, which everyone in their late teens or early twenties had to do, learning how to fight in case the country had to go to war again. It was abolished at the end of 1960, before I reached the necessary age. With the shrinking of the military, including the demise of the Dorset Regiment and many others up and down the country, fewer people know what it is like to be in military uniform. The traditions of the forces are now being handed down the generations by a smaller and smaller band. To this, many people would say 'Hurrah! Good riddance.' It is unfashionable to champion a reversal of this development, let alone the reinstatement of National Service; and from the point of view of western Europe several decades after the end of World War Two, the process was inevitable.

The act of deconsecrating such buildings, as it were, selling them off for civilian use, takes them out of the domain of war. So far from remembering, it gives us licence to forget. But many do remember, if only because of the name. 'Up at the Barracks': we see no soldiers there, though an ancient light tank still sits outside the military museum. If memory is to be preserved, it will be only through the continued use of that soubriquet by the people of the town; and then in time the reason will be forgotten, and we will say 'by the sorting office', some of the buildings having been taken over by the Royal Mail.

*

Whilst the careful preservation of some of the places where the victims of war met their fate enables us to remember them the better, and the folk-memory of 'the Barracks' and such buildings is also still in us, other sites of military activity are in principle unidentifiable. If you are killed on land then visitors can go there, and get a handle on what happened; but if you die at sea then there is no such thing as a visit to the site, one which will enable you to see the topography of the place, and understand.

One part of the ocean is much like the next. Invariably, then, memorials to sailors are on dry land.

Prominent on a ridge in Somerset, between Glastonbury and Somerton, stands a cylindrical stone column, perhaps eighty feet high. If you look at it from the nearest road, about a hundred yards away, at the top you can see the sails and the poop of a ship; rising from the centre is something akin to a mast, although perhaps it doubles as a lightning conductor. On one side of the cuboid plinth forming its base is the inscription:

IN MEMORY OF
SIR SAMUEL HOOD
BARONET
KNIGHT OF THE MOST HONOURABLE ORDER OF THE BATH
AND NOMINATED GRAND CROSS THEREOF
KNIGHT OF S^{NT} FERDINAND AND OF MERIT
KNIGHT GRAND CROSS OF THE SWORD
VICE ADMIRAL OF THE WHITE
AND COMMANDER IN CHIEF OF HIS MAJESTY'S FLEET
IN THE EAST INDIES.

This was the man who gave his name to HMS *Hood*, of which more later. On the next side of the plinth, the eulogy continues:

AN OFFICER OF THE HIGHEST DISTINCTION
AMONGST THE ILLUSTRIOUS MEN
WHO RENDERED THEIR OWN AGE
THE BRIGHTEST PERIOD
IN THE NAVAL HISTORY
OF THEIR COUNTRY

One of the brightest of those periods, possibly. And on the far side:

> THIS MONUMENT IS DEDICATED
> TO THEIR LATE COMMANDER
> BY THE ATTACHMENT AND REVERENCE
> OF BRITISH OFFICERS
> OF WHOM MANY WERE HIS ADMIRING FOLLOWERS
> IN THOSE AWFUL SCENES OF WAR
> IN WHICH WHILE THEY CALL FORTH
> THE GRANDEST QUALITIES OF HUMAN NATURE
> IN HIM LIKEWISE GAVE OCCASION
> FOR THE EXERCISE OF ITS MOST AMIABLE VIRTUES
> HE DIED AT MADRAS DECEMBER 24TH 1814

'Those awful scenes': unlike many inscriptions on memorials to war leaders or to those who have been killed in battle, this one does not entirely glorify war. Even though 'awful' here may mean 'inspiring reverential wonder', rather than its modern meaning of 'very bad', there does appear here some recognition that war is not entirely a good thing. (And just what were those 'amiable virtues' to which Sir Samuel's colleagues felt it right to allude?)

On the fourth side there is no inscription, but there are steps to what looks like a bricked-up doorway. The base of the monument has been defaced, needless to say, by various inscriptions. *BMX rules*, says one. *Janet and Mark* in a heart shape. *Fraggle I love you.* There are iron spikes around two and a half sides of the column, but even if they had been around all four, they would present nothing but a challenge to unruly youngsters. Two hundred years old, this structure is neglected, little by little falling into disrepair; and the trees which have grown up around it allow only a brief glimpse as one drives along the shallow valley below.

It is possible it will be preserved. But I suspect that sooner or later, during the next few decades, lumps will start to fall off it. Then it will have to be declared dangerous, and someone will surround it by fencing stopping all but the most determined from approaching. Shortly afterwards, it will be pronounced in danger of falling down. And it will have to be dismantled, because although there will be a few people calling stridently for its preservation, no-one will be able to find the money. In a few short hours it will be removed; and people driving the road below will glance up to the trees, and feel slightly uneasy, thinking: I'm sure there was something sticking up there, wasn't there? – some monument or other. Wasn't there?

Sir Samuel Hood has another memorial. At Mosterton, just over Somerset's border with Dorset, stands an inn named the Admiral Hood. The pub sign says 'circa 1748', but the exterior provides little evidence of that age. Given the date of the Admiral's death in Madras, it cannot have been an inn from the start, at any rate not with his name. Unfortunately the descriptions of the various Admirals Hood, and the pictures of the two Royal Navy ships to have borne the name, occupy an inconspicuous location in the bar; and what would have been the best place for them, above the heavy stone lintel over the fireplace, is occupied by a bland picture of birds.

*

In the Quantock Hills, a few miles from the Hood memorial, lies the tiny settlement of Over Stowey. Like Chawton Cemetery in which Peter Ferris is buried, its graveyard, behind the church, contains just one war grave, with its distinctive plain headstone. This one is dedicated to H. Grandfield, lance-corporal in the Tank Corps, who died on 1st October 1918. Five weeks before peace was declared, then. They brought him back here, to his village, his home, his relatives, to lie in the earth of the hills he knew. On another gravestone are those poignant words from the Bible: 'The Lord gave, and the Lord hath taken away: Blessed be the name of the Lord'. They break me up, those words. Perhaps they are too truthful. They refer to a brutal God, at one moment bountiful and at the next merciless, whose people have no choice but to acknowledge his power, and who on a whim will take possession of a life, and end it.

*

For a moment let's forget the war, the wars. Graves, then, and gravestones. Do not most of them, eventually, become useless? As in all cemeteries, here, no doubt, the majority are never visited. No flowers are placed on them. The stones are slowly crumbling into the earth, following the bodily remains below. What will become of them? What will this cemetery be like in a hundred years' time? Five hundred? Why does one visit a grave, anyway? You could say, if no-one visits, there is no point in its being marked at all. Yet the fact that someone might know it is there, and that one could visit if one wished – is that not important?

Here, then, are visible graves marked by heavy, inscribed stones, planted firmly in the ground. Permanent? Semi-permanent, perhaps; weathering and human caprice take their toll. A grave and its headstone can last decades, centuries, far longer than its occupants lived, and is much more dignified than a mean little granite square laid on the ground covering an urn of ashes. That is not a proper memorial. Is a headstone, or a plaque on the wall in a church, better on account of being more permanent, more likely to be noticed by people who have no personal interest? Of course it is. Some people may not see much point in a grand memorial stone. But there is more point than in a mean one.

How long should a gravestone last? One answer might be: for the length of time that relatives can be expected to visit it. How long is that? Perhaps: as long as they feel emotionally engaged with the people buried there. So how long is *that*? I am emotionally engaged with my parents, even though they are no longer alive, so I should like the opportunity of visiting a well-kept grave that, during my lifetime, looks more or less permanent. I also feel emotion in connection with my maternal grandparents, whom I briefly knew – and, perhaps curiously, with my paternal ones, whom I didn't. But suppose I were to visit the grave of my great-grandparents, assuming I knew where it was? With them my emotional ties are more tenuous: I might be *interested*, but I doubt I would *feel* much. And relatives who are still more distant? If they were famous then I might feel some pride, or humbleness in their shadow, but I don't think I would feel I had much, indeed anything, to do with them. So perhaps you should expect to be able to visit the grave of your grandparents, but not necessarily anyone earlier. How many years after one's grandparents die can one expect, on average, to die oneself? Two generations, perhaps; thirty years a generation, that makes sixty. Add a bit for safety and some for modern-day longevity, and cold rationality might dictate the lifespan of a grave – its memorial stones, at any rate – need be no more than a century.

But in the case of war graves, is there another answer? Do the burial-places of people who have fallen on active service deserve to be seen by yet further generations of their countrymen? There is unlikely to be emotional involvement with the individuals. But emotion in the visitors is created by the visit itself, as they imagine what happened to the poor devils buried there. In Britain the issue is overlaid by the activities of the Commonwealth War Graves Commission (CWGC), whose website, on which you can look up the memorial of any serviceman or woman, states that the grave is 'in the perpetual care' of the Commission. Perpetual? All we can say is, as far as we are concerned it is perpetual: we cannot vouch for our descendants. We cannot bind them, and their descendants, and their descendants' descendants, to keeping this grave in good condition. In a hundred years these mass cemeteries, and the stones of individual servicemen in other graveyards, may well still be there, still cared for. But two hundred? A thousand?

What is certain is that, even a hundred years after the war that spawned the CWGC, the Great War or the First World War as it came to be known after the still more enormous Second, people in their thousands visit the mass sites. Many do so in order to see the resting-places of their own forebears. George Laing, the Surrey doctor who took in Rea Leakey and his siblings, did not fight in that war but, as a doctor, took turns with his partner in his medical practice to travel to the battlefront in eastern France to work in the field hospitals. At that front, on the Somme, happened to be his younger half-brother Alexander, or Alec. Although Alec was a Church of England chaplain rather than a soldier, like George he was commissioned as an officer into the Northumberland Fusiliers, and close enough to the fighting to be in danger.

The family script, the oral tradition, goes like this. When one hospital tent was full, the wounded had to be taken to the next; if that too were full, then elsewhere. On one such day in 1916, a couple of orderlies approached Dr. Laing to tell him there was a casualty outside needing admission.

'We're full,' he replied. 'You know we're full. The orders are to move any more down the road.'

The answer came, 'We think you'll take this one, sir.'

It was Alec. As soon as George saw him, he knew he would not live. The script does not record what words passed between the brothers on that matter, but Alec was passed down the casualty chain, eventually to reach the hospital at Rouen, some 70 miles from the front, where, three weeks later on 24th July 1916, he died.

Alexander Laing is buried at St. Sever Cemetery, on the southern outskirts of the city. Like many others, this is a graveyard that has one local section, another for Commonwealth war dead. The instigators of the Commonwealth cemeteries intended to establish an equality in death of those who died for their country, and, in terms of the simple headstones, which are all of identical size and shape, they succeeded; but some distinction has crept in, because according to the listings of the graves, his is in the officers' section.

The year before the war broke out, George Laing had paid his brother the compliment of naming his second son after him. With what might have been recognised as an omen, but only in retrospect three years later, the infant died at six months from meningitis.

*

On holiday in the Lake District I ride my bike from Keswick, its northernmost town, south-west to Lorton, then alongside Crummock Water to Buttermere, through the Newlands valley and back. The growth and demise of trees on these hillsides is governed by human activity. We plant them, and later, cut them down; but they are in strictly limited areas, and on the fells where we do not intend to grow them, we install sheep to eat not only the grass but also any new tree-seedlings, which would otherwise grow to cover the landscape. Left to themselves, without human or animal intervention, the hillsides would no doubt be entirely wooded, as they were before the advent of mining, when the trees were burned for smelting the ore. Like most people, I prefer the hills in their current state, their shapes against the skyline clear, and the rock-formations exposed. Occasionally there is an exception, such as the managed plantations of conifers on the slopes bordering the Whinlatter Pass. In places here the trees have been newly cleared, leaving a mass of stumps and twigs through which it would be impossible to walk with any comfort, and on which neither bracken nor heather has had time to establish itself. Roads surfaced with hardcore run through the area. Built as they are for wheeled or tracked vehicles, they too are inimical to feet, and with trees on both sides there is no view. You might equally well be walking through the conifers of Wareham Forest in Dorset or the Black Forest in Germany. This one, Thornthwaite Forest, may be known by a slightly more charming name, but is no more attractive for that.

On the little road into Lorton from the Whinlatter Pass I stop by a teak seat, facing south-west towards Sowerfoot Fell. Fixed into it is a brass plaque:

> ERECTED TO THE MEMORY OF TWO GALLANT YOUNG MEN
> OF LORTON VALE
> WHO GAVE THEIR LIVES DURING THE 1939-1945 WAR
> JAMES E. LENNOX – RICHARD N. ROBINSON

At each end of the seat, beneath the horizontal arm rest, is a small flat panel with a hole cut out in the shape of a clover leaf. In the back of the seat is a larger one, but brand new and of oak. The cross-members upon which you sit are newly riveted to the supporting pieces underneath. Evidently, people have been looking after this memorial. Thus do English villages continue to remember their own.

From here the most striking sight is of Mellbreak, an isolated double-topped fell with two peaks of almost identical height. I find my way to the Kirkstile Inn near Loweswater and drink Bluebird Bitter from the Coniston Brewery. This is low in alcoholic content, but like the beers drunk at lunchtime in past centuries by farmhands, shipbuilders, steelworkers and sailors it is a manual workers' ale, useful for replacing the energy used in the morning, ready for the challenges of the afternoon. For my part, I'm hoping it will get me up over Newlands Hause. I emerge into bright sunshine and take a bridleway through a wood of beech, ash and oak, in which – unlike the conifer plantations – the light filters delicately through the leaves, and there is a pleasingly irregular profile of trunks and branches.

Near Littletown, where Lucy in Beatrix Potter's *The Tale of Mrs. Tigglywinkle* lived, I call at the tiny Newlands Church. One plaque on the wall reads: 'In loving memory of John and Alan Clarke of this parish who gave their lives in the world war 1939-1945'. Underneath are the words: 'To the stars by rough roads, O valiant Hearts'.

*

At the top of Castle Crag is a fine green-slate slab set into the rock. 'Castle Crag was given to the National Trust in memory of John Hamer, 2nd Lieutenant, 6th KSLI[1], born July 8th 1897, killed in action March 22nd 1918. Also of the following men of Borrowdale who died for the same cause … ' There follows a list of ten more. On one corner of the stone has been placed a string of blood-red fabric poppies.

*

Provence in late summer: Vaison-la-Romaine, on a river crossed by a splendid stone bridge dating back centuries.

---

[1] King's Shropshire Light Infantry.

What characteristics of this part of France distinguish them from England? In the countryside, the interminable sound of the cicadas – which you hardly ever see, because when you search for them, they stop. In the town, shallow roofs of the simplest tiles, rows of upturned half-pipes half a metre in length, covered with corresponding rows of *la même chose* but inverted. Made from a pale orange-brown clay, in places they are bleached even paler by the sun. They are laid loose, with only the lowest ones cemented in place. Every roofscape, however apparently random in its angles, has an easy, unpretentious elegance.

The old part of the town, Hauteville, rises – as its name suggests – above the new. The houses are of an almost white limestone. I love this rough stone; there has been no need to prettify it, and only sporadically has it been rendered, with cement of the same colour. The buildings rise tall on both sides of the narrow streets, to three, sometimes four storeys, their windows shuttered against the sun. Some are the haunt of artists, and a pair of double doors announces a theatre. The square outside the little cathedral is on the edge of the cliff, above the gorge, and you can look out from it over the river to the newer part of the town. Touristy it may be, even twee, but Britain can boast nothing quite like this. The narrow streets wind upwards to the château, its square keep perched on a huge outcrop of rock above the town. Down to its west, on a sloping plateau of the rock, is a nasty overhang. This would have been a desperate place to which to have to retreat. It is almost unassailable, but would be equally difficult to relieve if besieged. A notice tells me it is named Le Château Comtal, that it stands at a strategic point in the valley of Ouvèze, and symbolises the authority of Raymond V, Count of Toulouse. The soldiers lived in the castle, its *capitaine* in the town below. He, clearly, was not going to forgo fleshly pleasures. It dates from 1180, but was gradually abandoned after the sixteenth century. Four or five hundred years is good going. Which of our own present-day buildings will last as long? And that invites the question: Is longevity in buildings a virtue? Maybe only if they remain useful. Otherwise, you could argue, it is a positive hindrance, unless there should be other criteria besides usefulness. Beauty? But then what is the value of something beautiful which was intended not as a work of art (whatever *that* is) but of practical use?

In spite of the shade from the thick-trunked plane trees with their mottled cream and grey-brown bark, the sun makes it impossible at this time of year to do anything outdoors between half past ten and five o'clock. Instead, evening street life flourishes. It is so much more relaxed, energetic, elegant and civilised than anything permitted by the weather in England. The colours of Provence are yellow and mauve, lavender and sunflowers, infused by the Provençales into their table linen, their paintings and postcards.

And now here is the war memorial, elegantly carved into the rock opposite the bridge, bearing a hundred or so names from the First World War. Those from the Second are almost exclusively from 1944 and 1945, and are divided into several categories: the general ones, the *victimes civiles*, the *déportés politiques*, the *déportés STO* and the *FFI*[1]. The war experience of this part of France of course was quite different from that of the north where the Allied invasion took place: little direct fighting, and little destruction of buildings.

*

Back in England, approaching Fovant on the A30 from Shaftesbury towards Wilton, you see on the hillside to the south what look like curious patterns. As you come closer and see them face-on you realise what they are: huge insignia of Army regiments, four or five of them, cut into the chalk. Fovant Badges, these are known as. For decades this area has been associated with the British Army, and there are several camps close by, forever engaged in infantry and tank movements. Usually, one associates chalk cuttings on hillsides with prehistoric civilisations. Here, it is as if the armed forces have hijacked this ancient tradition for altogether baser purposes which have nothing to do with ritual or religion. When you see cuttings in the chalk hillside you expect them to be of horses, or well-endowed men with a club like the Giant at Cerne Abbas. White horses of unknown date are emblematic not of the modern military but of ancient peoples, hundreds if not thousands of years in the past. The Fovant Badges are somehow shocking: not memorials, but a bold announcement of the militarism of their age.

---

[1] STO: Service du Travail Obligatoire (people subjected to forced labour). FFI: Force Français d'Intèrieur (the Resistance movement).

*

The business meeting in London finished unexpectedly early and I had three or four hours to indulge myself at the Imperial War Museum. The visit ended in disappointment. Just before closing time I climbed the stairs to the art gallery on the top floor. On another occasion, in another place, the pictures might have had some power. But after the immediacy of the actual artefacts of war – the 16-inch naval guns mounted outside, the Lancaster fuselage, the bullets, the uniforms, the servicemen's letters – each of these images was exactly that. Someone's interpretation. A representation. I found them impotent. They had none of the reality even of the photographs. It was if they had been painted from a hundred miles away, through so heavy a filter as to remove the essence. If art is supposed to engage the emotions, in my case these examples of it failed. I quickly left.

Elsewhere, at Daniel Libeskind's Imperial War Museum North, in Manchester, the emotions of war have been washed away by an over-self-conscious design. One of the most significant recent buildings in the UK, we have been told. Perhaps. But whilst you are in it, the building seems to overpower the contents. In one way that may not be wholly a bad thing; it does succeed, by the discordant juxtaposition of its curves, sharp angles and unexpected slopes, to disorient you from a settled life and to express the pity of war.

*

On the fiftieth anniversary of D-Day, or rather the weekend closest to it, I took Helen to Weymouth in the rain for a weekend sailing course. After dropping her off I drove back along the seafront. The hotels and amusement arcades were bedecked with British, Canadian and American flags. Rows of coaches disgorged their elderly passengers into hotels. Small groups of baseball-capped bespectacled North American war veterans walked uncertainly around the harbour. A large cruise liner sat in the bay, and the Channel Islands wave-piercer ferry massively occupied a berth in the harbour. Much had been written about the occasion in the newspapers during the previous few days and weeks, with endless supplements; the television had been full of it as well. It was all there, in every word one read and heard: the greatest seaborne invasion in history, the streets in practically every town in southern England jammed with tanks, armoured personnel carriers, lorries, field guns, supply vehicles and hundreds of thousands of soldiers; and statistics of the thousands on both sides who were killed. Fifty years on, many of these ex-servicemen were taking the ferry across to those ports – Cherbourg, Caen – closest to where they landed on the beaches all those years ago when they were young. Fifty years! I hadn't even been born; but, such is the power of the words and images – the word-pictures painted by any old soldier willing to talk about it, the black-and-white photos in the books of the school library as well as those on my parents' shelves, the war films we saw at the cinema or at school on Saturday nights – that it seemed like last week.

For most of these people who went as soldiers across the Channel to invade the Continent, against the might of Germany, this was an interlude in their lives they had never bargained for. We sometimes think of soldiering as a profession, a job, taken up in the same way as engineering or nursing or landscape gardening; but only a very few of those people were regular servicemen and women. The others saw it as their duty to volunteer, or were called up, and suddenly found themselves doing things they had never done before and never would again. Those who survived are coming back now to look and marvel at it all. *Did I really do this? Was I actually here?*

But for me there were other things to do that day. I had my daughter to take into town shopping for clothes, one son to help with his last-minute revision whilst waiting for the other son's tennis tournament result. Two hours later the tennis-player phoned. 'I won!' he said, excitedly. 'I went three-love down, then came back to win, six-four six-three. I played really well. Got to go. I'm being called for the doubles. Bye. I'll ring you tonight.' I punched the air.

*

The Royal British Legion is the organisation for all ex-Service personnel. Anyone who has been in the Forces, in wartime or not, is entitled to be a member. Its club premises provide space for ex-soldiers and sailors and airmen to reminisce and drink cheap beer. Youth football teams and other clubs are affiliated, adopting names such as Blandford RBL. It is most in evidence on the Sunday in November which is designated Remembrance Day. Then, veterans of WWII (but, today, none from WWI, the last having died in 2012), shuffle proudly, in as close to a regimental march as their aged limbs can manage, along a short pre-determined route ending at the local Cenotaph of their town. A brief religious service is held, the words of Laurence Binyon ring forth ('They shall not grow old as we that are left grow old'[1]), and a single bugler plays the Last Post. In the weeks leading up to that day in 1995 the Legion, together with those newspapers which felt their readers, or at least their owners, would approve, mounted a campaign to persuade the country to once more commemorate the day on November 11th as well as on the nearest Sunday.

The Armistice ending the Great War in 1918 was signed at the 11th hour of the 11th day of the 11th month. The phrase 'the eleventh hour' derives from the Bible, the parable of the vineyard owner. Just what meaning Jesus intended to impart might be thought somewhat obscure, since the story entails a labourers' wage scheme in which those who arrived at the last minute, only just before knocking-off time, were paid the same as those who arrived earlier. All the workers were paid one penny, whether they worked the full twelve hours or arrived at the third hour, the sixth, the ninth or the eleventh. The vineyard-owner justifies himself by saying to the complainants: 'You agreed the daily wage with me. I choose to be kind to these others. Why should you grumble about the way I use my money?' One suspects that, unless the entire job were completed on the first day,

---

[1] *For the Fallen*, first published in *The Times* a week after the outbreak of the Great War in 1914.

there would have been chaos the following morning, but there the story ends. 'The eleventh hour' has come to mean 'just in time'. The phrase perhaps took on an additional meaning, namely 'before the young men of all our countries become even more comprehensively decimated'.

The following year, at the same time and on the same date in the calendar, and for years afterwards, everyone ceased what they were doing. People stopped on the street, they stopped in the shops, they stopped on the road, they stopped at school, and they stopped whatever they were doing at home. Cars, buses and trams drew to a halt. Business transactions were suspended. No telephones rang. There was silence. The country came to a standstill. For two minutes the country remembered those who had given their lives for it in what was, at the time, the biggest conflict the world had known; a war whose scale and particular horrors had, by most people, been entirely unexpected. (The second world war, bigger still, at least had the dubious merit of being not unexpected either in its size or, until the atomic bombs fell on Japan, its dreadfulness.)

At least, that's what I'd always understood. When she was very old, I asked my mother about it again.

'Do you remember the day when the Armistice was signed?'

She had been aged ten at the time. 'Oh yes. We were given a holiday from school. There was one girl there who didn't want a holiday, because she preferred being taught.' (What a swot, I thought.) 'My father asked me if I'd like to go up to London. So of course I said yes. And we went up, and we walked along the Embankment, and there were hundreds of soldiers marching along, and everyone was cheering.'

'And the next year, and for years after that, on the same day, people stopped what they were doing, didn't they, and stood for two minutes in silence?'

'Yes.'

'And the traffic stopped?'

'Yes. But then of course there was far less of it than now. I ... I can't be sure.'

'What about the trains? Did they stop?'

'No,' she said decisively. 'They couldn't really, could they? Well, signalmen couldn't stop what they were doing, and the drivers – ' Her voice trailed off.

And although there were few aircraft flying, they would hardly have stopped, either. So it wasn't as universal as it's sometimes made out. Perhaps some factories did cease production for two minutes, at any rate those where it was possible to do so without too much disruption, and where the management saw fit; but many production methods would have made that unworkable.

'So what do you think of this idea of going back to the two minutes' silence on 11th November?' I asked her. 'Eleven o'clock, everything stopping, even if it's a weekday. It happened between the wars, didn't it, but it stopped after 1945, and transferred to the nearest Sunday.'

She thought for a moment. 'I'm not sure. Would people, these days, would they do it? Does it mean as much to them?'

Since there is a credible campaign going, I thought, perhaps it does. But do these traditions not always die in the end, or become unrecognisable? Granted, it was more of a national event than it is now, but, sad or not, traditions have to be adapted to the conditions prevailing at the time. Time, the great healer, has also caused the collective memory to fade, and, because the march of technological and therefore social progress has been so rapid, inevitably the act has lost its central place in the nation's consciousness. Can you imagine the M1 grinding to a halt voluntarily for two minutes? Yet within a year or two of the campaign starting, numerous large employers, including the major supermarkets, observed the silence.

I cannot see this re-established ritual becoming any more than a limited success whose effects will trail off as the years roll past. More likely, the tradition will in some way become adapted, absorbed into some other celebration, its title perhaps changing too, rather like the takeover of one company by another, in which the name of the resulting organisation is often an amalgam of the two. A little later, when people have begun to call it by its first name only (because it's too much of a mouthful to say the whole thing), the lesser one is quietly dropped. Few complain, except perhaps the relatives of the founder of the now largely-forgotten firm; but no doubt they have sufficient shares to cushion the hurt. Likewise, the descendants of the war dead will still have their photographs, their medals, their certificates. Most of all, they will console themselves that the memories will not die whilst they themselves still live.

*

Alongside a few hundred others in my own small provincial town I stood and watched the parade. I found it impressive that here, and therefore in every other town and village the length of the country, a sizeable group of people, not only the old who lived through one or other of those wars, but also the middle-aged, the youthful and the very young gather in a large group around the war memorial and stand silent and still. There are no other circumstances in which anything remotely similar takes place. Within this public, collective act, a private one is enacted. I also found it moving. During those two minutes, yes, people were looking around a bit; they were certainly not all keeping their minds fully concentrated for all of that time on their memories of the dead: they were hoping the automatic oven had turned itself on at the right time to cook the lunch, they were thinking about the offside decision that denied their local football team a victory in yesterday's game – but overriding those inevitable small human failures was the reason they were there, which was to remember. On this occasion my emotions were fragile. One son and his school work, another and his football, both having worries; my own work too, the difficult meeting I had to arrange the next day ... I recalled my father marching with others of the British Legion (another little cause for regret: I shall never be able to join, membership being open only to those who have served with the armed forces) on that last occasion before his death, looking as smart as he could muster, with his campaign medals: that brought tears to my eyes, too ... As an act of national cohesiveness, an acknowledgement of collective history, this honouring of the dead is both a socially unifying force, and a private act of homage.

*

Just outside the town, on the London road, is a twenty-yard stretch of carriageway which had recently been resurfaced. The fierce fire from a burnt-out car had melted the tarmac, and the work was done after a mother and her two small children had been killed in a head-on collision with a van, in which a teenage boy was also killed. It was early one morning as she drove to work. She ran a corner shop in the town. Afterwards, bunches of flowers were placed on the grass verge to mark the spot. Flowers were placed, too, by the wall in the next village into which two teenage tearaways crashed at the T-junction, the culmination of a high-speed chase with a police car. Flowers are for the dead. As soon as you cut them, they too begin to die. When my father died, my mother hadn't wanted a wreath for the coffin, but at the last minute she decided she'd like a little bunch of flowers on it. My father had always liked daffodils, and so that was what she chose, but I was saddened because the only ones in the shop were still tightly closed, and although we put them in warm water, they would have needed much longer to open; and when, hesitantly, she did place them on the coffin, they were still closed.

We give flowers to the dead. Why? Because. Because there is nothing else we can do. We place them where they have died. We throw wreaths into the sea for sailors who have drowned; and when Helen and I were driving to Lymington for my sister's funeral on the Isle of Wight,

I stopped in the New Forest and picked some heather to drop from the ferry as we crossed the Solent to Yarmouth.

But the quintessential flower for the dead is the poppy. It is not just for any dead. It is reserved for those killed whilst on military service. The reason for its adoption as the symbol of war dead is, we are told, that it was the flower which bloomed all over the fields of Flanders where hundreds of thousands of young men died in the First World War. But that is not what makes it peculiarly well-suited to the task of remembrance. Nor is the fact that its colour is that of the blood which was spilled so freely. The reason the poppy is ideal is that, when cut, it is the shortest-lived of flowers. The moment you remove it from its source of sustenance in the ground, it wilts. It becomes limp; it dies. Its longevity is like that of the young whose lives it represents. They lasted, some of them, barely into mature youthfulness, let alone adulthood. The petals of the poppy are delicate beyond those of other flowers. It is their fragility which represents young lives cut short.

*

Graveyards, cenotaphs, churches, village seats: the wartime dead are commemorated in sundry places. One other variety is the great public schools of this country. (I say 'great public schools' referring, in some people's parlance, to 'privileged private schools catering only for those whose parents are rich enough to pay the fees'. Whatever you think about these establishments, whether or not you believe they lower the standards of State-funded schools by denying them the influence of well-connected parents who would otherwise devote leadership and financial clout to their improvement, the public schools have seen to it that they preserve, and often extremely handsomely, the memory of their former pupils who have died in war. Needless to say, given their clientèle, most of those were officers; it is less common to see a dedication in one of them to a private soldier, rather than to a lieutenant or captain or major. But that is not to deny the force of the memorials.)

I became aware of this during football matches. Or, to be exact, before them, during half-time and when they were over. What my elder son enjoyed more than anything when he was growing up was playing football; and I used to spend Saturday or Sunday afternoons watching. Years later, he began playing for what is called the 'Schools XI' of the Corinthian-Casuals, a club based in South London whose principal historic claim is that it was the exporter of football around the world – to Brazil, amongst other countries. (Notably, a contingent from the club travelled there in 1914, intending to play a series of exhibition matches, but, on arrival, immediately turned around without kicking a ball and caught the first boat back home – because war had been declared, and they saw their duty elsewhere.[1]) The club has maintained the tradition of what might now be seen as the redundant task of popularising football, by 'taking the game', along with – supposedly – its Corinthian spirit, i.e. the essence

[1] A century later, the club returned to complete one of the abandoned fixtures, an event commemorated in the film *Brothers in Football*, first shown on UK television in 2018.

of fair play, to 'the schools'. When the club was formed, in the 1880s, those were, inevitably, the public schools. Today, given the club's location, those it plays are within an hour or two's travelling.

So it was that I found myself at Charterhouse School, near Godalming, its well-spaced buildings displaying sharp, angled gables and tiled spires, in enormous grounds whose sports fields stretch as far as the eye can see. The match took place on a billiard-table of a pitch with not a weed visible. At half-time I strolled to the Memorial Chapel. Anyone who has seen the Anglican cathedral in Liverpool might correctly guess it was designed by the same architect, Giles Gilbert Scott, and although hardly as large, it does have an imposing presence given its position. Erected to commemorate the 700 former pupils killed in the First World War, it is now a memorial also to the additional 350 killed in conflicts since then. Engraved in the porch is the injunction 'YOU WHO ENTER THIS CHAPEL THINK UPON THE CARTHUSIANS IN MEMORY OF WHOM IT WAS BUILT WHO DIED FOR THEIR COUNTRY ... '; and on a series of stone panels in the antechapel are the hundreds of names, arranged according to the year they left the school.

The memorial to the war dead of Winchester College is just as impressive. This one is not a chapel but a cloister. In the narrow street between the rust-red brick buildings of the school, after the football had finished and the teams had listened to the obligatory homily from the Corinthians captain on the traditions that the fixture aims to uphold, I walked through a low stone archway. Beyond it is a quadrangle, bounded on its four sides by roofed cloisters. The cloister walls are set with stone tablets bearing the names of those from the First World War, this time arranged according to the year they entered the school, and stating their regiment and any decorations awarded; and, on a series of columns, similar details are engraved of those from the Second. Running around all four walls is an ornately-carved inscription, thanking God for their service and, like that at Charterhouse, providing, if it should be needed, an earnest exhortation to the reader: ... THOU, THEREFORE, FOR WHOM THEY DIED, SEEK NOT THINE OWN, BUT SERVE AS THEY SERVED, AND IN PEACE OR IN WAR BEAR THYSELF EVER AS CHRIST'S SOLDIER, GENTLE IN ALL THINGS, VALIANT IN ACTION, STEADFAST IN ADVERSITY.

These are magnificent memorials. Prodigious care, and no doubt expense, has gone into them. 'Their name liveth for evermore' is the mantra associated with them, whether or not written in stone. At Winchester, the stonework of the tablets honouring the dead of the First World War is noticeably more weathered than that of the Second. Will they eventually be repaired, re-engraved, replaced?

Or will these dead be remembered only electronically? On their websites, both schools have searchable lists of those who died, with short biographies. These sites give far more information, more accessible to more people, than can be contained on a memorial stone or a gravestone. But stone is not ephemeral, as an image on a screen is. You can be there in person, you can stand and look at it, for as long as your time or that of your companions will permit. At best, you can touch it. You can run your finger along the grooves which form the letters of your dead ancestor's name; and then the memory is etched into you more surely than by any other way. And if the name is too high on the tablet to reach, the act of imagining it will suffice.

10

Rest in Peace

RIP. *Requiescat in pace*. Rest in peace. What does that injunction mean? Ostensibly, that the individual commemorated should have no more troubles – which, needless to say, he or she will not. But what is also behind it, perhaps, is the wish that those left still alive can also somehow find peace, now that the event they most feared has come to pass; and associated with that, sometimes, is an abyss of guilt.

*

Whenever I enter the Digby Tap in Sherborne it seems to be occupied by schoolmasters. Schoolmasters from the Fifties and Sixties, it seems, wearing sports jackets with leather patches on the elbows. That is fitting, for Sherborne has a large number of private schools. There are two major secondary schools there, for starters, one for boys and one for girls, and numerous prep schools.

But the pub serves good beer, and is agreeably stone-flagged and wooden-panelled.

Framed on the wall was a yellowed front page from *The Times*, Friday December 5th 1941. In those days, and until the mid-1960s, the newspaper did not have news on the front page. Instead it bore classified advertisements in very small print: Births, Marriages, Deaths, Business Offers, Stamp Collecting, Personal, Legal Notices, Situations Vacant, and Cars For Sale – amongst which, on this day, were several Buicks and a Cadillac. The Deaths column had a sub-section entitled 'On Active Service'. The first entry was more poignant than most.

> EDE. – Missing, H. M. S. Glorious, 1940, now officially presumed killed in action, Flying Officer Herman Francis Grant Ede, D.F.C., R.A.F., younger son of Engr. Lieut. E.G. Ede, R.N., killed in action, 1917, and of Mrs. Ede, of Hamilton, Bermuda.

So the mother had lost her husband in the First World War; she had (perhaps) emigrated to Bermuda to escape her sorrow; and now another war had taken her son. The father, probably, had been killed in the trenches, the son as a pilot aboard an aircraft carrier. HMS *Glorious*, which started life as a cruiser but was later converted into a carrier, was sunk by the battlecruisers *Scharnhorst* and *Gneisenau* in June that year while covering the Allied withdrawal from Norway. It took six months, therefore, for Mrs. Ede to receive the official pronouncement that her son was presumed dead.

*

191

Conventional wisdom has it that the loss of a child is the worst event that can befall a parent. It is against the natural order of things. I am quite sure it shortened the life of my own father. His death was hastened perhaps not by that of my sister in itself but because it was from his own sailing yacht she fell. He never said as much to my recollection, but it would not be surprising if one of the uppermost self-reproaches were 'I should never have lent them the boat'. The kind of grief into which one descends is particularly acute. And perhaps one of the best ways of signifying you are in this state is to do what was done by the mother of Adrian Drewe.

Not far from Okehampton in Devon stands Castle Drogo, a 'country house masquerading as a fortress', as the publicity material has it; it is a forbidding-looking granite house in a commanding position on an escarpment above the river Teign, designed by one of the foremost architects of the early 20th century, Edwin Lutyens. His client was Sir Julius Drewe, the founder of a chain of grocery shops named Home & Colonial. (My mother bought many of the family provisions from our local branch during the 1950s, thus playing her part in the profitability of the enterprise, though by that time its founder was long since dead.) He is said to have lost heart after the death of his son, Adrian, a major in the Army, killed in the First World War at the age of 26. That was long before the eventual completion of the house in 1930, and one wonders whether Adrian ever actually occupied the room at the house that is said by the tour guides to be 'his'. Whether he did or not, the room is kept as a shrine to his memory. His mother lovingly assembled his possessions, and arranged them in a tableau. To this day, Adrian's room can be seen by visitors just as his mother left it.

What did Adrian's death demonstrate? It may well have hastened that of his father; whether he had had hopes of his son carrying on in the family business (Sir Julius had retired as a millionaire at 33, and clearly there was a great deal to inherit), and whether he saw the great house as the beginning of a dynasty of Drewes, I do not know. But the striking attempt at the retention of his memory, by the creation of the reliquary, tells us something else.

If the worst thing that can happen to a parent is that their child should die before them, then *ipso facto* it is also the most feared. Constantly in the back of the minds of parents is the image of the child dying without reaching our Biblically-allotted threescore years and ten, or at any rate completing life in some satisfactory way that entails the experience of all its principal phases from infancy to old age, each of which has its consolations and pleasures as well as its hardships. The fear accompanies parents from the moment a child is born. What parent does not dread the phone call from the school to be told there has been an accident? Or who, travelling home from work, does not every so often imagine a police car or ambulance outside the house, and being informed that in their absence Something Has Happened?

The protectiveness of adult humans towards their young is continued from birth not merely until the child is capable of independence, as in the case of other species, but for much longer – throughout life, indefinitely. But when the parent acquiesces in sending the child to war, a mental leap is required. The protectiveness is submerged beneath something called Duty, or possibly Necessity. A conscious switch of priorities is attempted, involving the acceptance, on the part of the parents, that their child may die. It is the same mental leap that the soldier himself takes in settling up ahead of time. But the soldier does it as a responsible individual, on his own behalf. Parents who accept or encourage it are doing something else. They are abdicating the responsibility of continuing to protect the child, whatever he or she has decided.

That, in turn, will entail at least a temporary guilt. If the young man, or the young woman, returns unscathed from the conflict, then the guilt is negated, there can be satisfaction that duty was fulfilled, relief that it did not come at the cost of the life, and a quiet forgetting that the original imperative had been shelved.

But what if he or she does not return? The overwhelming emotion is grief. Yet it is underpinned by that guilt, which now turns out to be permanent. Guilt that he or she, the parent, has taken it upon themselves, on behalf of the child, to settle up ahead of time – that they have embraced the possibility that the child may die. They may even feel they encouraged it, and that is very different from accepting the everyday risks that we all take. In an endless loop in their consciousness and their dreams they will hear that accusing voice: *I allowed this to happen. I did not merely allow his death, I encouraged it. He may have played his part in consenting to go to war but I am his mother, I am his father, and I could have stopped it. Instead, I acquiesced. I connived. Parents are supposed to protect their child. I did the reverse.*

And thus, perhaps, Mrs. Drewe, having contributed to her son's death by not preventing him joining the army, no longer had to deal with the fear that he might die, but, worse, had to live with the guilt of letting him do so. Possibly, she will have tried to prevent him going to war. Much more likely, she acquiesced in the prevailing opinion of the time, captured in the recruiting poster showing a middle-aged couple saying to a young man, 'Go! It's your duty, lad'. When she found out he would not return, then, in an enactment of the fantasy that she was wrong, she wrapped up the parcel of his possessions and put them on permanent, which is to say static and lifeless, display. Perhaps this helped her, somehow, deal with her emotions; but Sir Julius, we are told, 'lost heart', that heart of his no doubt pierced by the twin daggers of grief and guilt. Grief at his son's death, the unfulfilled promise, the uncompleted life. Guilt that he himself had not merely failed to prevent it, but abetted it.

Dulce et decorum est pro patria mori: it is sweet and honourable to die for one's country. Wilfred Owen, the poet who gave the most prominence to that line, and himself died in the Great War, called it a lie. But they are fine words, and no doubt the more so for being Latin; and people tend to believe fine words. 'Words are, of course, the most powerful drug used by mankind', said Rudyard Kipling[1], another whose son was killed in that war.

---

[1] Speech to the Royal College of Surgeons, 1923. The full quotation is worth repeating: 'I am, by calling, a dealer in words; and words are, of course, the most powerful drug used by mankind. Not only do words infect, egotise, narcotise, and paralyse, but they enter into and colour the minutest cells of the brain, very much as madder mixed with a stag's food at the Zoo colours the growth of the

Closer to the probable truth, which is that, in all wars, individuals fight for their comrades, are the words of Jesus Christ found on war memorials in towns and villages throughout the country: 'Greater love hath no man than this, that a man lay down his life for his friends'[1].

*

I'd always known that during the Second World War thousands of children were moved from their homes in the industrial cities to villages and towns remote from areas likely to be bombed. But it was only when my daughter wrote to my mother for help in a school project on the evacuation that I found she had been a volunteer involved in the transport. I told my daughter she might *know* something about it; I hadn't known she'd *done* it.

She escorted groups from London to Brighton. Most of the children had never been away from home before. There was a good deal of secrecy, and absence of information. Only when they boarded the train did they discover its destination. Each volunteer had been provided with a list of addresses. These were the families that had offered to house the evacuees. With a little gaggle of small children in tow, my mother would ring the bell of the first house on the list, then the next and the next. The householder would look the group over, and say: 'I'll have that one', or 'We'll take those two', and the

---

animal's antlers. Moreover, in the case of the human animal, that acquired tint, or taint, is transmissible'.

[1] Gospel of St. John, chapter 15, verse 13.

group would move on down the list until only the scruffiest children were left, to be deposited in whatever household remained.

In the context of life now, this fate seems, if not to defy belief, then to be quite unacceptable on an emotional level. How could *I* do that to one of *my* children?

Quite easily, is probably the answer. Had I lived, as the parents of those children did, at a time when the government told us it knew what was good for my children, and if I'd swallowed this line – which I probably would, given the lack of other information, and the relative absence of today's habit of questioning authority – then I would have done the same. The bombing was real enough. Perhaps the fact that those parents allowed their children to be taken far from their homes to places out of reach even by telephone reflected not so much an uncaring attitude but the peril the country and its population was facing. Policies of this nature were born of necessity. Even so, many children returned to their homes within a short time, often before the threat had receded.

Thus did my daughter succeed in evoking from my mother a description of the war which she had never told me. She had hitherto kept quiet about those years. She left the talking to my father. He it was who told the stories, who lent colour to my understanding of those events from before my time. She would add the intermittent footnote; but, like most women of my acquaintance, then and since, she hated war, and everything connected with it, with a passion.

But she did acknowledge, even if by default, that whilst she did not choose to hold important the sundry

197

reminders of it in the house, these might nevertheless be felt to be of significance by the next generation.

*

For decades, before the advent of e-mail and fax, the principal means of urgent written communication was the telegram. If the message had originated abroad, it was sent by radio to a receiving station. It was then typed into a land-based teleprinter system and sent via a telephone landline to the receiving post office. There the words were printed out on a continuous narrow strip of paper, about a centimetre wide. The strip was torn at convenient places and glued on an official telegram form. This was inserted into a small brown envelope, ten centimetres by seven, and the address pencilled on the outside. It was immediately taken by a delivery-boy on a bicycle or motorbike to its destination.

In my father's desk after he died I found two telegrams. I would like to have these, I said to my mother, and to frame them. She said yes. 'I wouldn't have thrown them away,' she added, 'but ...' The 'but' meant: I'd not thought of them as having much importance. No; maybe not to her, because she was of the generation that completed the business it was set. Perhaps that generation was able to move on, precisely because history provided its people with a job to do, which they did, whereafter there was an end of it. To me, from the generation that looks back, such artefacts are crucial. For us, paradoxically, they represent unfinished business. Business that will, in fact, never be finished. We have not had such a job to carry out, and all we can do is look back and admire those who did theirs.

Both telegrams were to my father's parents in Bristol. They had been evacuated from the centre of the city, with its factories and docks, and were staying with his sister Ivy in a suburb where they were less likely to be bombed. It would also have been cheaper for them all to live in one house. The first is date-stamped 19 September 1944. With typeface, spacing and other idiosyncrasies reproduced approximately, it reads:

```
170 7.15 PM LIVERPOOL Y OHMS PRIORITY
(- PRIORITY-CC )- A H AUSTIN 17 STALBANS ROAD
                    WESTBURY PARK BRISTOL = 6
= NOTIFICATION RECEIVED FROM NORTH WEST EUROPE THAT
  LT A V AUSTIN ROYAL ARMY SERVICE CORPS WAS REPORTED
  MISSING ON 9 TH SEPTEMBER 1944 THE ARMY COUNCIL
  EXPRESS SYMPATHY LETTER FOLLOWS SHORTLY =
UNDER-SECRETARY OF STATE FOR WAR + 17 6 9 1944 +
```

The second is stamped 25 September 1944:

```
 +   250 6.10 LIVERPOOL OHMS PRIORITY CC 77
PRIORITY CC A H AUSTIN 17 STALBANS RD WESTBURY PARK
                   BRISTOL 6
  FURTHER NOTIFICATION RECEIVED FROM NORTH WEST EUROPE
  THAT LT A V AUSTIN ROYAL ARMY SERVICE CORPS
  PREVIOUSLY REPORTED ISSING NOW LOCATED IN HOSPITAL
  . ACCIDENTALLY INJURED ON 12 TH SEPTEMBER 1944
  CONSUSSION FRACTURED LEFT CLAVICLE RIGHT FIBULA
 LETTERS MAY BE ADDRESSED TO HIM AT 107 BRITISH
  GENERAL HOSPITAL BRITISH LIBERATION ARMY BUT NOT
   TO HOSPITAL AUTHORITIES . LETTER FOLLOWS SHORTLY
   = UNDER-SECRETARY OF STATE FOR WAR +
17 6 12 107BRISTL 6 TW 1944 +
```

A letter confirming the details was sent dated 30th September, giving the date of the incident as 12th

September – a full week before the first telegram. Reconstructed from what my father had told me, the story runs as follows.

Operation Overlord, the D-day offensive against the German forces occupying France was launched across the English Channel on 6th June 1944. My father sailed to France some weeks later with units from his regiment, the Royal Army Service Corps, which was responsible for organising supplies to the front-line troops, such as vehicles, ammunition, fuel and food – all the requisites for servicing the needs of an army fighting a lengthy campaign. Stationed in Normandy, he was acting as a messenger between one unit and another on the night of 12th September, 1944. He set off on his motor-cycle. The message was never delivered, and he did not return to his unit.

The fact that he was missing was reported, and in due course that message was picked up at the receiving station in Liverpool. The telegram dated 19th September was sent to his father.

'Missing', in those days – as in the First World War – sometimes meant not merely 'dead', but 'blown so comprehensively to pieces we haven't been able to identify any body parts'. And, as with Peter Ferris, no-one could be reported as killed until positive proof of identification was found. So a message saying that someone was missing would, more often than not, be followed eventually by another confirming that the person concerned was dead, or presumed dead as in the case of Herman Ede.

At that time my father had been married for seven months, and his wife was expecting their first child. His records had evidently not, however, been altered to show her as next of kin, and his parents were still identified as his closest relatives. Notification of the fact that he was missing was therefore sent to them. At the time, his wife was living with her parents in Surrey. His father and mother did not tell her of the first telegram; probably this was to avoid unnecessary concern until firm confirmation was received of what had happened, but also because it is unlikely they had a telephone, and messages would have been complicated to send. One can only speculate as to what went through their minds as they considered whether to pass on the news. Their daughter-in-law therefore remained in ignorance of what had happened until after the second telegram had arrived. This, dated nearly a week later, shows that, contrary to what the family must have feared, he had been located, alive and relatively well.

He woke up in hospital, but remembered nothing of what had taken him there. It is possible that he was hit a glancing blow by a bullet from a German sniper's gun, and lost control of the machine. Another possibility was a wire stretched across the road, which would have been invisible to a speeding motorcyclist. A third possibility was a land-mine buried in the road. Any of these causes would have been enough to throw him off the bike and deposit him in the field at the side of the road, where he was eventually found by the search party sent to look for him.

*

My father never did tell us the nature of the mission he was on when he was injured. I always supposed it was getting some message through to another unit. It was only years after he'd died that I began to wonder whether it was something rather less directly crucial to the war effort, and more to do with the morale of his commanding officer – or, to be exact, his gastronomic preferences.

In our larder in the Fifties we had nothing like the exotic varieties of cheese you can buy now. Mostly, it was simply Cheddar, although my father was partial to the occasional small wedge of Danish Blue. But when stationed in northern France he had discovered there was something else.

'It was disgusting. Ugh! But the C.O. used to like it. Camembert, it was called. But he called it Postman's Feet in August.'

'*What*?' my sister and I said, while our mother pulled a face.

'Because that's what it smelt like. Haha! And whenever anyone was going near the village he'd ask them to get him some. He'd say, "Slim!"' (My father was tall and thin.) '"Slim! Don't forget the Postman's Feet!"'

So when he came off his motorbike, and ended up in hospital, had he been on a quite different assignment to what I'd always imagined? Had the village shop run out of Postman's, and he'd been sent further afield?

11

A Sense of Community

The fantasy is that I will call in at the pub on the junction at Beckington down in Somerset, and the old landlord, or a grizzled local on a bar stool, will eye me curiously and say, 'You're an Austin, aren't you?' and when my mouth drops open, will nod sagely, and say, 'Yes; thought so. Your father was Victor, wasn't he? The one who did all that running. Yeah. Oh, we remember him 'ere in this village. And his father before him. He had a brother, too, din't 'e? and a sister, and his brother went off and joined the Navy in the war, and didn't get sunk, did he, though he should have done, because 'e got posted to another ship at the last minute, didn'ee, and the ship he oughter've bin in, it got torpedoed in the Med. So some other poor bastards got it instead, 'scuse the language. Yeh, we know the old stories, that time he came down when he was a kid and tried riding the donkey, and the donkey cantered up to the hedge and stopped, but he didn't. Over its head into a bed of nettles. Yup, the cousins still live there in that farmhouse, out on the

Warminster road. And the last contact we had was when he had a puncture in that old green car. Yeah? He came down to the garage, and we lent him a jack. Was you there with him then? *Was* you! Well I never. Now then. How long ago was that, now? Thirty years? Thirty-five?'

Surely, somewhere around there, perhaps in several places, I am known, my history is known and my family is known, in spite of the fact that I have never lived there. I have a place, and roots; and roots, do they not, grow deep, and give rise to indelible memories.

So I stop at the pub, which is called the Woolpack; and of course the fantasy dissolves. Landlord? Two young people behind the bar, one male and one female. Grizzled local? Three suits discuss business over a bottle of red wine, before moving through into the dining room. Another business couple sits at a table in the bar. I'd seen their cars in the car-park – a new BMW, a large Audi and a Mercedes with personalised number plate. Not, I think, a place where the locals gather, and recognise long-lost cousins.

Up a lane behind the building (which does have the redeeming feature of a pleasant stone exterior, comfortably solid) is the church. It is compact outside and intimate in. Straight away, I feel at home. Does the churchyard contain any Austins? Or a Green, perhaps, my father's mother's surname? I walk slowly past the rows of gravestones. Edgell. Hillman. Sadler. Phippard. Owen. Warren. Watts. Mitchell. Gunning. Humphreys. Sadler. Cruttwell – Ah! But no; Austen with an *e* ... The wind is high in the beech trees, and the long grass shimmers between the gravestones.

We'd had the puncture just up the road. At weekends we used to pass through Beckington on our way to Southampton, where my father kept his boat. Sometimes it was just him and me, sometimes with my sister as well or with my brother or with both, and occasionally with our mother. Just outside Beckington my father would gesture over one of the fields to a farmhouse and say, 'That's where my cousins live.' One of us would reply, 'Why don't we go and see them?' My father would shrug, and say, in a way which told us he didn't mean it, 'Ah, well, perhaps I ought to, one day.' It didn't matter to us; it was just one of those occasional rituals which were a part of the journey. On this occasion we were on the journey home, a hundred yards up the hill from Beckington Motors. We got out, and sat on the wall, and my father rummaged in the boot and found the jack; but as soon as he tried to lift the side of the car with it, the rusty sill gave way and the jack went clean though the metal. He cursed, and walked down the hill to the garage. The rest of us stayed. We children took our cue from our mother; we knew she did not especially care for his origins and his relatives. He trundled back up the hill with a large industrial jack to fit under the differential.

'Oh, yes, they recognised me,' he said. 'Sort of, anyway. After all these years ... When was I last here? Must have been about 1936, I suppose.'

The dream persists ... I stop at the house, and do what we never did in the past: I go in, and say, Here I am; and they say, Welcome. Welcome, member of our family whom we have never met before but with whom common blood unites us. Do you remember? I ask, do you remember? and the old lady says, I remember; I remember your father. He was one of us. This is our place, but it is yours too, because we are one family. Have a cup o' tea.

Why are these images so evocative? It is the pain of loss, the loss of something I barely possessed. It slipped from my grasp before I had obtained a proper purchase. Where do I find that lost domain? How do I get there? Who can take me?

*

Driving through Bristol, it seems as if some of the lost domain has been found. Here are the views, here are the buildings I knew, the trees to climb and the grass to tread. This is where I cycled; this vertical rock-face rising from Bridge Valley Road is the one beside which I swept down on my bike, absorbing the view opposite towards the grey mud of the River Avon. That is the small wooden gate from the cul-de-sac on to the Downs. If you do not leave a place, do you still have those feelings of loss? 'One should never go back.' What fool voiced those words? Of course you should go back. You have to. If you do not go back, sooner or later your imagination, mind, or heart force you to do so. There is the school my sister attended, where she and I played tennis in the holidays: just through the gate are the very courts.

And at last, here is Canford. The cemetery: the final place to which, one day, all of us must come. The funeral of my Aunt Ivy, who was in the house when the telegram arrived about her brother, my father, was here, on just such a day as this: sunny, warm, still. I dropped some earth in the grave after the coffin had been lowered, but the sun had caked it hard, and the few lumps I threw made a hollow sound on the wooden lid. She was the last of the four of my family who occupy the grave; it is full, and I shall need to be put elsewhere. Her husband Reg is beneath her; and my father's father, who died when I was an infant, who told my father that one day I'd be good at football, because my head was as big as one; and beneath them all my father's mother, who never knew of me.

When I die, I should like to be buried in the ground. Cold wet earth against my face. What expresses the essence of being alive? It is the warmth of another's cheek against mine. In death, the cheek pressed against the cold, damp, lifeless, but comforting earth. From whence we came.

I walk away from the grave. I do not say goodbye to my forebears beneath, because I am merely walking from this room into the next; because before long, in one form or another, I shall be back. They know I am here; I know they are there, and soon we shall be together.

But family, and a sense of one's family's territory, is not all, in spite of the famous words of Mrs. Thatcher.

*

'There is no such thing as society. There are individual men and women and there are families.' The words attributed to the Prime Minister from a *Woman's Own* magazine interview in 1987 have been widely quoted since then as an example of the uncaring attitude of her Government. There were claims that the remarks had been taken out of context by a hostile press, and misunderstood. But although she may not have meant exactly what her words were later construed to have said, the meaning they conveyed had to be taken in the context of her other words, and the actions of her administration. The cap fitted. Whatever benefits her government might have brought to the country's economic wellbeing, at times it gave the impression of wholehearted support for the 'me, me, me' society, in which it was every man for himself and his family, and to hell with duty to one's neighbour.

The fact is that men and women do live in societies. As individuals, they have responsibilities towards other individuals, and groups of individuals have responsibilities towards other groups. They always have done.

If you are a doctor you are a member of the community of doctors, healers, nurses. The hospital movement, the curing professions. If you are a social worker or a helper in a home for the aged you are in the caring professions. If you are a police officer or a firefighter you belong to the community of police or firefighters and you are also a member of the community of emergency services. If you are a train driver or a hairdresser or a farmer or a car mechanic you are also a member of a community, and when you meet others from it, you talk the same language. You use the same conceptualisations. Operating from a particular framework of ideas is one of the corollaries of being in a community. The same kinds of things are of interest to you all, and you look at them from a common point of view, which may be different from the way others would.

And if you are in the armed forces, it is not only your point of view that binds you to others of your ilk, but your life, and, as part of the deal, the possibility of your death.

The words of Mrs. Thatcher suggested she had forgotten the achievement of Churchill, a predecessor of hers as Prime Minister, who bound the nation together in a common cause in which acting together was crucial to success. But forgotten also were the armed forces' role in the Falklands conflict five years previously, into which they had been thrust by the determination of Mrs. T. herself, and in which the binding together of individuals to form a unified force with a common aim was, as it always is in war, crucial. Not for nothing is a group of soldiers referred to as a 'unit'. They are interdependent, and that interdependence holds them together in a bond that is far stronger than one would ever see in other groups of people doing the same job. What was striking about the televised remarks of Captain Salt of HMS *Sheffield*, interviewed after his ship was sunk in the South Atlantic during that war of 1982, was the sense of loyalty. Clearly emotional, he emphasised how high morale was, and how exceptional the teamwork. 'I'm sure every captain would say that his ship's company was the best,' he said. 'But I know that mine is.' He did not state this in a cool and rational manner. He was speaking immediately after the fire had swept through the ship, and his emotion was palpable. If the force with which he spoke was any guide, then the bonds within the crew, twenty-four of whom died, were something quite outside the experience of most people in civilian life. It was the sense of community, of everyone being in it together, that impressed.

*

And when you die you become part of the community of the dead, existing only in the minds of other people. Whilst you are still alive you have some control over people's perceptions of you (including your own), but when you are dead you do not. Your identity has already been determined by the actions you have taken in your life, by the view of them held by the communities of which you were known as a member when you were alive. For a time at least, those communities grant you continued existence; but they themselves are subject to change, not least because people leave, or indeed die. The community of the dead of World War Two is recalled by their comrades, their families, the ones they left behind, the ones who, with them, lived through that time.

But it is recalled also by the people who did not live through the war, who have no stories of their own to tell of it, whose only stories are the ones told them by those who did, their parents and aunts and uncles and friends of their parents and their next-door neighbours. Allied to those tales are the ones told them at another remove, by the historians and film-makers and comic-strip artists. It is the sum of all these tales that provides not only the continued validation of the community of the dead of that War, but also of us, the children of our parents, whose identity as individuals and as a community rests in significant measure on our status as Post-War. Like our parents, we are defined by the conflict of 1939-45. The difference is that, not having lived through it, we are compelled, in our minds at any rate, to re-live it.

*

Nowhere has the sense of community of those who fight been expressed more forcibly than in *Das Boot*, the long German film about the men of a submarine, and *Band of Brothers*, the even longer American series following a company of paratroopers dropped into France in 1944. *Das Boot* is fictional, although the type of experiences it records are undoubtedly close to the truth. *Band of Brothers*, based as it is on events all of which, so far as the producers could ascertain from the histories and from the survivors themselves, actually took place, gives a picture which is not only factually accurate but which has the force of emotional truth as well.

'The point is,' said Nick, 'in the Army you get a group feeling, a camaraderie, and when you're training, this is directed against the sergeant major. He's playing the bastard, and you all join together in hating him, because of what he makes you do.'

'And then,' added Pete, 'that hate is transferred to the enemy when you're at war.'

I protested at this, or at any rate at Nick's premise. 'You do the training in order to get you to obey orders automatically. All right, you hate him. But he shouts at you so that when he says jump, you jump, and you get into a habit of it, until it becomes automatic, and the theory is that you'll then do it automatically in a war situation.'

'No, it's not only that, it's to develop the team spirit directed against a common enemy,' said Charles.

'It's like when I was at my prep school,' said Nick. 'What a harsh regime that was. But then when I went to Uppingham, there was all this freedom, and you didn't bond with anybody. That's why I don't keep in touch with anyone from there. Everything was liberal.'

'Ooh!' said Pete. 'I bet you had duvets, didn't you?' (Instead of threadbare sheets and prickly blankets, as he had at Rugby a few years earlier, and I at Hereford.)

'Yes, we did, actually,' said Nick.

'Oh, Christ! And I suppose you could choose which main course you had for lunch?'

'And you didn't have to wear your uniform all the time,' added Nick. 'You could wear a woolly jumper if you wanted.'

'Oh God!' shouted Pete. 'It's hardly worth going to a public school if that's what they let you do!'

*

Not long after this I heard a discussion on the radio about the First World War. There was discussion of shell-shock, the reducing to nervous wrecks of countless previously well-balanced young men who were incarcerated for months in the trenches, and so many of whom simply disappeared: buried alive or, more likely, blown to bits – into so many fragments that they literally disappeared. And for those who survived, either the whole war or a part of it, seeing one's comrades reduced by gunfire to this was enough to make them mad.

In the second world war there seems to have been less of this, though perhaps that is because the notion of shell-shock had become more familiar, and people were inured to it. But even in the second, some who took no direct part in close or sustained battle did not escape mentally unscathed. My father was one. Although his injuries were not from a front-line battle involving shooting at the enemy or being shot at, for years he retained an acute susceptibility to sudden loud noises. I recall his violent reactions to banging doors when I was a small child. If a door were left ajar and the wind slammed it shut, he would involuntarily squeeze his eyes closed, draw his breath sharply in through his teeth, throw down the newspaper, uncross his legs and jump out of his chair. 'Who left that damn door open? Keep it closed, for God's sake!' Or if a car or motorcycle backfired in the street (a common enough occurrence in the 1950s), for a moment a look of wildness, and panic, would pass across his face. These were hardly extreme reactions, and with the passage of time they subsided. For one thing, we children became accustomed to making sure the doors were shut. But to me they were just a little more evidence that, back in those times which were before my time, something important had happened.

That something significant had happened to the sense of community was apparent, too, if only from some of the remarks of the adults that we children used to hear.

'Things aren't like they used to be during the War.'

'People use to help each other, didn't they. Even if they didn't know them.'

'Everyone was more friendly.'

'You don't get that now.'

'You'd pull together.'

'Not now, that's all gone.'

'There isn't the spirit any more.'

'Shame, isn't it.'

There was a shared understanding, a commonality, a bond between people, even if those people were not well acquainted. They all seemed to have gone through the same experiences, and to be held together by them. They had lived through The War and done things in it. I knew they had Done Things, because whenever the question was asked, 'What did you do?' or 'Where were you, then?' there was always a ready answer. I even acquired the habit of asking my father, when he came back from seeing a friend of his, or some relatives, 'What did *he* do, during the war?' And he would say, 'Oh, he was in destroyers. Doing the Atlantic convoy run', or 'He was out in the desert. Tanks. Same as Rea'. Or, less approvingly, 'Says he was in Intelligence. But he never tells you much about it.' (Which, I suppose, you wouldn't.) One of his near-neighbours in later years was Dennis Wheatley, the thriller writer. My father scoffed at his claims. 'He might have written a few books,' he said (in fact Wheatley wrote dozens, many of which sold very well), 'but he's not very popular in these parts. Always boasting. Says he was on Churchill's staff during the war. Well, so he might have been. Three thousand people were on Churchill's staff. Probably some desk job safe from the bombs.' Whatever their claims, the war bound people together not only whilst it was happening but for decades afterwards. They had been through a great mission; they had all been in it together, and their sense of community was not merely local, but national. The whole country was a village. You knew what made someone tick, because it made everyone tick: the need to hang together in the same cause, which, via his oratory, found its champion in Winston Churchill.

*

Community spirit sometimes arose, perhaps, via dubious means – not so much engendered by the people themselves but engineered by the government. When I was aged, perhaps, seven or eight, I asked my parents about one particular feature of the low stone walls which fronted the pavement outside many of the houses in Bristol, including that of my Aunt Ivy. At intervals along their top surfaces were small squares of iron, sometimes flush with the stone surface and sometimes protruding an inch or so. What were these?

'Oh, there were railings there. They were cut off during the War.'

What?

'They were all cut off. All taken down. To make … warships. Guns.'

And later I found, visiting other towns and cities up and down the country, that this removal of iron railings and gates was not just widespread, but, it seemed, almost universal. Wherever you walked you could see the evidence. By mid-1943, to provide scrap metal from which munitions could be manufactured, the wrought iron gates and railings were removed from three and a half million houses, as well as hundreds of public parks, gardens and cemeteries.

This was not, however, the outcome of a voluntary sacrifice on the part of the people. The railings were removed by Government requisition. The local authorities zealously obeyed orders and sent gangs of workmen out with their oxy-acetylene cutting equipment, who systematically denuded the streets of their ironwork.

A suspicion grew, if not at the time then later, that the scheme was considered by the authorities a means of keeping up morale. Whether or not that succeeded, there were certainly some unintended consequences. Asking a question in Parliament, one Lord Hemingford stated

> To my own personal knowledge there has been tremendous loss of garden produce through gates and railings in front of houses and gardens being taken away and cattle, while being driven through the streets, naturally getting in and trampling down the good stuff in the gardens. Added to that there is a really irresistible temptation to a large number of children – some of them, I am sorry to say, are rather a nuisance to the places to which they have been moved – who go into gardens which are left open without gates or railings round them and steal the fruit ...[1]

No doubt those naughty children were the evacuees, evidently ungrateful to the citizens of the towns to which they had been moved. (Or maybe they were hungry.) But later evidence was that much of the resultant scrap metal

---

[1] *Hansard*, 13 July 1943, Lords Sitting.

remained unused, left to rust in council depots and railway sidings. What will be certain is that none of it was returned to its original owners to re-protect and re-decorate their property; and whilst cattle may no longer be driven through our streets, the wrought-iron stubs of the railings erected to deter them can still be seen in their hundreds of thousands.

*

'We're fifty-five soon,' said Pete. 'It's a milestone, that.'

'Halfway to 60.'

'I don't think 60 will be very nice, you know.'

'You think we're on the plateau, do you, heading for the edge?'

'We're in a canoe, heading towards the waterfall, and we've lost the paddle. Out of control. I could cope with the others, 40 and 50. But 60? No, I don't think so.'

'So you think it's the beginning of the end, do you?'

Later Nick was there, and then Iain. Nick, whose children are a good deal younger, was talking about getting a Scalextric for them.

'The best one,' said Pete, 'was a really cheap one I got for about a tenner. It was a figure of eight. The point was, it didn't go too fast, so the cars didn't come off like the proper Scalextric ones do. And also you didn't have all that frustration with the track not working.'

'Well I had a Scalextric,' said Nick, 'and it was well sorted out. But my brother, of course,' he added, with not a little vehemence, 'he smashed it up. He fell over it. Whether by accident or design wasn't established at the time. But I had my suspicions. And then, for good measure, he trod on it.'

'Whooh!' said the rest of us. 'Whorrgh!'

'And that wasn't the only thing,' Nick went on. 'If only! He was always falling over things of mine. Breaking them. It makes you wonder how much of an element of deliberateness there is, when there seemed to be so many so-called accidents.'

I said, 'So you became an anaesthetist because that was what you wanted to do to your brother, and he became a psychiatrist because that was what he wanted to do to you.'

'I think we'll change the subject, shall we?' said Nick.

So we talked about *Band of Brothers* again. I admitted I hadn't seen any of it. With predictable incredulity, Pete said, 'You're not watching *Band of Brothers*? You've missed the most fantastic television event.'

'It's so realistic,' added Iain. 'Based on fact. With interviews of the people it's about.'

'It's the one thing I've been watching every Friday,' said Nick, who always claims never to watch television himself, or listen to the radio, but just happens to be in the room when someone else in the family has it on. 'Come back home from work. Watch the Simpsons. Go to the gym. And then come back for *Band of Brothers*. It's perfect. My idea of heaven.'

'Yes, well, up to a point,' said Pete, 'but I do think you've got it a *little* bit wrong. Okay, *Band of Brothers*, fine. And the Simpsons? – yeah, okay, that gives you an alternative view of life,' he added, putting out his hand out and wiggling it from side to side. 'But who's this Jim bloke?'

'You can do without that, far as I'm concerned,' said Iain. 'Ten episodes of *Band of Brothers* does a helluva lot more for me than ten visits to the gym ever would.'

'One of the things that's good about it,' went on Pete, 'you've got people leaving the group, they go off on leave, or they're injured, and later on they come back in, so you've got that agenda of, you know, they were once members, but they've been away, and it's just slightly different. And you've got new people joining as well. There are just those subtleties, you know. Nuances. And then there was a bit where you just heard a snatch of music from the German lines, it was at Christmas, and if it had been any other film, they would have said, "Gee, guys, they're singing Christmas carols, well perhaps they're human after all", or something. They would have made something of it. But you got just the faint sound of it,' he said, putting his thumb and forefinger almost together, 'and they just sort of glanced at each other. They didn't say anything, and that was it. It's exactly like it would have been.'

'And the characters,' said Nick, 'they've aged so much. At the beginning, they were fresh-faced, and now you can see how much older they are. At the end, in the last couple of episodes, their faces are lined, and grey.'

A month later we talked of it again. 'You'd enjoy this,' said Pete. 'One of the people Nicky knows – '

'Your son Nicky, you mean.'

'Yes. Not Nick. Nicky. One of the people he knows is a bloke who was an actor in *Band of Brothers*, and when we went up to see *The Graduate*, that one that all those middle-aged actresses are in, playing Mrs. Robinson, he was in that. He was the Dustin Hoffman character, you know? We went to see him afterwards, round to the stage door. What he said was, when he was in *Band of Brothers*, it was bloody hard work, having to run across those fields, with full battle kit on, and to do it again and again. But there wasn't as much grumbling as there is normally on film sets, because it was all based on real people and some of those people were there, they met them, and everyone thought it would be a bit churlish to whinge. Because these blokes, they'd done it for real, just as many times as the actors had to. More, in fact. And,' he added, 'they'd had the Germans trying to kill them. So there were distinctly fewer complaints on that film set than there usually are.'

*

When you read a novel, particularly one focusing on the development of a family over time, then, as the story unfolds, the meaning of events that have already been described can change. A minor incident early in the book is later revealed as seminal. Characters are shaped by what happens to them and what they make happen. But because the words are written down, the view they present of what has taken place cannot be subject to much revision in the reader's mind. Sometimes there may be slightly different ways of interpreting what has been said, but the words are unchanging. Nor is there anything beyond the single account, presented in the book, to challenge the delineation of the surrounding circumstances. Admittedly, with a narrative that is in print for longer than a few years, succeeding generations will make their own analyses according to the spirit and customs of their own times. But there will not be huge differences. The same is true of plays. Current interpretations of *Hamlet* are never going to stray far from those of previous decades and centuries, though the nuances may alter a little.

A real family is different. A series of stories is told over the years by the senior members of the family to one another and to the junior. Each story may be told by different individuals, on numerous occasions, with different emphases at successive times. The understanding of the listeners develops as they become older, enabling them to place the tales in a context which they grasp imperfectly at first but better later on. Photographs help, though they may give undue prominence to particular aspects. There is a process of synthesis, in which aunts, uncles, parents and grandparents all fill in sections. It is never-ending. There are central characters, and others who flit in and out. When the stories are told well, by a member of the family who can give a picture of the essential aspects, who can dramatise by adding inflexion in the right places, then a creation arises which has an independent status in the family. If the storytellers die without a successor taking on the mantle, the tales begin to be lost. The listeners who remember them recall only some of the details, and are able to pass on only the outline, missing some particulars which embellish the story and others that were essential to its meaning. Others they forget entirely. The shared memories recall the houses that were lived in, the friends and neighbours, the local politics perhaps, the geography and history of the area, and myriad incidents – these form an essential backdrop. As the younger family members become older, they tell the tales to the next generation. But, crucially, they are mediated through a new experience of the world. Their meaning changes. One might even say it is distorted, but I am not sure the suggestion that the inevitable process of Chinese whispers denudes the tales of their original meaning is necessarily fair. Each generation must decode its legends with its own eyes. Who is to know how the events seen through the eyes of the third generation differ from the view of the first? The folklore, like the family itself, must be continually re-created. It is part of what it means to be a family. It is one of the varieties of glue that hold the individuals together in a unit.

Similar folklore arises in groups of friends. Their place is a village or town or suburb, the pub or club. Experiences are shared and later recounted, photographs are produced, letters or club records are shared. Thus is another reality constructed in retrospect. When, through the passage of time, the mythology begins to be forgotten, then one of the purposes of living begins to disappear. When one's friends and acquaintances, the people with whom one has made stories and carved out a reality, die, and there is no-one else with whom to make a story: then, perhaps, it is time to die oneself. But, before one does, if one can still contribute to the stories that sustain the younger members of the family or the neighbourhood, which give a depth and a history to their self-perception, then the richness of the family stories and hence that of family life is enhanced, and the process of re-creating the family continues.

Into her late nineties, disabled, immobile and needing physical care for much of the day, my mother's sister

Betty continued to tell the stories. Her memories were sharp, her descriptions of the events clear, her opinions of the protagonists uncompromising, and the energy which, with faltering voice but unfailing laughter, she brought to the telling was as great as ever. I thought: She is the last of that generation, and when she is gone, there will be no-one who can give voice to them; they will cease to exist. But they have been uttered. The sound of her voice may have died away; but I try to believe her words have a memorial that transcends the minds of men. Their traces, if only we could measure them, are still there, somewhere in the ether, confirming and validating her encounter with life on this earth.

*

For decades prior to The War, the landscape of Britain hardly changed. During that period the country was importing over half of its food. But in the early 1940s German submarines succeeded in sinking vast numbers of the ships carrying our supplies from North America. The attrition rate in the convoys brought the country uncomfortably close to starvation. When the war was over, the decision was made to reduce the risk of the same happening again, and to encourage farmers to bring us as close as possible to self-sufficiency.

'Years ago all this would have been grassland,' said Martin, in his soft Lincolnshire burr. 'Pasture. Mainly grass, which would have provided a bit of grazing, with a bit of clover and a few wild flowers. It would have supported, maybe, one sheep to every acre. You could grow legumes, like clover. Peas. Beans. They have the bacteria to fix nitrogen from the air to form the substance of the crop. Then after harvesting, if you plough the remains into the ground, and rotate the crops, there's enough substance for the next year to sustain wheat. Wheat doesn't have those bacteria, and otherwise it requires artificial fertiliser.'

We were on the bare rolling hills of the South Downs. 'And then after the war,' I said, 'during which we'd almost been starved into surrender, the policy was developed, wasn't it, to get the country self-sufficient in food, instead of importing so much? So, all right, they decided to cultivate land like this. But presumably the only reason you can grow these crops like wheat on it, year after year, is that they use fertilisers on it?'

'Yes. The whole reason we've been more or less self-sufficient in food is down to artificial fertilisers – and chemical sprays to get rid of diseases. Without those, the soil wouldn't support anything other than grass.'

'Where do they come from, these fertilisers?'

'Ammonium nitrate is manufactured. Potash is mined. Big companies like Bayer and ICI make the ammonium nitrate, and the stuff that's mined comes from various places. South America for instance. We might have been close to self-sufficiency in food – '

'Apart from bananas,' said someone else.

'Oranges.'

'But we were certainly dependent on other countries for the fertilisers.'

'Tell me this. If nothing was put on the land, no sprays, no fertilisers, if it was left as it always was, how much of the land in this country which currently supports crops would still do so?'

'That's very difficult to answer. Depends on all sorts of things – '

'Well, roughly what? Half?'

Martin took a deep breath. 'Yes. About that, I'd say. If you took away all the fertilisers, pesticides, all the artificial things put on it, then about half the land currently used for crops would be fit for growing them. Needing a shower of rain every day and a shower of shit on Sundays.'

He bent down to pick a bright green sprig of the wheat, still in its early stages. He pointed to a faint brown discolouration. 'If this isn't treated, the yield will be about two-thirds of what it would be if it were healthy. And down here,' he said, holding the plant lower down, 'this dark discolouration is another disease, and when the plant with the corn at the top approaches its maximum height, because it's weakened, the whole thing will just fall over,' and he moved his forearm from the vertical to the horizontal in a sweeping movement. 'He'd better spray this lot, and he'd better do it pretty quick.'

We descended to a wood, and Martin spoke about the two old countryside skills of pollarding and coppicing.

'Both are carried out for the purpose of producing long straight lengths of wood, up to an inch or so in diameter, for making hurdles and fences. Pollarding is what you do to willow trees. Six or eight feet above the ground you cut off the crown of the tree, leaving it to send out new shoots from the top of the stem. Coppicing is cutting off the tree at the base, from where, again, new sprouts arise. You do this to hazel, which is good for thatching, because the newly-grown sticks can be bent double before they start to break. If you leave them to grow thicker, they make good walking sticks. My grandfather used to wrap copper wire in a spiral around the top of a likely-looking shoot, and leave it for a couple of years, and come back to it when the wire had become nicely embedded, and then cut it.'

We passed a plantation which was coppiced years ago, but was now neglected and overgrown. 'There's no living to be made now, in those old country crafts. But if there was, I'd be there like a shot. There's nothing I'd like better than to work in the open air on a variety of tasks like that. I'd be perfectly happy. You don't have to earn a lot to be happy. To me that would be wonderful.'

The walk finished at Burton, where there was a little church and the George and Dragon, which sold Woodforde's Norfolk Wherry, at 3.8 per cent alcohol a good mid-day beer. Grilled this-and-that for lunch; the day was sunny and the pub was crowded inside and out. We murmured our appreciation of the village, the walk, life in general. Julian took up the refrain. 'I've been rather pleasantly surprised by Sussex,' he said, too loudly. 'It's really quite a nice place.'

On two or three neighbouring tables the conversation hesitated. I leaned forward and wagged my finger at him. 'Julian!' I hissed. 'They're all locals around here for godsake! They all *live* in Sussex!'

'Well, I do think it's quite nice,' he said, not lowering his voice at all. He turned round to a chap on the table behind, who was already purple and looked as if he could explode any moment. 'We come from Dorset,' he said, as if that were back on Earth, and this was somewhere on the far side of Mars.

226

'It's his first outing this year,' I said, attempting to crave the indulgence of Mr. Purple. His colour lightened slightly. 'Ah. Let him out of prison, have you?'

This, of course, was exactly the wrong thing to say. Julian is a probation officer. 'I *work* at the prison,' he said. 'Worked in them for years.'

'Worked? *Been* in them, anyway,' said Iain.

'Don't let on what he was in for,' said Pete.

'Everybody leave now,' said Martin.

But eventually the bloke realised Julian was harmless, and to the relief of the rest of us they succeeded in chatting together without coming to blows.

*

A Sunday walk on the Somerset levels, following narrow roads and the rivers Parrett and Yeo. The land was flat and the wind completely uninterrupted by trees or hills. The longest stretch of the walk took us into the teeth of what was almost a gale. Had it been raining, or colder, we'd have perished of exposure. Eventually we reached the Rose and Crown at Huish Episcopi, with a series of linked rooms. On the wall was a large framed monochrome photograph of a soldier from the First World War, standing with his arms folded. From a distance he looked smug, but on closer inspection it was only the effect of his upturned moustache; take that away and he looked solemn. Under it was an inscription:

'He whom this scroll commemorates was numbered among those who, at the call of King and Country, left all that was dear to them, endured hardness, faced danger, and finally passed out of the sight of men by the path of duty and self-sacrifice, giving up their own lives that others might live in freedom. Let those who come after see to it that his name be not forgotten. Serjeant Reginald Philip Slade, Coldstream Guards.'

'Passed out of the sight of men ... ' The evocative language in which official commemorations are expressed. It is partly designed, no doubt, to help the grieving process of the next of kin, and make them proud. With its solemn celebration of lost lives it is intended, too, to combat any lurking anti-war sentiment, and draw attention away from the suggestion that hostilities might be regarded as unnecessary, or a mistake.

*

The first Tuesday tennis of the season was nearly rained off. I phoned Pete at ten to six.

'I take it we're not playing in this.'

'I'm halfway through getting my shorts on.'

'Maybe you should take them off again.'

'Well,' he conceded, 'if you phone the others and tell them we're not playing, I'll be happy not to come.'

'Oh, all right then. See you in a minute.'

In the event, the rain stopped immediately. As usual, Charles's play was wildly erratic. His shots varied from brilliant to abject. In one service game he threw the ball up several times and caught it again before serving.

'You having trouble with your toss again, Charles?'

'Not that time,' said Pete, as he responded weakly to Charles's next effort. 'Came fast that time. Came very fast.'

In the pub Paul, who is an architect, told us that the most pleasing aesthetic effect is produced by buildings which are constructed from as few kinds of material as possible. He cited the Taj Mahal, which meets the ideal of being built, inside and out, of one only, namely white marble.

'I was in the planning department down in Weymouth, and I pointed at that development by the car park – do you know it? They've done this bit out of concrete and that bit out of brick, and there are clay tiles in some places and slate tiles in others, and I said, "Who the hell designed that thing over there?" And they all put their heads down under their arms, and looked at the next person, and one of them said, "Oh, I had a bit to do with it to start with, and then I went away on holiday, and so-and-so finished it off", and so-and-so came in, and he said "No, no, by the time I got to it you'd done most of it, and there wasn't a lot I could do, and anyway, *he* had quite a hand in it as well", and he pointed his thumb to some other bloke, and I said, "So this is how you do it, is it? Who's got a set of dice? You roll one, and he rolls another, and she does the next, and whatever comes up from the first we'll use for the walls, and the second is for the cladding, and the third is the roofing material. That's what you did, isn't it? You said to each other, let's put together all this random different stuff and make an unholy mess of the whole lot". It is goddamn awful.'

Dick was there, and Pete repeated the story of how he used to interview candidates applying for the job of dental nurse in his surgery.

'Haven't you heard this one?' he asked. Dick hadn't.

'Oh! I thought everyone knew. I used to ask them if they liked the Moody Blues.'

'*What*?'

'And if they said yes, then I wouldn't employ them.'

'Why not?'

'Well how can anyone who likes the Moody Blues be taken seriously?'

Dick looked nonplussed.

'So bloody pretentious,' Pete went on. 'Are *you* a Moody Blues fan?'

Dick evidently felt it better to remain silent.

'Anyway,' said Pete, 'none of the people applying to be my dental nurse nowadays has heard of them, so that question's rather gone out of fashion.'

Then he began to tell the story about the German woman patient who'd been in that day.

'She was aged fifteen at the start of the second world war – '

'And she married a U-boat captain,' I interrupted, guessing, 'and we widowed her, is that right, did she tell you all about that?'

'No,' he said, 'and you'll be sorry when I tell you what did happen. She was fifteen when the war started, and when it ended she was in Berlin, she was with her mother, and she had to go and join some relatives outside Berlin, and it was the Elbe which was the dividing line between East and West Germany, wasn't it? – and the Americans stopped at the Elbe, and waited for the

Russians to reach the other side. Anyway, she was on the far side of the Elbe then, and they were spotted, her and her mother, by these British soldiers, and they came across the river, they were off duty, and they just came across, and they raped her.'

'Jesus.'

'Yeah. And then a bit later on there was an official patrol boat which came down the river, and she waved at it, and she got taken across, and she told them what had happened, and there was a court martial, and anyway, she came back to this country.'

'Did they get done, or what?'

'I'd had enough by that time,' said Pete, 'I was trying to get her to stop. This was just between a scale and a polish, she was telling me that.'

'What on earth made her come to Britain?' asked Charles.

'Oh, I didn't get that far.'

'Christ, anyone in that position, you'd have thought they'd have hated the Brits, wouldn't you?'

He shrugged.

'What you've got to do,' I said, 'is send her an appointment for three weeks' time, telling her there's some other bit of treatment she needs, and then get the rest of the story.'

'I went down to your part of Weymouth the other day,' said Nick, 'and I managed to find your premises, and I have to say I was a bit disappointed.'

'You have to remember,' said Pete, 'I don't have any trouble getting patients. In fact there's a whole lot I really could do without. So there's no need for me to make any effort at all. No-one has ever come to my premises and said how nice they are. I can tell you that for absolutely definite.'

I said, 'What you'll have to do, all your patients, you'll have to make them reapply for their places on your list, and you'll have a questionnaire like 'What is the most interesting thing that's ever happened to you?' and if they say, "During the second world war I flew a Hurricane and shot down three Messerschmitts", you keep them on your list, and if they say "I once went to a Moody Blues concert' you say "Out!".'

We agreed the beer was especially good that night. It was a little warmer than usual, and had a mellow, soapy texture.

*

Pete and I had both seen an old *Hancock's Half-Hour* on television before meeting in the pub. It was the one where he takes a seven-hour train journey with Sid James, spending the whole of the time irritating the other passengers by trying to engage them in conversation. Occasionally, between scenes, there were exterior shots of the train, leaving a station or puffing through countryside.

'What I thought it would be good to do,' says Pete, 'is to make a model train in black and white. You can imagine it. It would look just like the old photographs.' Most photographs of steam trains, of course, are in black and white, because by the time colour photography was widely used they were obsolete.

'It's the same with war pictures,' I said. 'Those ones you see of Kosovo, it's difficult to think of it as a war, because the pictures are all in colour.'

'Vietnam was in colour.'

'Yeah, but we didn't see as many of those,' said Charles. 'We were at college, and no-one had the time to waste watching television.'

'Even if we *had* a television.'

What we were brought up on were pictures of the first and second world wars, all of course in monochrome.

*

After a meeting in London I sat in the George IV in Portugal Street, near Waterloo Bridge. This is a typical central London pub with high, ornately plastered ceiling, dark polished wooden bar in the middle from which the staff can see all parts of the room, and mirrors. I ambled through a few more pages of *Five Days in London, May 1940* by John Lukacs.

Just upriver of the bridge as I crossed to the railway station stood the London Eye, the wheel, changing its aspect as I walked. Seen end-on from the north side of the bridge, it is a slim pencil, vertical against the sky, but it slowly becomes an ellipse, until by the time you reach the far side and glimpse it behind the Hayward Gallery, it is almost a circle. 'Ruined the skyline it has', said so many alleged aesthetes of London architecture, prominent amongst them one Norman St. John Stevas, respected though he might have been as a Conservative arts minister. Tosh. It enriches it, adding an unexpected geometrical variant to the profile of the buildings in this quarter, which are already heterogeneous, from the straight-edged concrete of the National Theatre, stark and unbroken by windows, to the curves of the new block above Charing Cross Station.

Later, at Tom's, I discussed the book with Nick, and Nick was obsessional. He cheerfully admits to being obsessional about lots of things, and the war years in particular. He talked about the bombings of German and French towns, precision attacks, Mosquitoes, two waves of planes, the first to lay down the markers. 'The second wave was incredibly accurate with the bombs,' he went on. 'They did this over some of the villages in France. If they'd applied the same principle to German industrial areas then they could have wiped them out in a much more efficient way than they did.' And I was telling him about the book, and how those five days at the time of the Dunkirk evacuation were crucial. Churchill had had to keep the other four members of the war cabinet on side. There were two Conservative (Halifax and Chamberlain, both experienced in government) and two Labour (Clement Attlee – Prime Minister after the war – and Arthur Greenwood). Being untried in government, neither of the two Labour men said much, but if Churchill had alienated any of the four of them and there'd been a split, his premiership would probably have foundered – and the outcome of the war might have been very different.

'All right, it's just one historian's interpretation.' I said, 'but it fits with other things I've read, and the general flavour of what Churchill was like. Okay, it's quite a short book but it is actually only about those five days, so it's pretty exhaustive, I mean everything that happened over that time, it's all there.'

Pete had been to the Tate Modern and told us about the blue canvas. Entirely blue. Nothing else.

'When I walk round an art gallery,' I said, 'with some of this modern stuff, I look at one of these things and I really don't know what to think. But quite often there are some words on the wall at the side, putting it in some kind of context, saying what the artist is trying to do. And sometimes it strikes me as pretentious nonsense. But it does often give a quite different view of the thing, so it *can* be quite helpful. But then I think: the picture should stand on its own. You shouldn't need to read a whole lot of stuff about it, in order to appreciate it.'

'Okay,' he said, 'I do agree, it can be important to have the words of interpretation adjacent to it. But that's because we haven't been educated in what modern art is. The only reason we don't need a passage of interpretation for other paintings in other galleries, you know, the older ones, is that we've already got the cultural background. We know what Christian religious paintings are supposed to be showing. *Our* generation does. But at art colleges, now, they're having to explain to the students coming in, the background. Like the Annunciation. The students simply don't know what it is. They see this picture of Gabriel or whoever, announcing to Mary she's going to have this baby, and they don't know anything about it. They don't know who the people are. They don't have that culture.'

*

235

I listened to Sue Lawley interviewing William Deedes on Desert Island Discs. For a long time he was the editor of the *Daily Telegraph*. He was the 'Bill' of the fictitious *Dear Bill* letters in *Private Eye* during Margaret Thatcher's prime ministership, purportedly written by her husband Denis, in true-blue Tory reactionary style. My father always enjoyed reading them. The magazine used to go to my parents' address whilst he was alive, and he would remove it carefully from its polythene envelope, read it, and replace it before re-addressing it to me.

'I know you don't like talking about this,' said Sue Lawley, 'but I would like to ask you if you don't mind: you won the M.C., and the citation says that your actions were taken in complete disregard of your own safety. What do you say about this?' Deedes replied that, in wartime, when a nation is fighting for its life, people do things they simply wouldn't otherwise do. He implied that, given the position he was in at that particular time, he could do nothing else. 'I lost a number of young officers whose lives would still be going, and be prosperous and successful no doubt, and I suppose I felt partly responsible for this, but you find yourself acting as you do … ' His voice trailed off, and, as so often in these conversations with people who have fought, there was nothing his interviewer could add.

12

Remember This Sky

'I'm glad we're doing this,' said Pete as we drove off. 'Excellent idea. The more I think about it, the more pleased I am we decided to do it.'

At Bournemouth Airport there was a much larger crowd than you usually get because an Antonov transport plane was due to land.

'What's the big attraction?' asked Iain.

'It's the largest plane in the world. It's Russian.'

'What? Bigger than a Jumbo?'

'Yes.'

'What the hell is it doing at Bournemouth?'

'Oh, I don't know. Some commercial deal. I'll just need to put on my other anorak,' he added as we drove in, 'my saddo anorak.'

We moved through towards the departure lounge and when I went through the metal-detector thing it beeped.

'What an unpleasant job, to have to frisk you,' remarked Pete.

On the plane were Mick and Colin, business acquaintances of Iain's. Hearing we had no tickets, Mick sounded reassuring. 'I think I might just be able to help you out.' He marked the place on the street map to meet at lunchtime the following day.

Pete leaned back expansively in his seat. 'This is a *good move*. I'm enjoying this. Haha!'

At Dublin, two double gins later, courtesy Mick, he jabbed his finger and insisted: 'From now on, everything is *sub judice.*'

We were on a boys' birthday outing. Iain, Pete and me, all reaching 50 in February. Pete had booked the flight, I'd found some accommodation, and it was Iain's job to get the tickets. In the end his contact had let him down. But we'd decided to go anyway. 'I've never gone to a rugby international without a ticket and not managed to get one,' we'd been told by Rob, who as a Welshman not only talks a good game but sees a lot of them. So we were confident.

We checked in to the hotel and went out. I'd never been to Dublin before, but its elegant Georgian terraces were nonetheless familiar, repeated as they were in various cities of Britain. (There was one slight difference, though, which I couldn't at first identify. Eventually I realised what it was. The buildings still had their railings. Ireland, of course, was neutral during the war[1], and there was no demand that the people give up their iron in the name of the war effort.)

---

[1] Thousands of Irish citizens did, nevertheless, fight in the British forces.

In a bar on Merrion Row, heaving, like every other watering-hole, Iain spotted a couple of South Africans he'd met sailing. They'd seen the Ireland/England 'A' game that afternoon. Like us, they were there with no tickets for the main international; but, like us, seemed laid back about it. And like Rob, they had never failed to get into an international when they'd arrived without tickets.

'The Hyne Bar in Lower Baggot Street,' they told us. 'That's where to go, up where the boys from Galway rugby club will be at lunchtime tomorrow. With business to be done.'

'Bloody good move, this,' said Pete. 'I'm really enjoying it.'

And in the eating house, it was good *craich*. Kitty's Kaboodle it was called, a crap name if ever there was one, though I suppose no more of a cliché than Mick's Bar or Paddy's Bar or O'Reilly's Bar. Between us we had the steak, the salmon and the steak and it was good.

'With every hour that passes,' said Pete, 'the better this is. I don't give a shit about the tickets. We're here for a bloody good time.'

In Barry Fitzgerald's, just north of the river in Marlborough Street, there was acoustic guitar and whirling violin. Pete said, 'I've always wondered what it would be like to get in a fight. Doesn't it fascinate you? That's the epitome of manhood. The ultimate thing for men. We're the only generation that won't have done that.'

'It would be over very quickly,' said Iain. 'And you'd be either dead or seriously injured.'

'Well, no I don't think you would. But I agree it would happen quickly.'

'How many of these do we have to drink?' I asked, as Iain brought me another Guinness.

Pete grinned at us. 'This is getting better,' he said. 'Whose idea was this? Bloody ace move.'

This pub had curved wooden sections to the window frames and a beer-glass shelf suspended above the bar and felt comfortable, but we moved on to the White Horse Inn, back on the other side of the river again, where there was cricket on the television high above the bar, out of focus. The average age was about twenty years younger, you could hardly hear the music being played in the corner, and we didn't stay long.

Under a street-light at a crossroads we pored over the map, trying to find our way back to the bed-and-breakfast.

'You lost, fellas?' asked a tall friendly Irish lad. It turned out he had a ticket – but no spares. 'I think you might have a bit of difficulty getting them this time,' he said, 'there's been a lot of interest created, with us winning against Wales. And the weather's going to be nice tomorrow, so a lot of people will be up for the match.'

Everyone I've ever met who's been to Dublin say the people are so friendly. Everyone. Too many for it not to be true. And it is. This bloke, now. You wouldn't have got that in London.

I knew the way back then. Down this road, straight over the lights, turn left. Ages since we had a piss. Every square we passed had thick black railings and no way in. 'Just stand up against the fence and pee through it,' I said to Iain. Up here, turn right ... This the street? Yes. Here? Key didn't fit. We went all the way down trying each door. They all looked the same. Eventually one of them opened.

'I feel good,' said Pete, as he woke up on Saturday morning. 'I thought I'd be a lot worse, after drinking all that Guinness. But it's all right.'

'It's like the adverts used to say, Guinness is good for you. And the more you have – '

'The better it is.'

We walked slowly around the town, looked at the rugby ground, asked a copper what the chances were, had a cappuccino and ambled to the place Mick had mentioned, Paddy O'Flaherty's at number 51 Haddington Road. It was almost empty at twelve o'clock but over the next two hours a lot of people came in and no-one left. At last Mick arrived, and during the next half an hour two tickets mysteriously turned up. Iain went off with him. Five minutes later he was back.

'Here. You have these. There's almost a dead certainty I'll be able to get another from this bloke upstairs and if he doesn't deliver then there's someone else.'

Pete and I skipped down the road amongst the crowd. This was the best moment of the whole weekend so far. There was not a cloud in the sky and life could not possibly have been finer.

The crowd slowed and tightened as we approached the ground and close to the turnstiles I was rammed up against the concrete wall. Inside, men were peeing up against the other side of it. The congestion on the terrace was just as bad and we couldn't free our arms from our sides to do the Mexican wave. 'Only the Mexican nod', said Pete.

For the first threequarters of the game things were fairly even, but England overran the Irish in the last twenty minutes, six tries. The view, you had to admit, did not allow for seeing much detail down the other end, but on the other hand you did get an idea of how ordinary, in a sense, an international game of rugby is. In some respects it is not very different from what we played at school: the space on the pitch, the positioning of your own team and of the opposition. Television makes the game look much more different from the rugby I played than it really is. Okay, the crowd was a bit bigger. And the expectation, the atmosphere, the wall of sound coming at you not just in stereo, but from left, right, down in front of you and up behind, sweeping through the stands, rising and falling away, was electric.

As we were waiting to make our way out, Iain shouted at us from behind. We hadn't seen him since the pub. It turned out he very nearly didn't get in. The bloke from whom he'd bought his ticket had originally reserved it for his boss but his boss wasn't there at the appointed time and he sold it to Iain. But then as they made their way down the road a car toot-tooted and there was his boss. So Iain had to give it back, and was preparing to go back to Number 51 to watch the game on telly when he saw a couple of chaps sitting glumly on a wall, and only one of them was holding a ticket.

'Do you want to get rid of it then?' Iain asked.

'Yeah, maybe.'

'How much do you want for it?'

'A hundred.'

'Give us a break! I've got me two mates inside and I'd like to join them but I'm not paying that much.'

'Give it him for face value,' said his friend. 'Go on.' And Iain was in.

'Bloody hell,' said Pete as we made our way out of the ground. 'I'm so glad you got in. God! If us two had been in there with those tickets, and you'd had to sit in the pub and watch it on telly, I'd – I'd have felt awful for the rest of my life.'

The Burlington Hotel was where Mick had said he'd be afterwards, a big concrete-and-glass job near the ground with an extraordinary film-set of a bar inside, with supposedly half-built stone pillars and sections of wall. Guinness, Guinness and Guinness lined up on the table, one of those high ones encircled with a brass bar to hold on to and another to rest your feet. There were Mick and Colin, and a bloke who was introduced as Paul Noyes ('Ever seen the name before?' 'Yes. Alfred Noyes, the poet.' 'Right. Read anything by him?' 'No.' 'Nor have I. And have you come across anyone else with the name?' 'No.' 'There aren't any,' he said).

When we got there it was barely five o'clock and I thought, we can't possibly stay here all night; but the Guinness gradually put me on fast-forward, and although I was conscious of Iain and Pete getting restless (they'd had only one sandwich each since breakfast and I'd had two), by that time I'd got into conversation with a bloke called Callum about the Northern Irish. He had no time for them, he said, neither Catholics nor Protestants. 'They're different from us. They're crazy.'

'All of them? Both sides?'

'Yes. All of them. They have a different way of thinking.' Was his attitude typical of his countrymen? 'It is, yes. Look at the vote Sinn Fein gets in the South. Five per cent? It's nothing. As far as I'm concerned, they should be no more a part of Ireland than a part of Britain. Look at what they did to that poor boy the other day. He was only doing his duty.' He meant the latest British soldier killed by the IRA. Suddenly I understood what he felt. It was the same in England, I said, when that French student hitched a lift last summer from a lorry-driver and was murdered by him. I felt ashamed, I said, ashamed that a foreigner could come to my country and be treated like that, because it diminishes us all.

'That's it,' he said. 'Okay, I'm in business, and it's not good for that, because everyone assumes it's us as well as them. And it's not. But I am proud of my country, and when those bastards up North carry on the way they do, we are all tainted with it.' (I thought: That's conflict for you. Whatever its origin. Conflict and its history and the beliefs associated with that. They make people behave differently.)

Eventually we made a move. The crush in the loo was as bad as in the bar and on the way to find an eating-house Iain and I peed in the canal.

'Just watch it,' shouted Pete, 'it's nearly full already and I'm not staying here if you two are going to make it burst its banks.'

Lots of places were closed and in the end we decided we could do worse than old Kitty's Kaboodle.

'Bloody good, this is,' says Pete. '*Such* a good plan. Eh?'

On Sunday morning I woke about the same time as the others and lay in bed, squirming a bit, waiting to go to the bathroom. 'Come on,' said Pete. 'Get up and stop pretending that's Pamela Anderson you've got there.'

Our return flight to Bournemouth wasn't until the evening, and Pete had a plan. We checked out of the hotel and hired a car which we could later leave at the airport. We drove north to Drogheda, more Guinness and lunch for a tenner each in a prim hotel dining room, and a few miles on there was the huge tumulus of Newgrange, where we crouched in its prehistoric stone burial chamber. Then at the monastery of St. Patrick at Slane we hazarded a treacherous spiral staircase up its ruined church tower, and finally there was a cup of tea and a scone at the Hill of Tara, apparently an ancient capital of Ireland, a slight rise looking over miles of the shallow saucer of the interior. As we approached the central part of the henge, Pete said:

'Look at that sky. I want you to remember it.' Thick grey clouds in horizontal layers were drifting across the horizon in the February wind.

'What for?'

'I just want you to make a mental note of it now and then forget about it. You'll know what I mean in a week's time.'

What's happening in a week's time? I thought. My birthday? He's going to give me a picture he's painted, and he's done the sky like that. Or – it's a diorama of HMS *Hood*, the plastic Airfix kit he gave me ages ago which I never put together and which he took back again, saying he'd do it for me. That's what it is, a background of grim grey Atlantic cloud as the great ship plunges her stately way through the high seas, symbol of the Royal Navy, the Empire, of British engineering and the maritime tradition of centuries.

A few days later a package was waiting on the doorstep. The mighty *Hood* it was, and the background sky was exactly like the one Pete had pointed out in Ireland. There was no ship's name, just a little brass plaque he'd engraved with the date and the time of her death, and the latitude and longitude of the position she lies, 'deep in the waters of the north, washed by the cold currents of the Denmark Strait, 500 miles north-east of Cape Farewell'[1].

*

The evening of my birthday I had an 'At Home' in the pub. In the end there were twenty or thirty people. I told Pete the model of the *Hood* was *just* the biz. On the horizon he'd painted tiny images of *Bismarck* and *Prinz Eugen* firing at her.

'And did you notice the sky just above the horizon? It's slightly paler. That's because there's a reflection off the white of Greenland. And I spent quite a long time studying those books.' (I'd lent him a couple[2].) 'I've been wanting to give it to you for ages,' he added.

Julian gave me a tube of Dunlop tennis balls, with the trade name 'Fort' emblazoned on the tin.

'I think they've got the wrong name,' Graham said. 'They ought to be called 'Fift'.'

Everyone was very kind. The sandwiches were huge; I was glad I'd ordered them. After twelve o'clock there were eight or nine of us left, but when, some twenty

---

[1] *The Mighty Hood* (1959), by Ernle Bradford.

[2] ... and *Pursuit: The Sinking of the Bismarck* (1974) by Ludovic Kennedy.

minutes later, someone wanted another drink, the aged Austrian barmaid Eve told us pleasantly that unfortunately the bar was closed. After that it seemed a bit silly to wait until we were thrown out, with our glasses empty; and when, around half-past, Jennie told Pete she thought it was time to go home, that was the signal for a final drifting away.

*

Rob S. is my car mechanic. He's lived in Weymouth all his life. A couple of weeks later he brought the car back after doing some work on it. He came into the sitting room with his bill and glanced round.

'Here. Who's been making models of HMS *Hood*, then?'

I was astonished. 'How do you know that? How do you know it's HMS *Hood*?'

'I know a lot of these ships. I like them. I'm interested in them. I recognise all of 'em.'

'Brilliant,' I said. I told him the story of how Pete had given me the kit years ago and when, after several months, I'd made no progress, had taken it back and then presented it to me for my fiftieth. 'I'll tell him,' I said.

Should I have been surprised? No. He's *from* Weymouth. Born and bred. If you're brought up on a farm then you'll know tractors, corn varieties and milk yields of cows, even if you grow up to be an accountant. Born in a Naval port? You'll absorb the history, the folklore, names of ships present and past. And especially if you become a mechanic, because complex machinery is your bread and butter.

*

Tennis. Pete and I managed to win the first set comfortably, in spite of a long first game on his serve in which the few contacts I had with the ball were almost totally unsuccessful. My one fortuitous touch came when I lifted an easy lob to Graham. Normally he puts anything like that away with ease. He netted it.

'You wouldn't have bet on that,' said Pete.

'You certainly wouldn't. Not a penny.'

'The odds against that happening were about the same as the odds against the *Bismarck* getting hit by a torpedo from a Swordfish,' he said. 'Or even a Swordfish actually finding the *Bismarck*.'

Which they didn't, of course. Or not at the first time of asking. The first time they flew off from the aircraft carrier *Ark Royal* they found only the British cruiser *Sheffield*. Mistaking her in the murk for *Bismarck*, they attacked. *Sheffield*, with commendable restraint, refused to fire so much as a warning shot back, and dodged them; and with their second sortie, the Swordfish came up with the torpedo strike that jammed *Bismarck's* rudder. 'Stringbags, they were known as,' my father had told me, and indeed, with their double wings flimsily held together with struts and wires, these obsolete-looking planes seemed hardly an advance over anything built by the Wright brothers. But they were blessed with those two slices of luck. They missed their own ship and they hit the enemy, thereby avoiding a horribly embarrassing, not to say tragic, outcome for the Royal Navy – and the nation.

It was to be some years before I saw a Swordfish fly myself, incongruously in tandem with one of the Navy's present-day helicopters; but the juxtaposition on that occasion was fitting, and sombre.

*

When my infant teacher asked us to draw a picture, mine would always be a ship. Why does one child habitually draw one thing, another child another? Probably because, having chosen a first subject arbitrarily, and been praised for it, the child thinks: That seemed to please them, so I'll do it again. 'Not *another* ship, Nigel!' groaned Mrs. Green; but by that time the habit had been ingrained, and I found no other inspiration.

'Perhaps he'll be a sailor,' said my parents to one another. 'Join the Navy.'

'Like Jim,' said my mother. (Her brother, who was an officer.)

'Or Harry,' said my father. (His brother, who was only a petty officer.)

Before the war Jim had served in the *Hood*. She probably rivals Nelson's *Victory* as the most famous warship in British naval history. Apart from several books, she has been the subject of a feature film and several television documentaries. Her fame rests not only on her spectacular demise, blown literally out of the water by the German battleship *Bismarck*. She was famous long before that. She had already, for two decades, been the best-known contemporary British warship. She was beautiful to look at, well-proportioned, long and sleek in the water. She possessed awesome firepower. And she was fast. In 1923, leading a squadron of seven British warships, she embarked on a world tour. According to Ernle Bradford's book, consultations between the Foreign Office, the Admiralty and the governors of the British overseas dominions ended in the conclusion that

> it would be a wise cementing of old friendships to send an important British squadron around the world ... Such a gesture of 'showing the flag' would fulfil two purposes: it would strengthen the links of the Commonwealth at every level, and it would serve to remind the people of the new countries that the price of Admiralty was a heavy one.

And for the *Hood*, ultimately it was to prove heavy in blood as well as cash. But that was in the future.

> By the time the squadron reached Fremantle ... what had started as an experiment in Empire relations and an exercise in training men and ships, had become a triumphal procession ... A hard-bitten Australian journalist found poetic prose coming from his typewriter ... : 'The picturesque has yielded to the terrible. Her mailed might appals and exalts – appals because of her sheer size and strength of armament; exalts because, in her, England is still England.

*

'England is still England'. Those were the words I took to heart, when I first read the book, which my father had borrowed from the library when I was eleven. The nation *was* its warships. England, a seafaring nation, resided in her ships; lived, moved, had her being through her mastery of the seas. I was English, and therefore a seafarer; I was a son of the people who lived by, and through, their relationship with ships and the sea.

Except that I wasn't. I never went to sea. Ships might have fascinated me but when I was ten it was discovered I was short-sighted. My parents took me to a consultant who told them they should discourage any idea of joining the Navy because although my eyes weren't that bad, they might get worse and I would be rejected at the first medical. So I put on my glasses and thought no more about going to sea. I was a bit sad, though not for long. Sure enough, my sight got worse.

I still had my nose in books about ships, but when I was fifteen and my father bought a sailing yacht, I spent much of the time on it bored and quite a bit of it being seasick. I found little romance in sailing, because the sea was always and only the sea, and when you were out in it, especially when you were not in sight of land – why! there was nothing to look at and nothing to do. In the words of a popular song: 'We joined the Navy/To see the world/But what did we see?/We saw the sea[1]'.

Another verse begins: 'We joined the navy/To do or die/But we didn't do/And we didn't die'. But during the Second World War a lot of people did do; and many of

---

[1] Lyrics by Irving Berlin, sung by Fred Astaire in the film *Follow the Fleet* (1936).

them died, on both sides of the conflict, in merchant ships as well as warships. Of course, a lot fewer *died* than merely *did*: unless, that is, you were a German submariner, in which case your chances of surviving the war were twenty-five per cent. In other words, three out of every four men who set sail in a U-boat during the Second World War perished. And half the time, being in a submarine, you didn't even get to see the sea. (Large numbers of sailors in surface ships didn't either, such as those manning the engine room.) In a small boat off the Isle of Wight I might well have been bored. If I'd been in a German submarine thirty years previously, I would have been not only bored but frightened, and soon, probably, dead.

*

A *world tour*? Who does *world tours*? Rock stars. Monarchs, sometimes; or they used to. But *ships*? Why would a *ship* do a world tour? It wouldn't. Not now. But we are talking nearly a century ago. Then, it cannot have seemed unnatural. Of course, as far as the sailors were concerned, the world cruise became a world booze, and although they had to dress up and look the part when visitors came on board, and behave themselves when they went ashore, there was partying and dancing and no doubt much else. HMS *Hood* visited Cape Town, Singapore, Wellington, Auckland, Honolulu, San Francisco, Panama, the West Indies, Quebec. People were in awe of the British Navy and particularly of the *Hood* not only as its representative but for herself. But she was not only respected. 'For nearly a quarter of a century the

Hood was the most famous ship in the world – a living legend', says Bradford; 'for twenty-one years the pride of Britain's Navy, the biggest warship in the world', echoes Ludovic Kennedy. It seems to me from these accounts, from the affectionate way of which she was spoken and written, that she was *loved*.

Loved? How can a warship – indeed any ship – be *loved*? You cannot cuddle a ship. Nor even a model of a ship. I discovered that myself one Christmas when my Aunt Betty gave me a big black-and-white plastic model of the famous passenger liner *Queen Elizabeth* (86,000 tons, and thus twice as heavy as the *Hood*). It floated in the bath all right but when I dried it off and took it to bed with me it was cold and hard and bumped unpleasantly against my head, and quite soon I put it down on the floor. But I still loved it; and I did so for months, until it began to leak, and in spite of my father's efforts to patch it up with glue it kept shipping water, settling lower and lower; and eventually I no longer loved it enough to stop it being broken up for scrap, or rather being put in the dustbin.

But people loved the Hood, all right. I doubt that she was loved by women. But she was certainly loved by men. It is of course not only ships they love. They love aircraft, and cars, and steam engines. They love static pieces of machinery and individual examples of machined metal or wood, though perhaps with not quite as much fervour, and not in such numbers. Nonetheless *love* is not too strong a word to use for the feeling some men sometimes have for an old clock or a gun or a sword or even a set of particularly well-made chisels. But the strongest of this kind of love is of a piece of machinery, made up of a dozen or hundreds or thousands of moving parts: machinery which efficiently does what it was designed to do, and whose individual pieces fit snugly together to make the whole; which works almost silently, with a hiss rather than a scrape, a clanking not a banging, each piece of brass or steel moving harmoniously on or against or within the next, kissing it through a translucent film of oil. It will do this properly only if it is cleaned and oiled and looked after and ... *loved*.

But a ship, though a piece of machinery, is more than that. You have to look after it, yes: but you are *in* it, you sleep in it and are succoured by it. *It* looks after *you*. You love it, and it loves you; the relationship is a symbiotic one, and the ship's fate and yours are entwined. If you use her well and succeed in what you are trying to do then she will protect you and allow you to continue in her; but if her fate should be to die, then as often as not yours will be too.

If you love something, you cleave to it; you want to merge with it, you want your being to be absorbed by it, so that you are one. If you *love* a ship, you want to be in it, and, if it should die, you wish to die with it. And if that ship is already dead, what then? Somehow, you want to have died with it.

It is a peculiar kind of nostalgia, this.

*

One of the reasons warships are not loved by women, I suspect (or shall we say not as much), is that their primary purpose is destruction. The apologists for war – amongst whom, sometimes, I count myself – would cavil

254

at this, and say their primary purpose is deterrence, and only when that has failed is the secondary purpose, killing, implemented. Yes; but you do not achieve the first without being able to do the second. First, you construct a device that is able to wreak enormous damage on an enemy. Only then do you decide whether to wade straight into using it for that purpose, or, instead, to use its threat as your weapon. My mother abhorred the violence associated with the war, and with the films about it or indeed any other war, and would change the subject when it arose, if she could; and, generalising – no doubt dangerously – from a sample of one, I came to think that perhaps the truth was that women dislike war more than men because its violence is in direct antipathy to one of their primary biological impulses, which is the giving of life. And because they have a continued role in the nurturing of new life which is more crucial than the role of men, they can less easily countenance its destruction.

Yet the partners – and they are still mostly women – of people in the armed forces are fiercely loyal to them, if less so to what they get up to. They will banter with them about tanks and guns and aeroplanes, and join in with the belittling of the enemy that is often an essential part of the mental preparation for war. To an extent they are humouring them: big boys' toys. But there comes a point when they will shy away from such talk. Perhaps it is no more than what occurs when men go on too much about the football or the cricket. But I think there is more of a distancing.

*

Many of the men who served in the *Hood* before that last voyage were still alive for many years after the war. There are their relatives, and those of the sailors who died in her. The Hood Association has an annual dinner. And these days, of course, there is a website.

But the most poignant aspect of the love-affair with the *Hood* is the memorial service at the church in the New Forest at which Admiral Holland, the commander of the force when she so shockingly exploded out of this world and into history, himself had attended. The service is held every year, on the Sunday closest to 24th May, the date of her demise. Unless you arrive early there is standing room only. In 1998 I decided it was time I went.

'Why are you going?' Helen had asked me.

Oh dear. Why, indeed? All the answers say too much and too little. Because I have been fascinated by the story since I read *The Mighty Hood*. Because it is important to acknowledge those men and I owe my life and my freedom to them. Because I feel guilty about not having fought a war. Because I never went to sea. Because I had an uncle who served in her and another who was also in the Navy during the war (and narrowly avoided being sunk in one of its ships, being posted to another days before she sailed). Because those ships were the biggest and the most awesome fighting machines there have ever been. Because the *Hood* was the naval symbol of British history stretching back through years which were also lived through by my forebears. Because I have a familial affinity with those who have been lost at sea. Because with both my parents dead I no longer have a reason to visit the New Forest and this provides one, and one which is also a link with the most seminal historical events that have shaped my life.

Even at ten o'clock, an hour before the service, cars lined the narrow road outside the church and people were making their way slowly inside it. At twenty to eleven, extra chairs were brought in. Apart from the National Anthem, we sang *O God our help in ages past, Thou whose almighty word,* and *Eternal father, strong to save.* Many of the attendees were old, ex-Services, with rows of campaign medals and decorations on their lapels.

The order of service required that the act of commemoration ('Age shall not weary them, nor the years condemn') should be said 'by one of their number'. There was only one person this could be. Three men, only, were pulled from the cold North Atlantic waters after the ship had sunk. All survived the war, but by 1998 two had died. The one remaining, Ted Briggs, had been a young Ordinary Signalman at the time[1]. His voice shook, as it had on a television documentary I had seen some months before when he spoke about his experience of the sinking. And of course I too found it moving, with the bugle calling the Last Post. Tears did more than fill my eyes, they ran down my cheeks.

Outside after the service, scores of people chatted to one other in the green of the churchyard. Briggs was the central figure, surrounded by little queues of people wanting to be photographed with him. I managed to attract his attention, and shake his hand. I congratulated him on his performance in the service.

---

[1] The other two were Midshipman William Dundas and Able Seaman Bob Tilburn. Ted Briggs died in 2008, aged 85.

'It doesn't get any easier,' he said.

But why not? You would think that with each passing year the memories would fade, and tasks like this would become more automatic. Evidently not; and you see this kind of reaction frequently in ex-servicemen recalling the events of battle, indicating that raw emotions which have been buried for decades lie only just beneath the topsoil of composure. Perhaps that small shrine in the corner of the church, with the fine oil painting of the ship and the book of remembrance inscribed with the names of the one thousand four hundred and eighteen who died in her, and the presence of hundreds of people filling the church, not only revitalises his memories of what happened, but also impresses on him the effect the ship, and those events, have had on countless people whose connections with them are tenuous to say the least.

Not everyone, of course, can be as steeped in the story as me (and no doubt most of the others there); and I was reminded that the number of such people will relentlessly diminish. How many years more will this service continue after Ted Briggs himself has gone? He was eighteen when the ship was sunk, so at the time of that service he was 75.

The Hobler at Battramsley, just down the road, seemed a sensible place to stop for a drink on the way home. The garden is a popular place for Sunday lunch. I made a decision not to visit Lymington to look at the site of our old house. There is only so much melancholy I can cope with in one day.

*

A year later I was there again, this time with Pete. We found a seat just in time. There was room in the pew for one more person. An old man entered. Like most of the other old men there, he was wearing a suit with a row of medals hanging heavily from the left lapel. He had been a Chief Petty Officer. 'I lost a lot of my mates on that ship,' he told us. But he himself had missed her last voyage because he was on leave. Had he known any of the three survivors? 'Oh yes, yes. Knew Tilburn.'

He'd been in minesweepers before the *Hood*, coastal patrol. 'When I got posted to the *Hood*, I couldn't believe it.' He shook his head in admiration.

'Different?'

'Oh, completely different, compared to a minesweeper bobbing up and down on the waves. Mind you, she was a wet ship. Practically a submarine it seemed sometimes. She was still capable of thirty-two, thirty-three knots. But – '

'All that armour,' I said.

'Yes. Added afterwards.' ('That's why, when I did the model,' Pete told me later, 'I had her lower in the water than most of the photographs show.')

His speech was a bit slurred, and I nodded and grinned hopefully in various places; I did learn that after the *Hood* went down, he was in the crew of *Penelope*, a cruiser which took part in relieving the siege of Malta. Every year, he told me, he also goes to the service for the *Penelope* in Blackpool. Perhaps there's a service for every ship that was sunk, somewhere in the country? Hardly. That would be far too many services. Hundreds ... I found out later, via the Internet, that *Penelope* was sunk in the

Mediterranean in 1944, with the loss of three-quarters of her crew of 500.

After the war he settled at Dibden Purlieu and worked at the Esso oil refinery at Fawley.

'I quite enjoyed working on those tankers. They sent me over to Milford Haven in 1970. Just before I retired. Worked on them there. Yeah. Enjoyed it.'

The elderly preacher rambled a bit, but spoke evocatively enough about the sense of sheer desolation in the destroyers despatched to pick survivors from the *Hood* when they found a mere three men, a few items of wreckage, a little oil on the surface, and square mile upon square mile of empty ocean; and of the nation's, and his own, utter disbelief at home when news of the sinking came through: the *Hood*, the most famous ship of the Royal Navy, on whose graceful lines as she lay in the Solent he, fourteen at the time, had gazed.

I watched the flags being marched into the church, and out again afterwards, each of heavy cloth, lovingly embroidered. What are flags *for*? They are representative. They represent the ship, and the campaign, and the people in the ship and maybe abstract notions such as courage and self-sacrifice and duty. Afterwards Pete and I talked about what the service was for; what churches are for. 'Whenever I hear that word 'church',' he said, 'I try to substitute for it, 'temple'. And that just brings out the proper meaning. The people going into their temple and indulging in their strange rituals.'

We drove to the yacht club in Lymington for lunch. Pete was still a member there, in spite of, like me, no longer having his parents living in the town to visit. A good roast, and a good pint.

13

Messing About in Boats

On the seashore I watch our children from a distance. Rich, ahead of the others, steps rapidly from rock to rock, allowing the spring of his muscles, the flex in his joints, to take him from one to the next, balancing briefly on each before moving on, or taking three or four together in a series. Small waves splash close by, and there is a deeper roar of larger ones beyond. The salt breeze fans my face and I can feel the hardness of the rock underfoot.

Juliet and Joggan follow. Each one acts at first individually, finding anemones, seaweed, multicoloured pebbles, driftwood. But as soon as something interesting has been found, the occupation becomes a social one. A new discovery must be acknowledged by someone else. 'Look what I've found! Come here!'

It is a dull day, but the orangey brightness of the lichen, contrasted with the grey-green rock and the green-grey moss sprouting from its crevices, almost hurts the eyes. I keep within sight but only just, and they take no notice of me. At one level they probably know I am there, lagging behind by twenty, fifty, a hundred yards; occasionally I see all three busily crouched over a pool. At other times, one bobbing head is all that is visible. They are drawn by something entirely other than what we, their adults, have given them. It is a thread that comes from the centre of the earth, via the rocks, through the water, through mouths of fishes and the waving tentacles of sea anemones, the spirit of the deep, the ether ... It is a siren-song borne on the wind, half heard: heard not at all if ears are not open to hear. The fear held by us, the adults, is that, like the Pied Piper, the strains of that music will take them far away. It will take them out of our world, to which we strive so hard to shackle them, and give them wings to fly ... Is there a power possessed by children, an unconscious, unselfconscious and natural power of sight, but which one can recognise only in retrospect, by passing out of it and into the concrete and unmysterious world of adulthood? Or are these thoughts and actions all derivative, arriving unembellished from the adult world? Is the notion of a vision possessed only in childhood merely the sorry illusion of grown-ups? Perhaps the truth is that the land through the hill to which the Pied Piper leads the children is one to which the adults know themselves to have been, in some dimly-recalled past.

... Now they have found an old wooden pallet, and are heaving it over and over, down the rocks towards the water's edge. They carry it the last few feet to the sea, and it becomes a raft. Amidst shouting and laughter, one of them eventually succeeds in standing on it for a few moments as it floats. It has become a co-operative exercise, where the social dimensions of the task are dominant.

They wend their way back, sometimes looking after one another as they scramble across the rocks, every so often finding fish and crabs in pools the receding tide has left. The mood changes. The world changes, and now we are in a different one. A family one, and time for the picnic ... We are on a different planet, and the pull of the sea is forgotten. But it will show itself again, as surely as the tide turns.

Only the sea can do this, only the waters of the sea and its disciples, the rivers and the streams. It is only water that can thus absorb us and our children. Entirely unselfconsciously, we are drawn to it. Only the sea, in perpetual and rhythmic movement and sound, gives us the ability to lose our self-awareness, to lose ourselves. If Darwin is to be believed, if we indeed evolved in the way he suggested, our forebears struggled up out of the mother sea and thenceforth made the dry land their home. To return, back to the shallow waters, the beginnings of our being, to live and play there for all time: is an unconscious wish to do that the source of its magnetism?

*

One morning Charles rang to ask if I was on for the next sailing weekend on the Norfolk Broads. Iain would be going, Martin G., Brian, Michael, Julian perhaps, as well as a contingent from his in-laws in Wales. I told him I'd let him know in the next day or two.

'What did he want?' Helen asked, chopping beans.

'Sailing,' I said. 'Eleventh of October, probably.'

'Are you going to go?'

'I don't *think* so.'

'Why not? Go if you want to.'

The demands of the morning, breakfast and getting off to work, and making arrangements for looking after the children after school left me insufficient time to say why. It was the kind of question to which the answer, in spite of requiring few words, nevertheless needs a long time in which to say them. Or perhaps I chose not to find the time ... It was this: If I were to go, all the time I would be thinking: My sister died of this. She went sailing and she drowned. Nor was she the first family member to have met her death in the sea. My mother's eldest brother Jim, having ironically spent his working years in the Navy, had drowned after a presumed heart attack whilst swimming, on holiday in Crete. I did not wish to contribute to that particular grim family statistic.

The arguments on the other side, of course, were those of rationality. That had been a chance in a million; it was sheer bad luck; you take more risks each time you go on the road than you would sailing on the Broads; the weather would be warmer than when that happened to her, and even if I did fall in, there was no chance of becoming paralysed by cold; I would be with several other people, all of whom could swim and could pull together to rescue someone; the number of drownings from small boats around our coasts is minuscule. In any case, I'd forget about all that. I'd enjoy it.

Then there was another voice, a more pointed one, that said: You're afraid! Show you can overcome the past! Shrug aside the fear! You a man or a mouse?

Yes, if you ask the question, and if that is the way you wish to frame it, I admit I am afraid. Yes, words do hurt me. But, in this case, not enough for me to act on them.

I would have gone if I had had to. Since I did not have to, there was no need to subject myself to it. Would I have enjoyed it? In part, yes. Would I have enjoyed enough of it to warrant going? I didn't know. There was group pressure to go. What was the impetus for a decision not to? It consisted of reasons which some people, surely, would easily brush aside. They were tentative reasons, all to do with feelings, with perceptions. They were these: 'I have a respect for the past. That says to me: there is no need to go the same way. Do not put yourself in that position'. Hers was a death by water which told me to take care, if I could, to avoid it. It was an ancestral voice which spoke, weak because it had no reason yet strong because ... Because what? Because I let it? Perhaps. It was real nonetheless, in spite of its weakness. And the voice also said: You would be thinking about it all the time if you went; it would be like a sore spot you would be unable to ignore, and which, irritating little thing that it might be, would spoil the weekend by constantly making its presence felt. I refrained from going, in memory of her. Out of respect, if that is not too inflated a notion.

*

The urgency of The Ancient Mariner to tell his story is readily understandable. In a ship, on a boat, if something goes wrong you have nowhere to go – except the sea. The sailors whose ships were torpedoed by submarines had no choice but to strive to keep it afloat by whatever means they could: and if they couldn't, then commit themselves to a much smaller boat. Or a lifejacket, and if that was all you had, then you would be lucky to survive. As for the submarines themselves, if they were caught, and depth-charged, then you had even less chance of living than the sailors on the ships you had sunk.

'At the going down of the sun, and in the morning, we will remember them'. Those are the words spoken when we remember the dead of the last great War, and the one before it; they are apposite, because they are an understatement. We do not remember them only at those times, but also at sundry other times and in sundry places; a small event, of trivial significance in itself, triggers off the memory. I stand in the kitchen making coffee for family members, after supper. Today they went for a walk on the cliff-top to Old Harry Rocks, the chalk-stack mainland sisters of the Needles on the Isle of Wight where with my sister's husband and I walked around the coastline and searched for her. I'm looking in the cupboard for mugs; and whenever I do that, I see those two blue-grey ones with depictions of Salisbury and Winchester cathedrals they gave us one Christmas ... my sister, who that night fell off my father's boat and inhaled not the life-giving night air but gobs of black salt water, filling her mouth and throat.

The coastguard search and rescue helicopter flew out early the following morning, clattering low overhead as we looked along the shore. The sight of it imparted a curious sense of elation, perhaps at the fact that even though the possibility of finding her alive was nil, all that was possible was being done to find her remains. She was washed up five months later, on a narrow beach on the island, and found by a man from Orpington and his young son walking their dog; she was identified from dental records. After the inquest I wrote to him, thanking him for his part in her laying-to-rest. I received an elegant letter in reply, in which he said that of course he could have done nothing less than what he did, which was, presumably, reporting his unpleasant discovery to the police. Words, spoken or written, can be helpful at times like this, especially when well-chosen as these were. There is little enough else that is, God knows.

Years later, a helicopter would be the object not of elation, but heartbreak.

*

For a short period, small boats were a part of my life, and for a few years at the end of my teens I was on the way to being able to describe myself as a sailor. But I hadn't been brought up in it when very young, and by the time my father did acquire that first boat, I was at the wrong age. I wanted to do things myself, and disliked being told. But on a boat you *have* to be told. For perfectly obvious safety reasons, someone needs to be in charge. My brother John on the other hand, five years younger, was happy to obey orders, and developed into a competent navigator. So my father found him useful. I was merely an extra pair of hands, and only when not being seasick. Whatever the reasons, I never had a boat, and never would; and for that, I felt sorry. I was from a nation of seafarers. Britain had built its strength upon the command of the seas, and I was sad not to have shared more in that, even as a weekend sailor of pleasure-craft. To be sure, I did find out what the phrase 'sea-legs' meant. I knew what it was like keep your balance bobbing about in a small boat for two or three days, and then be unsteady on reaching the shore. It was the loss of my sister that put an end to any such possibility. She fell off my father's boat one night in March when the sea was at its coldest, and within a few brief nightmare minutes her husband had discovered for himself the impossibility of one person both sailing a boat and pulling another out of the water.

Shortly afterwards my father sold the boat. He did talk of buying another, a smaller one, just for messing about in occasionally; but the talk was half-hearted, and then he died. And I, too, set my face against sailing again.

Messing about in boats. The phrase is from *The Wind in the Willows*. There is of course a good deal of messing about to be had in boats, raising and lowering the sails, stowing the ropes, tying up and casting off, tightening and loosening the rigging depending on the wind strength – and checking the engine is in good order. In a small cruising yacht, if the wind is too light or indeed too strong then you are likely to need a reliable motor. But good reliability was never, in my limited experience, a characteristic of small marine engines, and especially outboards. Hardly surprisingly, the innards tended to become waterlogged; and salt water is worse than fresh.

*

Pete's sailing boat is an old wooden one, built in the 1920s. 'We were thirty miles off the French coast,' he was saying. 'There'd been hardly any wind, all the way across, and every time a large ship got close enough, which was quite often, we had to start the engine and scarper out of the way as fast as we could. And then the alarm went off on it. Low oil pressure. We'd been putting fresh oil in it a bit more than we normally have to, and we'd run out. But we couldn't find the leak. And by this time, we were out of the shipping lanes, but you know what that French coast is like, there are rocks all over the place. So we decided to wait for wind, but we had to drop the anchor, because the tide was quite strong and we'd just have drifted on to the rocks. There was a hundred and sixty feet of water and we just had enough chain. It was absolutely taut. And then we got a bit of a breeze, so we pulled up the anchor and sailed a bit further in. Then the wind dropped again, but we managed to get closer to the coast by using diesel as a lubricant.'

'Wasn't that dangerous? Wouldn't the heat of the engine ignite the diesel?'

'We didn't think it would. But we had to stop using it because there wouldn't have been enough left for fuel. By this time we were in sight of the harbour. The only thing we had left was a bottle of extra virgin olive oil. And that got us into the harbour and on to a mooring.'

'Result.'

'I was telling this story to Snowy,' Pete went on. 'You know, the artist, who rents the studio above my surgery. And he said – you know, in that sardonic voice of his – "Extra virgin olive oil? Well! – so there are *some* advantages to being middle class. I mean, you wouldn't have got very far on *lard*, would you?"'

*

So I wished I were a seafarer, or at least a sailor. The thing about being a sailor is that you can talk about it at any time, and people will be interested. You won't have to force the story on them, like the Ancient Mariner. That underwater obstruction you hit which nearly sheared off the rudder. The characteristics of different shapes and sizes of boats. Tacking, tides, wind conditions. Extra virgin olive oil.

On one occasion Pete told us about another local dentist, who earns his bread and butter doing locums, but whose real interest is sailing. He has crossed the Atlantic several times, at least one of them single-handedly in the regular transatlantic race inaugurated in 1960 and won on that occasion by Francis Chichester. At the end of one trip when he arrived back in Portland Harbour, having sailed from America with two of his teenage sons, a race was about to start out of the sailing club. At which point, he didn't put ashore, thankful to be on dry land after weeks at sea. He joined in the race.

*

But I did absorb enough of the sights, sounds and smells to recall some impressions of being on the sea. Ripples lapping against the sides of the boat. Greyness of sea merging into sky, chilly in the early morning. Rigging wires slapping rhythmically against the mast in the breeze. Other boats moored, gently bobbing, awaiting use. Birds' footprints on brown-grey flat mud. The complex aroma of fishiness and diesel fuel. A watery sun; the coolth of the wind on your cheek. And you will learn to judge whether a wind is a force 3 or a 5 or even a 6 or

7, because you have been out in them all, and the wind strength has dictated what you do with your sails, how quickly you need to spill the wind from them, how much of a reef you need to take in the foresail; and ever afterwards you won't think, 'This wind is a bit strong', you will judge it in terms of the Beaufort scale. You go out to play tennis, and it's a force 4, and you know it will be a completely different game to when it's a 2.

*

Death at sea, in the case of most of those in the *Hood*, probably came quickly. She went down within three minutes. But the sailors in the ship that sank her, the *Bismarck*, had longer to contemplate their fate.

The *Bismarck*, and her sister ship the *Tirpitz*, were the most modern and most powerful battleships in the war at the time. To the convoys bringing vital food and other supplies across the Atlantic to Britain, they posed a massive threat. The *Bismarck* had to be sunk. After the *Hood* disaster, she duly was, following the disabling of her rudder by the torpedo dropped by Swordfish aircraft from the carrier *Ark Royal*. Two torpedoes hit the ship, one of them amidships where it did little damage against the thick armour-plating, but the second exploded astern in the steering compartment and jammed the rudder fifteen degrees to port. *Bismarck* could therefore steer only in circles, she was low on fuel, and partially flooded. By that time, in spite of being a formidable fighting machine, with highly accurate gunnery systems, she was a sitting duck to the overwhelmingly superior numbers of ships and guns hurriedly assembled by the Royal Navy. Eventually, she was pounded to pieces.

The aspect of the battle I find the most sobering lies in the knowledge each of those German sailors must have had, over a period of several hours, that they, or at least many of them, were about to die, and probably by extremely unpleasant means. They were doomed, and they knew it. Of course, many men going into battle on land, sea or air know that they *might* lose the battle. The German sailors will have known for certain that they *would* lose. It was clear even before the first shot was fired that their position was desperate. What kind of fear is it that a man encounters when this knowledge comes upon him? What comfort might there be from the presence of one's fellows? The traditions of battle at that time demanded that you fought at least until the position proved not merely desperate, but hopeless. The crew of the *Bismarck* fought beyond that point. Could they not, without dishonour, have surrendered? The answer is probably no. With the rudders jammed, Admiral Lütjens had signalled Berlin: 'Ship unmanoeuvrable. We fight to the last shell. Long live the Führer.' When *Bismarck* was sinking, the order was given to abandon ship; but an order to do that is not an order to surrender. When she went down, she did so with her battle ensign flying. With all the main armament out of action and the ship ablaze from stem to stern, the order was given to scuttle her. (The usual reason for scuttling a ship, by means of opening seacocks and setting explosive charges, is to prevent it falling into enemy hands.) That was after an hour and a half of intense fighting, during which large numbers of men must have been killed and still more wounded.

It seems to me an astonishing act of collective bravery of the crew to have done their duty under such circumstances. Their duty was, simply, to fight as long as they could move a muscle, and then to die for their country. These were trained sailors, but they were also ordinary people, with mothers and fathers and wives and girlfriends and children. The traditions of the German navy might not have been as long-lived as those of the Royal Navy, but they were as proud.

Had the boot been on the other foot, had it been a British ship presented with overwhelming odds against her, then no doubt the decision would have been the same. At one time I had some e-mail correspondence with Alastair, a Royal Navy officer who had been in HMS *Sheffield* when she was sunk in the Falklands. I'd been enquiring about whether or not naval ships carry white flags for the purpose of surrender. He put me right.

'First of all,' he said, 'RN ships don't carry white flags! Secondly, white flags don't mean that you want to surrender, they mean that you want to call a truce and talk. If any warship wants to surrender, they "strike their colours" i.e. take down their ensign.' In the unlikely event of a white flag being needed, it would have to be made by cutting up some of the signal flags which have white as part of their design.

Alastair went on to tell me about an incident from the Battle of Coronel, a naval gun-battle off the coast of Chile in 1914. Badly hit and effectively wrecked, the one remaining British ship that had not either escaped or been sunk was HMS *Monmouth*. 'The German light cruiser

Nurnberg came alongside the *Monmouth* and demanded that she should lower her flag (i.e. surrender), but the crew refused, and therefore she was sunk by close range gunfire with the loss of all 600 men – the Germans didn't lower any boats to pick up survivors as they considered the seas were too rough. Otto, the son of the German Admiral in charge of the force, Vice-Admiral Maximilian von Spee, later wrote home to his mother "It was dreadful to have to fire on the poor devil no longer able to defend herself, but her flag was still flying". I spoke to someone who had been the Captain of the modern Type 23 frigate HMS *Monmouth* and he told me that he'd heard the story that the *Nurnberg* called out via loud hailer asking her to strike her colours and the reply from *Monmouth* came back "Fuck off Fritz!"'

*

Numerous accounts have been published of the sinking of the *Bismarck*, some of the more recent containing descriptions of the discovery of her remains, as well as those of the *Hood*[1]. But the most evocative remains Ludovic Kennedy's in *Pursuit – The Sinking of the Bismarck*. As a young sub-lieutenant in HMS *Tartar*, one of the destroyers in the group pursuing *Bismarck*, Kennedy himself was witness to the battle.

> Young men with bits of their faces blown away,
> limbs separated from bodies, splintered bones

---

[1] For example: *Bismarck: Germany's greatest battleship gives up its secrets* (1990), by Robert Ballard; *Hood and Bismarck* (2001), by David Mearns and Rob White.

sticking through skin, blood gushing and flowing everywhere, men with stomach wounds watching their insides seep out and trying to shove them back, others vomiting with shock and disgust, the ghastly screams of the suffering ... they just sat there silent and bleeding, waiting resignedly for the end ... The tangled wreckage, smoke and flames, the piles of dead and mutilated, the moans of the wounded. Some helped to adjust the lifebelts of the less badly wounded, put them over the side: others found the screams got on their nerves, wanted to shut them up.

How would *I* have reacted? How would any of us? I doubt if we can even imagine. We can only hope we would have been brave. And what does 'brave' mean? By whatever means one might earn that epithet, it would need to entail the admiration of our fellows, whether for hours, or minutes, or for a few brief seconds before we all perished.

But we have not been tested; we shall grow old, and will never know.

*

I cycled back home from the pub quiz. This one we'd won, but we did have it a bit easy. In our team were Iain and Pete and Brian. One of the rounds asked you to look at photocopies of modern paintings and say who the artists were and what countries they came from. A doddle for Pete. Another round asked you to name the last ten mayors of Dorchester. For years Brian was a town councillor, so there was no difficulty with that one either. The prize was three bottles of cheap and nasty wine. Iain took one, Brian the next, and Pete and I tossed for the third. He won the toss, so I went home with the bottle.

I swung the garage door up, giving it just the right amount of heave to cause the catch to engage, and wheeled my bicycle in. I stabilised the front wheel by hooking one end of a luggage-strap around a spoke and the other to the bottle-cage. With my right hand I took a grip of the seat-tube, a third of the way up from the bottom bracket; bracing my back, I hoisted the machine upwards, lightly supporting the front of it with my left hand under the down-tube. As with the door, the momentum achieved with the initial lift was just enough to get the machine up to the required height, and I hung it neatly from the crossbar on its two brackets on the wall. I took pleasure in the grasp of my hand on the cool metal, the stretching of the muscles of my arm, the ability to grip and move and turn and judge everything just right, not too tight or too loose or too far or too short, each movement in harmony with the preceding one and the next; and I thought of Henry and the wolves in the forest.

When I was nine my aunt Betty took my sister and me to visit our grandmother, and we all walked down to the little bookshop in the village. A volume in a plain green-and-white jacket was picked out for me. 'You'll enjoy this,' they said. 'It's about a dog.' I wasn't over-excited. But they seemed to want me to have it; and during the next few years I read it at least half a dozen times. *White Fang* was the second book Jack London had written about a dog. The first was the better-known (if only because its title has become a common phrase) *The Call of the Wild*, published in 1903. The hero of that book escapes from his comfortable domesticated existence to an altogether more dangerous and exciting life in the forest. In *White Fang* the opposite happens: a wolf which is, in reality, half-dog grows up in the wild but eventually becomes domesticated. At the beginning of the book, two men desperately attempt to survive in the Alaskan winter with dwindling supplies and a diminishing team of dogs to haul their sled to the safety of the next settlement. A pack of hungry wolves pursues them, and, at night, comes ever closer to the fire built to prevent them from enticing away, and killing, another member of the dog-team. One of the men, Bill, rashly leaves the safety of the fire in an attempt to drive the pack away, but the three rounds left in his rifle are not enough. The wolves make short work of him, too, and as they close in once more, his companion Henry sits beside the fire:

> As he piled wood on the fire he discovered an appreciation of his own body which he had never felt before. He watched his moving muscles and was interested in the cunning mechanism of his fingers. By the light of the fire he crooked his fingers slowly and repeatedly, now one at a time, now all together, spreading them wide or making quick gripping movements. He studied the nail-formation, and prodded the finger-tips, now sharply, and again softly, gauging the while the nerve-sensations produced. It fascinated him, and he grew suddenly fond of this subtle flesh of his that worked so beautifully and smoothly and delicately. Then he would cast a glance of fear at

the wolf-circle drawn expectantly about him, and like a blow the realisation would strike him that this wonderful body of his, this living flesh, was no more than so much meat ... He glanced at the hand that held the brand, noticing the cunning delicacy of the fingers that gripped it, how they adjusted themselves to all the inequalities of the surface, curling over and under and about the rough wood ... and in the same instant he seemed to see a vision of those same sensitive and delicate fingers being crushed and torn by the white teeth of the she-wolf. Never had he been so fond of this body of his as now when his tenure of it was so precarious.

You would have plenty of time to examine your body like this in the tedium of war. But when battle commenced it is unlikely you would think about it: until, that is, some part of your hitherto perfectly-functioning flesh were torn off, albeit by high explosive rather than wolves. And then, if you were still conscious, you might realise that all you most feared had begun to happen. Did those men on the *Bismarck*, waiting for the beginning of their end, look at their hands like this, and their arms and their legs, and think something similar to Henry? Who was it who said that in war you spend ninety per cent of the time bored and the other ten percent terrified? It would be curious if you did not spend at least a little of that ninety per cent contemplating what the ten per cent might bring to your flesh and blood, the shredding of the one and the shedding of the other.

*

The coast of southern Britain is littered with the remains of anti-invasion devices. Many are concrete pill-boxes, in which were placed guns that would, if required, be fired at invading forces. No doubt if the threat of invasion had been greater than it was (and it was serious enough, though thanks to the success in the air of the Battle of Britain pilots, never seemed imminent) they would have quickly increased in number. Others are larger concrete structures with semi-circular steel fittings on which anti-aircraft guns once rotated. On beaches lie the remains of lines of large concrete blocks, designed to make it impossible for tanks and other vehicles, discharged from landing-craft, to cross.

West of the main beach at Weymouth, on the far side of the town harbour but within the huge harbour of Portland, is another beach, much smaller, named Sandsfoot. At one end the rocks are sandstone, grotesquely eaten away and pockmarked by the sea, but hard, heavy, lava-like in appearance. When the tide is out a few rock-pools are uncovered. The ruin of Sandsfoot Castle teeters dangerously above. The beach is hidden from the road, and access to it is by a sloping path followed by a flight of wooden steps. At their foot is an object more curious than pill-boxes and tank defences. It is a solid wooden lump in the rough shape of a boat, perhaps twenty-five feet long and half that wide, consisting of stout lengths of wood held together with inch-thick iron pinions. I saw it first when I was five. Its boat shape was more obvious than it is now and the timbers were sound. I can remember realising it could hardly be a seagoing vessel, because you obviously couldn't get into it: it was solid. All you could do was climb on it, and jump off again. No-one told me what it was, or, if they did, I did not understand or soon forgot.

Each summer, for five years during the early 1950s, my father drove the family down to Weymouth for a fortnight's holiday at the Trelawney Hotel, at the top of the road above the beach. Each year I paddled in the little waves which, as always in the harbour, sheltered as it is by the great breakwater built by prisoners incarcerated for the purpose on Portland, broke not with a roar but a splash. And each year I spent some time jumping on and off that curious wooden construction, wondering afresh what it was. It lies there still; its wood is rotting and soft to the touch, and it has sunk a foot or so further into the sand. I have since learned it was a naval gunnery target. Along with another similar structure it was towed out to sea off Portland where the Royal Navy took pot-shots at it with whatever guns they were trying out that day. Of solid wood as it is, it was evidently unsinkable; but one might have thought that if the gunners had been accurate then even a thing of such robust construction would have been blown to smithereens.

I never did find out how it came to be dumped there.

*

Moored in Portland Harbour during one of those holidays was HMS *Indefatigable*, an aircraft carrier which had been completed a year before the end of the war. One of her officers had installed his wife at our hotel whilst the ship was stationed there. My father struck up a conversation with him, and he invited us on board. We were taken out in the ship's launch. My sister and I ran up and down the flight deck and looked at the one aircraft parked on it, a Seafire, the naval conversion of the Spitfire. I was lifted up on to the plane and was allowed to sit in the cockpit for a moment. I recall being astonished at how small it was. 'Is this a real aeroplane?' I asked my father. 'Does it really fly?' 'Of course it is,' he said, embarrassed in the presence of the officer. 'They gave you an enormous plate of jam sandwiches,' he said years later when reminiscing (again), 'in the ward-room. And you and Diana scoffed the lot.'

Another, tinier, beach lay just beyond Sandsfoot. Immediately behind it was a railway embankment. Little goods trains used to pass by on their way to Portland, and the engine-driver at the front and the guard at the rear used to wave back to us small children on the beach. The railway has long since gone; now the embankment is merely a path where in the autumn you can pick blackberries ... One day time will turn, and I will be brought here again and those trains will puff once more behind us on the beach, and we will wave to the driver again, and we shall exist in that fragment of time, that present, with no past except the descriptions of it given me by my mother and father, and no thought of a future. And one day too, another day, when our own children are young again, we shall bring them back to the beach and when the tide is out we shall take them to the rock pools at the far end, and show them how to find crabs under stones and pick them up. Then there will be no time. There will be no past. There will be no future. There will be only this, for ever.

*

I cycled to Weymouth to see *Endeavour*. This is a modern, full-sized replica of Captain Cook's square-rigged ship in which he sailed to Australia in 1768. What struck me most was the number of ropes. Ropes from the sails, ropes stretched up the bowsprit, ropes hanging from the cross-trees, ropes snaking up the sides of the three masts, ropes tied to anchors and to stanchions and to other ropes. Every spar was all but hidden by ropes. Ropes half an inch thick, an inch, two inches; and aside from the fixed rigging, every one of them was designed to be pulled, up or down or for'ard or aft or to the lee side or the windward. How on earth would you know which one to pull, and when? How many paragraphs of how many books of procedures would you need to know, in order to operate this ship? Here was I, living in an age of massively advanced technology, in which human beings are able to fly in a few hours to the other side of the world and even to the moon, and *I didn't know the first thing the lowliest cabin-boy would have to do in order to sail this primitive wooden ship!*

For a moment my imagination took me back a couple of hundred years ... I am the captain. The tide is up, the wind set fair. It is time to depart, to sail the ship out from the harbour and into the bay, bound for foreign parts. The vessel's owner is there, top-hatted and cigarred, his wife in her finery hanging on to his arm. Mothers of fourteen-year-old boys who have never been to sea before are dabbing their eyes with handkerchiefs at the prospect of their departure, and everyone is looking expectantly in my direction. Er ... Um ... *What, in God's name, do I do*?

In the pub later I described this little nightmare. Pete had the answer. 'That's easy. You say, "Carry on, Mister Mate! Take her out of the harbour. I am just going below to my cabin for a smoke"!'

We discussed the shape of her bows and stern.

'What surprised me was that she's not at all pointed.'

'How did they bend those timbers like that?'

'They must have used a lot of steam.'

'It would have been a lot simpler to have them come to a point.'

'Then she would have gone faster.'

'Maybe they needed to get as much volume into the given length as possible.'

'But also, speed depends on waterline length.'

'Maybe at the speeds she was going, it would make negligible difference.'

'Speed may not have mattered that much. She was built originally as a collier.'

She was, however, fitted with cannon for Cook's voyage, and the sailors did have muskets with which they not only defended themselves but also attacked the Aboriginal people they encountered, when they needed water and were refused it. Her ostensible mission was to study the planets from the South Seas, since the astronomers of the day knew there was to be a particular alignment of them which could not be viewed from Europe. But there was also a secret mission entrusted to Cook by the Admiralty, to find out if there existed a southern continent – and, if there were, to claim it for Britain.

This of course is the kind of ship Samuel Johnson was talking about when he said, 'Every man thinks meanly of himself for not having been a soldier, or not having been at sea'. Seamanship then required entirely different skills from those of today. But the essentials of the sea remain. You still have a very cramped place in which to sleep. And seasickness does not change much. Whether you are in a 500-ton wooden ship or a 44,000-ton battle cruiser, you will pitch and roll, if a bit more rapidly in one than the other; throwing up on the deck is much the same in both, and you will certainly be required to wash it off.

*

Later, the conversation took in the speed of aircraft in the sky. Should air be regarded as a fluid in the same way that a liquid is? If so, then isn't the power, and hence the cost, needed to propel aeroplanes at increasing speeds subject to a law of diminishing returns? In the air, is some principle at work similar to that relating to water, namely that the longer a ship is, the faster it can move through it? I told the story of Tom Griffiths, friend of my in-laws, who at one time ran a skip hire business. (During the war he'd piloted a Stirling[1]. He was shot down over Denmark, captured and sent to a POW camp, but this was near the end of the war when things were chaotic, and he escaped. He stole the commandant's car and drove it to the coast where he traded it for a passage to England. When he landed he sent a message to his wife that he was coming home by train but didn't know which one. She met several and eventually he arrived.) As part of some festival or other in Bristol, there was a makeshift boat race

---

[1] Four-engined bomber, similar in size to the Lancaster.

in the harbour for floating skips which had to be equipped with an outboard motor of a specified maximum power. Tom also sailed small boats, and he knew that maximum speed was a function of waterline length. He and his men welded two skips together, one behind the other. Although the resultant heavier vessel accelerated more slowly than the others, and therefore during the first part of the race trailed behind them, in the end it reached a higher maximum speed, overtook all the rest and won.

Graham turned to Paul.

'There you are, you see. Length does matter, after all.'

14

Out of time, out of place

.

When someone is getting on a bit, but when they're still active and unlikely to die in the immediate future although they'll probably do so before you do because they're older, and when you're a close relative of theirs, particularly their son or daughter, then it does occasionally cross your mind that when they do go, even though it'll be some way ahead and you don't know what your own circumstances are going to be, nevertheless you'd quite like to inherit this or that particular item, because you've always liked it. You feel slightly guilty at these thoughts, because you have absolutely no wish for the person to die; it's just that, being realistic in an actuarial sense, this object is going to be left with no owner, and you'd like it to go to someone who will cherish it, namely yourself. And your conscience is mollified by the thought that the person in question would, if asked, probably not mind your having the said object, in fact would rather appreciate it, since they would know it would be put to good use and that in some small way their life would be extended beyond their death, by the continued use of that object in the hands of someone who'd known them and would remember them when they looked at it or used it.

But when that person does die, all of a sudden you find that the objects he or she possessed lose their life too. The furniture, the jewellery, the pictures, even the books: those items which defined the person become a diaspora. Each of them is up for grabs by the relatives (who is going to get the ruby necklace? who the mahogany bureau? who the first edition of Beatrix Potter? who the box of garage tools?). They are spread out, separated from one another, and fall into a multitude of hands. But it is not only because of this they are no longer the items they were. Having been separated also from their original context, they lose their accrued meaning. On the surface they look the same. But they are not: not, at any rate, in terms of their spirit. The clay of which that is composed has lost all shape. It is formless, lifeless, void of consequence. The meaning of each item individually, and all of them as a whole, has gone. The books, for example, are no longer an agglomeration, on those particular bookshelves, in that especial order, looked at according to that habit. Some are thrown away, a few are taken by other people, the remainder may be unloaded at a second-hand bookshop.

And so when this item, on which you have set your heart for these many years past, is safely ensconced in your possession, your view of it changes. You discover that the object itself has subtly altered. The covetousness – for that is what it was – with which you regarded it when it was in the hands of its previous owner blinded you to the realisation that when removed from its proper situation, then the life which had left its owner would drain also from the object; that although it might be infused with some kind of new life, which you are now giving it through your possession of it, that life is the wrong one. In its new position, the object is stripped of its proper significance. Because there is nothing left of the essence of the person who has died, nothing remains of the essences of his or her possessions. Only when an item has been re-allocated to someone else can it begin to build its significance anew. But its meaning, then, is altered almost or quite out of all recognition, and the only connection with its former existence lies in the fallible memory of the person by whom it has now been acquired – you. And you are not putting it to the same use as that other person did, you are not looking at it in the same way, it does not mean the same to you as it did to them; it does not even mean the same to you as it did when it was in its proper place. It behaves differently. You behave differently. And the accompaniment to this discovery is the knowledge that coming to possess the object is absolutely no consolation for the loss of the person. Irrespective of any other feelings for them, on account of this alone you would actually rather they were still there, that the object were not in your possession but back where it belongs in that of the person who gave it its proper place, its proper use and above all its proper existence. All of a sudden, now, the object does not exist as it did previously, because that person is not there to perceive it.

And thus I discover that Berkeley was right after all. Bishop George Berkeley the eighteenth-century philosopher, that is, who, to my incredulity when I was a philosophy student in my youth, maintained that an object existed only in so far as human beings perceived it. To the question 'What happens when someone leaves the room, then, thus ceasing to perceive it? Eh? Are you telling me the object ceases to be, and magically comes back into existence again when you re-enter the room?' Berkeley would answer, 'No. And that is because the object does, in fact, continue to be perceived. Not by human eyes, it is true, but by God.'

To the sceptical minds of 1960s philosophy students this seemed nutty enough, but when we learned that Berkeley then went on to use this position in an attempt to demonstrate both the existence of God *and* the existence of objects, he lost us entirely. As our tutor pointed out, the good Bishop couldn't have it both ways. On his theory of the perception of entities, he could either first assume the existence of objects and then derive from that assumption the existence of God, or first assume the existence of God and then derive from *that* assumption the continued existence of objects. What he could not legitimately do was assume the one, and prove the other, and at the same time assume the other and prove the one.

Probably we only half-understood what he was trying to get at (and I can't claim to have re-read him since then), but thus it was that old Berkeley forfeited all credibility in the particular class I attended, and in our essays we referred to his crackpot views with derision; but now, older and maybe more tolerant if not wiser, I find that there was more truth in what he said than I was prepared to allow.

*

So it was that I found myself at my parents' house which I was trying to sell because they had both died, and one by one I had to remove the items which still populated it. When I had visited it a few days previously to cut the grass, there in the corner of my mother's bedroom was a box of her clothes. I thought: that's why the house hasn't sold. People have been into that bedroom, seen a box of old lady's clothes with a hat on top, a flat-topped blue hat with a rim, and the notion of buying the house has become tainted with that of the hat and her death, and lost its attraction. In the supermarket car park were the recycling bins, and I took them there.

Next, I unscrewed the loft ladder, because otherwise the two plywood chests of drawers up there wouldn't come down; and after I had loaded one of them – there wasn't room for both – into the car, it was time to leave, because I had arranged to have a drink with Iain back home, which suited my younger son because he wanted me out of the house so he could have a booze-up with his mates. But before I went, I glanced in the main bedroom; and still fixed to the pelmet above the curtains was a framed cloth badge from Gloucestershire County AAA[1], and another saying Somerset County AAA 1934, and wooden badges of the Royal Army Medical Corps and the Royal Army Service Corps, and a similar plaque with the coat of arms of the Institute of Administrative Accountants, which my father ultimately served as its Chairman; and a smaller metal badge of the St. John

---

[1]Amateur Athletic Association.

Ambulance Association, in which, between the wars, he worked a few evenings a week. (In those days there was no established state ambulance service, and the St. John and the St. Andrew Ambulance Associations, and the British Red Cross, relied on volunteers.)

And when I had taken these down, I put them in a little pile ready to take back to my own house where I would not know what to do with them, because they belonged not there but here, not at that moment but in the past, not with me but with him and with us as we once were; and I thought perhaps I should have had them burned with his mortal remains, or failing that then with those of my mother who died later, or at the very least on a bonfire in their garden, a funeral pyre of their possessions. Instead, I deposited them in the car; and then I walked out into the garden in which neither my mother nor my father, nor my brother, nor anyone else I knew would again sit in the sun, and out of nowhere there rose in front of me the images of people, mostly nameless to me, with whom he competed in the 100 yards and the 220 and the quarter-mile, sixty years ago; and I remembered him running even though it was before I was born, for he had told the stories with such vividness, and showed me the photographs. And those people from his past, and those events which occurred before I was on this earth were more real to me than the events and the people which had populated my own life. I did not understand why this should have been so. These things were past and I did not understand why they were still with me; they were real and I did not understand why I could not touch them again.

As I drove away from the house, I thought: Did I lock the back door? ... Yes. Yes, I'm sure I did. A hundred yards further on, I thought: I'd like a drink. But I promised Iain I'd be back for a drink with him. When I reached the traffic lights I decided I couldn't leave without going one last time to the Fisherman's Inn. I did a U-turn and returned to the house to phone Iain to say I'd be late. I checked the door. I hadn't locked it. I called in at the pub but the Flower's Original was tasteless and too fizzy. Three-quarters of it went in the urinal – before, that is, it had passed through my gut.

*

A few weeks before that, I had removed my father's collection of medals, which had been in another frame on the bedroom wall. Campaign medals from the war, more insignia from his running days, Civil Defence awards. The Civil Defence movement was initiated after the Second World War as an antidote to the potential effects of a nuclear attack, which, after the two bombs on Hiroshima and Nagasaki in 1945 had demonstrated just what would happen, was considered perfectly conceivable. Commercial and other organisations were encouraged to start their own voluntary Civil Defence squads, and my father became involved with the one at his employers, Ringer's tobacco company in Bristol. There were weekly training meetings, and regional and national competitions, and on one occasion his firm, even though small compared to most others taking part, made it to the national finals, where they were runners-up.

I thought: What use are those medals now? What function do they serve, with no-one looking at them? Hung on the wall, you do glance at them from time to time. Visitors do, too. You hope they will ask questions. If they do, you need to judge how much interest they really have. You have to start with a one-liner. If they listen attentively then you might add a sentence or two. If they ask another question, then it may indicate they are more interested than you had dared hope, and you can expand. If you are really lucky you can tell them the whole story, though of course in abbreviated form: few people will want to listen all evening. You need to finish just before their interest begins to flag, because then they may return later and ask you to complete the story, or even – oh Heaven! – question you on one of your other exhibits. When your audience is the same age as you, then you can assume their background knowledge of the context is roughly adequate. If they are younger then you may have to put in a few historical details. And if they are children, then brevity, and probably hyperbole, is essential[1].

---

[1] But, quite often, insufficient. In a *Times* 'Notebook' entry in March 2020, Max Hastings tells the following story: 'A precociously intelligent 12-year-old step-grandson strolled into my study and asked what I was writing. I responded: a tale about the Royal Navy in the Mediterranean in 1942, then set about enlightening him further. "Stop!" [he] said, raising an imperious hand, like an old-fashioned policeman at a road junction. "Don't tell me any more! It would go straight in one ear and out the other." He resumed scrutiny of his iPad, and I retired hurt. I should probably have thanked this decisive infant, for sparing both of us from wasting our time.'

*

One of the few documents I read in any detail on my psychology course at university was an account of the German ethologist Konrad Lorenz bringing up geese. With him was born the idea of imprinting. This is an automatic response to certain stimuli at an early stage in the creature's development when it is especially sensitive, during which it forms a permanent attachment to the first moving thing it sees. What a gosling sees when it hatches, or certainly the first thing that moves, is its mother's backside. At a crucial stage of its development, the imprinting of this image leads to the young creature following that object. When the mother gets up to waddle away, so does the gosling. In one experiment, Lorenz so manipulated things that what the goslings saw during that brief critical period was not their mother's backside but his own. There was a wonderful photograph of him walking over a field with a string of goslings in train behind, following him as if he were their mother. They were fixated on him.

During their own early years human beings become fixated on whatever aspects of their lives strike them at certain stages. When I first became aware of what my mother paid for a pint of milk, the cost was eightpence. That is what, to me, a pint of milk ought still to cost. It cost eightpence in 1956 and so it ought to cost eightpence now, or about 3½p in today's coinage. A sliced white loaf was elevenpence. A small balsa-wood glider, packed flat in a paper package, was sevenpence ha'penny. My father paid four shillings and sixpence for a gallon of petrol. How dare the price now be more than a pound a *litre*? It would be just as outrageous if the mechanism pushing up cash values did the reverse. The point is, things have their natural prices. There is a certain amount of money they *should* cost, which is what they cost when I was nine. There is a right time of day to have a cup of tea, too, and a right way of making it. There is a natural range of subjects to talk about, and amongst them the most important, because recognised and participated in by everyone, was the second world war. As a topic of conversation it cropped up almost as often as the weather. We became fixated on it. We have followed it wherever it has gone. We have listened to our mothers' and fathers' stories, read the books they brought back home from the library (and bought our very own, without reference to our parents), watched the television programmes and seen the films.

To us, when we were children, the war almost seemed still to be going on. It wasn't exactly *now* but it was still with us. Aside from the legacy of books and model aircraft, its consequences were present in the rationing of food and other essentials such as clothing and furniture, which did not finally cease until 1954. But the war had the great advantage that it had already happened. Having happened, it could not be changed: and therefore it could be used as a reference point. It was a landmark, or a series of them. Wittingly or unwittingly, our parents regaled us with tales of those landmarks, which to us became part of the substrate of everyday life. It was real. It wasn't history, because it was too recent. History was what had happened long ago. For us, the war wasn't the past, because we could still sense it around us. For our own children (and now grandchildren), by contrast, it *is* history. They do it at school. If it is also to some extent a reference point for them too, that is only because they take their cue from us.

*

The Digby Tap in Sherborne had a remarkably homogeneous clientèle that lunchtime. Again they appeared to be respectable bespectacled schoolmasters in their forties and fifties with a pint of beer and a plate of quiche and chips. They were mostly at separate tables but seemed to know each other. They greeted each other heartily and laughed uproariously.

On my previous visit, aside from the obituary of Flying Officer Ede, pinned above the bar I had noticed a newspaper cutting extolling the virtues of beer. It described English ale as a meal in itself. This was something I had long known. I had resolved to bring paper and pencil with me the next time I visited, in order to take details with which to regale anyone who started talking about the health-giving properties of red wine. There had been a lot in the papers about that in recent weeks. Why should the French and the Spanish and the Italians, and now the Californians and the Australians, be able to sing all the best tunes about the benefits of alcohol? None of them could brew decent beer, and it was about time someone put in a good word for England's finest product. It contains lots of useful nutrients and contributes handsomely to all the x pints of water we are recommended to drink per day. And the association with beer bellies is misplaced because those are developed not on account of drink but through eating a lot. Now, although I had brought the means to write it down, I was unable to do so because one of the schoolmasters was on a bar stool immediately below where the cutting was pinned, with his pie, chips and newspaper. Evidently I was destined to return, and return, until I had my information.

Halfway down my pint I quickly became absorbed in a book edited by Leslie Frewin in 1962 on the Lord's Taverners. This was a charity set up in what was then The Tavern at Lord's, the cricket ground. The book was an anthology, with an introduction by Prince Philip and pieces by well-known people, either writers or cricketers. One laconic piece, by Quentin Crewe, described the game: 'It is played almost everywhere where English is spoken, and also in Yorkshire and Lancashire. It is not played in America, which explains a lot.' But the piece that struck me was by Neville Cardus, the doyen of cricket writers so I understood, though I'd never read anything of his. It describes an incident immediately before the outbreak of war in 1939, just after Hitler had invaded Poland. The author is in the Long Room at Lord's. There is one other person in the room. A match is going on outside, with no spectators. After a while two workmen enter the room, take down the bust of W.G. Grace, cover it with a sheet and carry it away.

'Did you see, sir?' asks the other man.

'I saw, sir.'

'It must be war.'

*

297

One morning during a visit to one of the primary schools in Swanage I noticed a fat little book whose spine stood out from the others on the shelf. It was the wrong shape to be one of the earnest tomes on education, and too dull a colour for a children's book. In faint red print on the spine was the title 'All About Ships and Shipping', and the author's name, E.P. Harnack. Inside was the publication date of 1938, just before the outbreak of war.

Schoolchildren in the 1940s and 1950s might well have leafed through it, but I judged the likelihood of any of the current crop, or indeed the staff, being interested in it as not much above zero. Yet someone had faithfully, and recently, affixed a library classification number to it; somehow, the book had escaped the periodic purges of out-of-date and irrelevant volumes that any library with limited space must endure from its custodians. I waved it at the head teacher.

'I'll give you a fiver for it.'

She peered at it. The corners of her mouth went down. 'Done,' she said. 'I'll put it in the school funds.'

I stopped in a lay-by on the road back to the office and leafed through the book. The title was accurate. It had everything. It described the development of the steam ship. There was a table of the distances between important ports, and a list of all the lighthouses and lightships around the British Isles. It recorded the fastest Atlantic crossings since Brunel's *Great Western* had accomplished the feat in 15 days a hundred years previously, in 1838. It showed the Royal Navy officers' insignia, and, for good measure, told you their annual salaries: £2,650 plus various allowances if you were Admiral of the Fleet, £90 if you were a midshipman. A series of colour plates included the house flags of shipping companies, most bearing their initials. GSNC for General Steam Navigation Company Ltd. CSC for Clyde Shipping Company. A lone elegant K for Kaye Son and Co.

And CL for Coast Lines, in the Bristol office of which Aunt Ivy, my father's sister, worked for years as a clerk. She was astute enough; she simply had not had opportunities. Aunt Ivy was plump, and friendly and jolly, though often with an air of underlying sobriety. She remained at much the same social level at which she had been brought up, originating in a working-class family, and marrying – late – a small shopkeeper, Reg. He was small in every sense: she wasn't tall, but he was shorter than she, and his conversation was pretty small too. I always felt rather sorry for him. Of course he, and Ivy too, were aware that my father had married above his station, and they probably felt inhibited when in my mother's presence; she, in her turn, no doubt could not avoid looking down on them, and particularly Reg. Rarely, if ever, did they go on holiday, except to Weston-super-Mare, or maybe by boat to Ilfracombe; and I doubt if they ever went abroad.

More than once I heard Ivy reminiscing with my father about incidents during the war. Once during an air raid on Bristol she and Reg, and hers and my father's parents, took their routine places in the cellar for shelter. One of the bombs fell not far away, and the shock wave went through the house, disturbing the Westminster chiming clock on the mantelpiece. From the sitting room above them they could hear it start to strike the hour. One, two … six, seven, eight … eleven, twelve – but it didn't stop at twelve. It went on to thirteen, fourteen, fifteen. On and on it went, until finally, after they had counted a hundred and twenty, Ivy said, 'My goodness, Reg. Is that clock ever going to stop? I don't care that the air raid is still on, for heaven's sake do go up there and stop it.' And Reg ventured up the stairs and opened the back of the clock to halt the mechanism, before scurrying back down into the cellar.

Coast Lines was one of dozens of British shipping lines that began to die out in the 1960's, forced out of business by foreign competition and the rise of road transport, a process which continued savagely until, now, there is little left. Once I had a wall-chart of the company and its associated shipping firms, and several matching postcards, with pictures of dozens of ships, their funnels painted in the company livery. (Why were shipping companies called 'lines'? Perhaps it derived from the old sailing days: ships of the line, the line of battle, in which ships were drawn up to fight the enemy. The line of ships as you would see it in pictures of the Spithead Review, the Sovereign's periodic inspection of the fleet off the Isle of Wight, or the Portland review.)

I returned to the book and its gems of information. A Royal Navy sailor will always regard himself as 'in' a ship rather than 'on' her, whilst a merchant seaman will not care one way or the other. The Saturday night toast in a naval wardroom is always 'Sweethearts and Wives,' to which somebody usually adds, 'And may they never meet'. Naval officers who have been round either the Cape of Good Hope or Cape Horn may put one foot on the wardroom table, whilst both Capes carry the right to put both feet. The book lists the expenditure on the Royal

Navy, starting at £15 million a year in 1890, increasing to £100m as the first world war began, rising steeply to £347m in 1918, then falling to £50m before creeping up again in 1936-37-38, which brought the statistics up to the book's publication date. No doubt there was then another cost explosion in the years immediately following.

Finally, there was a list of Royal Navy ships, divided into categories: battleships, battle cruisers, cruisers, destroyers, frigates, minesweepers, minelayers, aircraft carriers, submarines, torpedo boats, support vessels, with simple black silhouettes to represent each type. Hundreds of ships were named, with their respective displacements, speeds, lengths and armaments. The book's previous owner had pencilled crosses by some of the ships, and sometimes annotated them: 'Sunk off Crete, May 1941' (HMS *Gloucester*); 'Sunk off Java, March '42' (HMS *Exeter*); or, starkly, a plain 'x'. This little book, with its line drawings and dry, factual text, its exhaustive prose and lengthy sentences, expressed the reality of the subject far more readily for me than the later large format volumes with their complicated diagrams and bold photographs and colours.

15

Portland Stone

From the southern outskirts of Weymouth, Portland is an irregular flat grey rectangle in the distance. Generations of sailors in Her – or His – Majesty's Navy have gazed on the harbour lying at its foot. For centuries, this harbour was never without a naval presence: latterly, sleek grey steel vessels, bristling with the weaponry of their day. The superstructure, the bridge, the guns of those modern ships mirrored the shape of Portland itself, rising straight-sided from the sea, adorned with masts and antennae.

One lunchtime I drove the short distance to the southernmost tip of the Island, known variously as the Bill of Portland, Portland Bill, or, most frequently to those who live on the island, just 'the Bill'. (Apart from 'the beak of a bird', the dictionary gives as one of that word's meanings 'a sharp promontory'.) In the car park facing the sea past the Trinity House obelisk, the wind buffeting the car, I glanced up. Just offshore, a Royal Navy destroyer was ploughing and pitching through the swell.

I grabbed my camera, and hurried through the spray to the rocks above the sea. A still camera will not capture the plunging and rising of the bows as a ship drives forward, but the photos would, at least, remind me of that movement. I stood with my coat fastened against the wind watching as the monochrome outline of the warship sailed away to the west. The scene filled me with a heady mix of yearning, romance, and unfulfilled wishes. My father's brother, and one of my mother's, sailed in such ships during the War. No doubt there was less discomfort in that ship than in theirs. Then, I did not doubt, the working environment was hard: seasickness, boredom, constraint, cold, using every ounce of one's strength to push onward into the unknown, apprehensive of dangers of both storm and enemy; and to my mind came the haunting sound of church congregations singing the lines of number 370 of *Hymns Ancient and Modern*:

> Eternal Father, strong to save
> Whose arm has bound the restless wave
> Who bidd'st the mighty ocean deep
> Its own appointed limits keep;
> O hear us when we cry to Thee
> For those in peril on the sea.

It is the tune that is haunting, full of threat and crescendo, like waves crashing on the shore; and 'peril' is the word encapsulating the whole of that sea-going experience, which for hundreds of years has been one of the essences of Englishness: and, come to that, Welshness and Scottishness and Irishness also.

I drove back down the hill overlooking the harbour and Chesil Beach. A helicopter was buzzing about; a few ships were anchored in the bay, and everything looked as it always had done. I switched on the radio to hear the news bulletin.

' ... The naval training establishment at Portland in Dorset is to close down, with the loss of fourteen hundred jobs ... Dorset County Council says this will prove disastrous for the area ... The operation is moving to Plymouth ... An end to the association between Portland and the navy which has existed since the middle of the last century ... It will raise unemployment levels in the Weymouth area from ten to fourteen per cent ... '

The announcement came on 12th November 1992. It was not a surprise. It had been anticipated for two years, but the news was still a shock, reported nationally and relayed in huge shrieking headlines in the local Evening Echo. Over the years the numbers of Navy ships present in the harbour had been diminishing anyway. A colleague at work, older than me, a native of the island, once scoffed when I referred to the Navy being at Portland; for him, a true Naval presence meant the enormous harbour – enclosed on three sides by the Weymouth coastline, Chesil Bank and the isle of Portland, and on the fourth by massive breakwaters built by prisoners – full of ships. By 1992, the maximum you would see there at any one time was four or five.

I suppose one might rejoice at the reduction in warfaring activities; but it was impossible not to feel sadness at the demise of a Naval port which has been the home of so many sailors. The 'Bygone Days' feature in the Echo was destined to have a field day or twenty.

*

The Eight Kings Inn at Southwell on Portland. The board outside said 'A Gibbs Mew house'. 'Oh, no, it's gone,' said the landlord. 'It was taken over by ... ' He couldn't remember, but his wife could. 'Enterprise Inns', she said. He was toothless, bespectacled, and apologetic for the absence of the Flowers IPA – 'I didn't know we'd run out last night. Did you?' he asked his wife. 'I wasn't in here last night,' she replied, 'so *I* didn't know.' I took a Wadworth's 6X, a good mouthful with a fine nutty taste. I felt it sinking to the centre of the tongue and the centre of me. This is what English ale does for you. That advert for Heineken, 'reaches the parts other beers cannot reach', was an excellent slogan. But it was for the wrong beer. It would have been so much better had it been invented for a proper English beer, or English ale in general.

Covering the walls were framed black-and-white photographs of ... The inevitable. This is Portland, after all. These were amongst the most famous of warships. There were at least three of the *Hood*, one of the *Bismarck*, one of the *Ramillies.* And another I thought I recognised – either the *Royal Oak* or the *Warspite*. I unhooked it from the wall to look at the back. *Warspite.* Elsewhere, a picture of the commissioning of the *Dreadnought* in 1914. This will have been a pub frequented by sailors. One of the many. For decades, all the pubs on Portland, or at least its northern end fronting the harbour, would have been frequented by sailors.

If you love Portland, you do so in spite of its bleakness. There are a few shrubs and bushes but – and this is surprising, for a plateau of land this size – almost no trees. And if you stop the car near the top of any of its cliffs you could be forgiven for being slightly puzzled at the view. It doesn't look natural. The cliffs are too jagged. Weather-worn stone is smoother, prettier.

Until you remember that this coastline is entirely man-made. The explanation is on an information board at one of the car parks. Much of the stone comprising Portland has gone during the last few centuries to the construction of London. St. Paul's Cathedral was built of it; Buckingham Palace, the British Museum, the National Gallery, the Bank of England, Somerset House – all clad with Portland stone. Municipal and commercial buildings in Manchester, Liverpool, Bristol, Dublin, the United Nations building in New York – and, not least, most of the headstones in the Commonwealth War Graves cemeteries of northern France, as well as those in the UK and the Cenotaph in Whitehall, consist of it. 'Until 1850,' runs the description, 'all quarries were confined to cliff edges. The stone blocks were then tumbled down directly to be manhandled into waiting ships'.[1]

Few of the cliffs of the Portland peninsula, then, are naturally-formed by the wind and rain over millennia. The lumpy, misshapen edges of this island are no accident; a few hundred years ago they must have looked quite different. What we see is not what our ancestors saw. Even the much-photographed Pulpit Rock, at the Bill down at the southern tip of the island, is an artefact, left there at the whim of the quarrymen.

---

[1] Millions of tons of stone were also deposited into the sea in the mid-19th century to form the walls of the harbour, but was hewn from inland quarries.

How far back from the original cliff-edges the present-day ones are now is impossible to say; but judging from the untidy collections of unused boulders lying on the lower slopes of the cliffs and along the shore, and bearing in mind the thousands of buildings of Portland stone which rise from the streets of the capital, nearly 300 miles away by barge, as well as elsewhere in the country and the world, the island must be quite a bit smaller than it used to be.

The little quarrying which takes place now is carried out in the interior, from a series of enormous holes in the ground. Portland is a place where the ravages of the past are written on it as starkly as a crater on the moon attests to a meteorite from space. You do not have to shut your eyes to imagine its history, because the scars are all too visible. When I had been in Ludlow a few weeks before, I had picked up a tourist leaflet for Herefordshire and the Marches. It proclaimed the beauties of the region and the fact that it was 'rich in history'. But the photographs were all of rolling countryside. There, the occasional castle provides evidence of the strife between the Welsh and the English, but the activities of humankind have not left the area desolate. On Portland, the landscape is testament to that one industry, the extraction of stone. The other businesses, the maritime ones, though they too have virtually ceased, can be remembered by the harbour walls. They can be remembered also by the innumerable inscriptions and photographs of naval ships and wrecks in the pubs, or those of them whose owners have troubled to display the history on their walls. That is where people are prompted to remember these things. It is at their bars and tables that they talk of them. They are the land base of the men whose definitive habitat is the sea.

*

Next to the dockyard is the Green Shutters Inn. 'With clientèle almost exclusively dockyard employees, it faces an uncertain future now the naval base is closed', says the local CAMRA guide. There is another pub immediately next door called the Sailor's Return, a third a few doors along named the Royal Breakwater Hotel, one next door to that known as Portland Roads Hotel, and a few paces from that is the Jolly Sailor. Over the centuries they will have done huge trade every time a ship docked: sailors in their hundreds pouring into them in order to get plastered, and some hours later staggering out, having spectacularly succeeded in their aim. No doubt there were as many brothels as pubs. Now, the island seems almost deserted: a community of ghost ships, ghost sailors. At five-thirty, this is the only bar open. Half a dozen men are present. Two, aged about thirty, are discussing how they joined the Navy.

'But what they didn't suggest,' says one in a Scots accent, 'was that I join as an officer. And I thought, "If feckin' Prince Andrew can get into the Navy as an officer, with five O levels, I should feckin' get in with eight".'

*

A little later I was there again, spending a weekend with friends at the youth hostel nearby. In the evening we walked a little way towards the old dockyard, to the

Green Shutters and back, where one of our number, a lady recently divorced, was flattered to be propositioned by a male a decade younger.

In the hostel the publicity for Portland was masterful. The coloured sketch map was predominantly bright green, whereas anyone who has spent five minutes on the island knows it is unremittingly grey. Its drabness, the savagery of its scarred cliffs, the bleakness of abandoned quarries and the sharp edges of those still in use, the plethora of brambles sprouting from every unkempt corner – no hint of this appeared in the leaflet.

Dominating the higher, northern end of the island are the brutal outlines of the Verne citadel, now a prison. Behind it are the derelict structures of the evolving and finally dying naval presence over two hundred years – roads, paths, bridges, walls, and, beneath the eastern cliff, a firing range. The painted canvas targets are long gone, but behind where they once stood is the man-made mound of earth and rock into which have thudded thousands of bullets. At the cliff top is another forbidding structure, whose imposing stone chimneys and fifteen-foot wall crowned with vicious coils of razor wire could signify nothing but another prison: this one the Youth Offenders' Institute.

If there is an attractiveness to Portland it probably lies in its juxtaposition with the bay into which it projects. Some people might regard the sea itself – any sea – exceedingly dull. It has waves, of varying size, its colour shifts depending on the clouds overhead and the depth beneath, and it has a horizon which is always a single line; but if you are surrounded by it then you will need to look elsewhere for your amusements. In the case of sailors, there is often little time for those, because sailors are concerned principally with surviving it – of struggling with its caprices and charting a route across it, in other words out of it. It attains interest only at its intersection with the land. Thus whilst the sea may be dreary, and this particular piece of land also, the interface between them is not.

The circuit around the perimeter of the island is fourteen miles. We had lunch in the sun outside the Pulpit Inn, at the foot of the peninsula, even though it was nearly November. Later, when it was dark, we took fireworks down to the beach. A group of local teenagers came to watch, sitting harmlessly a few yards away from us, oohing and aahing. The event was punctuated by a large woman marching up to us and saying loudly, 'Would someone tell me who's got the licence for these fireworks?'

'Licence?' said David, mildly. 'We haven't got a licence. We're just a group of friends enjoying ourselves on the beach. What do you mean, *licence*?'

'Right,' she shouted, and stormed off.

'Go and get the police,' one of the kids called after her. Needless to say they did not materialise, and nor did she reappear.

Portland had engendered starkly mixed feelings in me, and by the close of the weekend I had not had enough of it. I wanted to stay, in order to beat those feelings into some kind of recognisable form, to extract from them some understanding.

It was partly because the Navy wasn't there. It had been present for two centuries but now it had gone. The place used to be stuffed with naval pubs, but half of them were closed and the rest were struggling to cater for a thinner population. No off-duty sailors walked the streets. I dislike places which are so patently not what they were, and which have not yet found another identity. Nor did I like the signs of long-ceased stonecutting, overgrown and unused quarries, vanished traction engines. You could see them all in the old photographs and the books of Bygone Portland, but on the island itself there was only their absence.

Strange, that weekend. Before it had begun, I had had a sense of impermanence, and, throughout it, I had rarely felt more temporary about myself. Why should I have felt this regret for ways of life that exist no longer? Probably because they ceased only recently, within my lifetime, and perhaps because those men had worked with their hands and wore flat caps, and reminded me of the poses struck by my father and unnamed acquaintances in my own family albums.

'It does have a certain attraction,' said Nick later, when I described the weekend.

'Oh, I quite like Portland,' said Pete.

'Yeah, but would you want to live there?'

'I wouldn't mind. Some of those houses, the views are quite attractive. On the hill, looking down over the beach. It's like a Cornish fishing village.'

Perhaps. But to find much of Portland pleasing to the eye, I think, is hard. Hard, yes; it is a rock, and a hard place.

*

'On', note, is always the preposition associated with Portland. If you go to the country's largest city you will be *in* London; if you go as far north in England as you can, you will be in Northumberland; go a little further and you will be in Scotland. But go to Portland, and you will be on it just as surely as if you go to the Isle of Wight or the Isle of Man. Thus the language confers the perception that Portland is an island. It is not, of course. It is connected to the mainland by the causeway named Chesil, a huge natural bank of shingle whose stones, curiously, become progressively larger the further south you go. Sixteen miles away, near Bridport, they begin as apple-pip-sized bits of gravel, and when you arrive at Portland some of them are the size of a cricket ball. But although Weymouth has – or rather has had – its share of sailors' hostels and naval history, it is Portland which has the most direct and stark connection with the Senior Service. Weymouth represents the soft underbelly of naval life, Portland the business end. And in spite of the wide, straight road, which presents no difficulty to motor traffic except when the storms over Chesil are particularly strong, Portland might well be an island; its people consider themselves as a quite different race from the mainlanders of Weymouth, and are perceived as such in return.

*

Between my son's tennis matches on the indoor courts in Portsmouth I walked into the city centre. There were one or two impressive municipal buildings. The modern civic offices, fronted with panels of brown glass, were not out of sympathy with the town hall in spite of the contrast in styles. Facing them was a statue of Queen Victoria. Above the neo-Corinthian columns of the Guildhall was a frieze, topped, appropriately in this maritime city, by Neptune holding a copper trident.

And next to the Guildhall was a curved wall war memorial, erected in 1921, with hundreds of names in bronze lettering. At the centre of the circular area was a monolith, at the top of which were four scenes in stone relief. Two were of ships at sea, one of soldiers marching, the fourth of sailors firing a naval gun. I performed the smallest of rituals: a few of the poppy wreaths placed on Remembrance Day a month previously had blown over, and I carefully replaced them. 'From officers, adults and cadets, B company, Hants and I.O.W. Army Cadet Force'. 'Never to be forgotten. SAS – SBS and all special forces who failed to beat the clock. From the Special Air Services Association Southern Branch'. 'The Lord Mayor, the Lady Mayoress, Councillors and all members of Portsmouth City Council. In remembrance'. 'In memory of all our comrades. Portsmouth No. 10 Branch, Normandy Veterans Association, 1944'. 'Au mémoire de tous les combattants qui ont gardé l'ésprit de résistance'. And so forth. THEIR NAME LIVETH FOR EVERMORE, it said above the curved wall of names; and, centrally:

THIS · MEMORIAL · WAS
ERECTED · BY · THE
PEOPLE · OF · PORTSMOUTH
IN · PROUD · AND · LOVING
MEMORY · OF · THOSE
WHO · IN · THE · GLORIOUS
MORNING · OF · THEIR · DAYS
FOR · ENGLAND'S · SAKE · LOST
ALL · BUT · ENGLAND'S · PRAISE

MAY · LIGHT · PERPETUAL
SHINE · UPON · THEM

So, although this was originally a First World War memorial, like most others it also commemorates the dead from the 1939-45 war. Next to the monolith were four little flower beds, five feet by seven, one each for the Royal Navy, the Army, the Royal Air Force, and civilians. Planted in them were dozens of little wooden crosses with poppies, each inscribed with a name by relatives. '1914-1918. Battle Of Jutland. G.F. Cooke, HMS Queen Mary. C.F. Cooke, HMS Black Prince'. '2146301 Sapper J. B. Hopkins, R.E. Udine, 9th May 1945, age 23'. Another with merely the name of a ship. 'HMS Coventry, D119'.

*

Berthed alongside one another at Weymouth quay were twin sand-hoppers registered in Panama, named respectively Long Sand and Hope Sand. Their holds were open and I could see into the sloping interior of the nearest. These were not large ships by today's standards, perhaps a hundred feet long, but a massive presence

314

amongst the fishing boats and pleasure yachts. A thin strand of wire, threaded through flimsy stanchions, was no bar to stepping aboard; and the deck of the ship, at this particular state of the tide, was exactly on a level with the quay, and less than a pace away. On both deck and quay were wet patches, buckets, and haphazardly snaking ropes to trip over. The temptation to take that half-pace was almost irresistible. I would be stepping in to a maritime world, taken out of this skin, out of this life, out of this landlocked history of mine into a waterworld, a universe of ever-rolling seas, of wild waves and blessed harbours. Of standing in the prow, and listening and feeling the crash of the weight of water against the steel plates beneath me; of cargoes, and derricks, and oilskins and lashing rain; of shore leave, the strangeness of feet on dry land, quayside taverns and the relief of alcohol, the warmth of women and quick love in the afternoon. One small step for me, one giant leap for the imagination.

A harbour is the focus for one of man's oldest activities, and his oldest relationships, that with the sea; it is the interface between it and the town to which it belongs, to whose existence it lends meaning. Everyone congregates around it. There is no division between workplace and recreation: the ships are within spitting distance of the harbourside taverns. A harbour speaks of travel, where road and rail and sea converge; it speaks of arrivals and departures, greetings and farewells. It speaks of eking a living from the coast and the deeper sea, by means of fishing and of trade with other ports on the coasts of this country and others. It is through the harbour that these activities are channelled. This is where sailors come home after weeks or months at sea, to be fed, watered, and sexed. In *Heart of Oak,* by Tristan Jones, who sailed in the Royal Navy throughout the Second World War, is a sensitive description of the author's first experience with a girl, just a little older, in Manchester; and what he valued most, because it was what he needed most and it was what she gave, was kindness. Down countless centuries, sailors have returned from the sea to the arms and the kindnesses of women, some of them known to them and some never seen before. 'The kindness of women' is an apt phrase, used by J.G. Ballard as the title of a thinly-veiled autobiographical novel; it sums up a crucial aspect of the unequal relationship. Women know men need them; men's need for them and their love has no parallel in any need which women may have for men: and their kindness is bestowed with grace.

*

Fronting the main road down into Weymouth is the Swan. On its walls, too, are naval photographs. Some are recent, showing one of our current nuclear submarines being manoeuvred by tugs in the dock at Barrow-in-Furness: a huge, black, sinister, cigar-shaped thing, designed for warfare in a different league from its predecessors in the two great wars of the twentieth century. Then, it was torpedoes designed to sink single enemy ships. That, perhaps, was warfare on a human scale, if such a thing is possible: a scale limited to one thing at a time, a single target. Now they are equipped with nuclear warheads capable of devastating whole cities and killing millions, which is inhuman. Not that, if you were the victim of either, the difference would matter much.

Other photos are from earlier years: one of frigates, F107 and F114, probably in the 1970s, and another taken from the bows of a ship looking astern. This shows two forward turrets, whose guns are not large enough to be those of a capital ship; perhaps a light cruiser. Then there are carved painted wooden ships' badges. One is that of HMS *Starling*, another frigate, and one of the ships in which, besides HMS *Hood*, my Uncle Jim served. She visited Bristol in 1959, and I still have photographs of her, taken with my Brownie 127 camera.

'Someone with naval connections here?' I ask the thirty-something landlady.

'No; my husband collects that sort of pictures. Some of them left by the previous people.'

… It is just after the war, and a man comes to the end of his time in the Navy; he takes a living at a pub close to where he has been based, perhaps in the town where he met his future wife: a little inland, but not too far, still within a whiff of the salt sea in whose depths he has put down roots. On the walls he hangs mementoes of his naval career and its camaraderie. Every now and then an ex-shipmate comes in, but his sense of identity does not depend only on this. The traditions, culture, and awareness of the Navy is within every man, woman and child of this district. A pub with pictures of naval ships and other artefacts, frequented by Navy or ex-Navy men, extends its influence by subtle human means. A man will go home and talk about it: Guess who was in the Swan? – Old so-and-so, who was in such-and-such a ship with me. His wife will listen, perhaps mention it to a friend or two; the children will chatter at school. Names of ships, their length, size, armament, history, the battles they fought in; the advantages of one type of gun over another, the value of armour plating, the efficiency of radar and radio systems, the usefulness of submarine detecting equipment, the characters of captains and the attributes of admirals, the wetness of different vessels and whether they ride the waves or plough through them; and they will tell of men who served in this ship or that, of terrible deaths and lucky escapes, most never known beyond a small group of men but others recorded and published, like the story of the merchant sailor who was asleep in his bunk when a shell from the German 'pocket battleship' *Admiral Graf Spee* crashed through his cabin, and whose legs, had he not had them drawn up to his body, would have been shot off[1].

They come to know the ships as personalities. Everyone has either been in the Navy or knows someone who has: a brother or father or uncle or son, a friend or neighbour; and there are tales of the way the ship shudders when the guns are fired, and the vibration when she is at full ahead, and the interception of a suspicious vessel, and how shiny the brasswork has to be kept, and the way you finally get your sea-legs after two or three days out of port, and the fact that the Chief Petty Officer likes his boiled eggs done just so, and how, if you were to go up for'ard when the ship is at high speed in heavy seas you would almost certainly get washed

---

[1] *The Navy's Here*, the story of the *Graf Spee* and its supply ship the *Altmark*, and the Battle of the River Plate, by Willi Frischauer and Robert Jackson (pp. 105-6 of the Pan edition, 1957).

overboard, no question; and of the love the ship's engineers had of the oily whiff of their engines, and of a daily tot of rum, and of women in Gibraltar and Cyprus and Hong Kong.

The romance of the Navy has centred on the battleship and its supporting vessels, the cruisers and the destroyers, whilst the aircraft carrier, lopsided and uglier than the rest, is the object of some suspicion, because she is not quite in the mainstream of naval folklore. But now, post-war, there is a period of peace hitherto unprecedented in the twentieth century: forty, fifty, sixty and more years of peace in Europe, punctuated by brief if savage skirmishes elsewhere – Suez in the Fifties, the Falklands in the Eighties, the Gulf in the Nineties. The era of those ships has long passed. The so-called peace dividend, by which nations of East and West alike, no longer entertaining the threat of war between them, were supposed to be able to save money by spending less of it on their armed forces and more on health, education, social services and transport, which was predicted to follow the end of the military threat from the USSR and its allies, was partly instrumental in the erosion of naval strength; but the death knell of those huge battleships and cruisers with guns capable of hurling sixteen-inch-diameter projectiles, each weighing a ton, over twenty miles at an enemy ship on the horizon, had been sounded as early as the Battle of Jutland in the First World War. It took until 1941, and the sinking of the last of the Leviathans, as the *Hood* was dubbed, before their essential vulnerability began to dawn on naval strategists – or at least the British public.

Little by little the culture changes, and, over the years, the pub and its environs gradually lose their naval tradition. The knowledge seeps away, departs with the people who possessed it; and even of those who remain, their lives move on to other things: why should they live in the past? The Navy and its central role, not only in the defence of this country but also in its consciousness, all but disappears. In time the ships' names are forgotten, and with them the knowledge and the habits. The air breathed in this building by sailors, their friends and relatives, is still here, and the photographs on the wall remain, but the conversations are no longer about the Navy, the sea, grey skies and a heavy swell, about foreign ports and stokers and captains and guns, 4.5-inch and 16-inch and ack-ack, the sudden fear of an enemy submarine, the shout of 'Action Stations!' One by one, naval men leave the service, or die, or move away; and, amongst the clientèle with past naval connections, other preoccupations increasingly take the place of those stories from history.

*

The Belvedere Inn overlooks Weymouth harbour. The landlord told me he served twenty-five years in the navy, coming out in 1983.

'Most of the time I was in destroyers. I had a bit of time in the *Hermes*. Finished up in the *Intrepid*, just before she went to the Falklands. Joined straight from school. Ended up in charge of tactical training at Portland.'

Once more on the walls were dozens of old photographs, including a number of the old railway that, for a hundred years until its closure in 1965, operated between Portland and Weymouth. I told him I used to come on holiday to Weymouth when I was small. 'When we sat on that little beach beyond the far end of Castle Cove, the railway ran along the back.' I pointed to one of the photos. 'There it is, see? The driver and the guard used to wave to us.'

'If you were on leave,' he said, 'you could get the early train in the morning, take you into Weymouth, and then there was another one that would get you right back up to Portland, eleven o'clock at night.'

With the photographs was a black and white print depicting the naval review in Portland harbour of 1912.

'Look at all of those! Number of ships in the navy now, compared to that? Almost nothing, isn't it?'

'We've hardly got a navy,' he said, sadly. 'And the discipline's gone. It was going when I came out. You're not even allowed to swear. We used to have a good fight to sort out an argument. Go outside, discuss it with your fists. You're not permitted to do that now ... Spent about ten years of my navy career based at Portland. But that was all right, I come from Bournemouth. Just go back there on the train. Why they closed Portland beats me. It's a wonderful harbour. Best in the world. It's the road links, see. Place like Portsmouth, you just shoot down the motorway and there you are. But they've been arguing about a proper road into Weymouth the last thirty years. They'll never sort it out.'[1]

---

[1] They did sort it out eventually, though only because of the 2012 Olympic Games, when – to local pride and delight – Weymouth and Portland were selected to host the sailing events.

*

On the wall of the Weatherbury in Weymouth were two long photographs of several naval ships with, in the background, a built-up shore. At first I assumed this must have been a local naval review, but the buildings were grander than those on the sea-front down the road.

'Where's this?' I asked the landlord.

'Shanghai,' he said. 'HMS *Hawkins*. 1937.'

'And what are these other ships?'

'They're from other countries. Don't know what they are. It was a free port. Jean's grandfather, he was a midshipman, and Louis Mountbatten, he was on the ship at the time, a signals officer. She was a cruiser, the *Hawkins*.' I didn't say, 'I can see that', because it would have been (a) impertinent and (b) dishonest, since I'd have had to look at the photo more carefully than I'd had time to do, and think before making the judgment. The ship, no doubt, was named after the Sir John Hawkins of Spanish Armada fame, a cousin of the more famous Sir Francis Drake – and needless to say there have been numerous HMS *Drake*s down the centuries.

On guard by the fireplace, one either side, were two six-inch shell cartridges of polished brass, standing nearly three feet high. Care and precision, not to mention a good deal of high-quality brass, went into their manufacture. After their use they had evidently been lovingly looked after by decades of elbow-grease and Brasso. Thousands of them, alongside others larger and smaller, were used in anger by the Navy, at huge expense. But torpedoes, containing an engine for self-propulsion as well as high explosive, cost far more. I remember my father telling me that each torpedo fired in the war cost £1,000. A *thousand*? This was in the late 1950s, when a thousand pounds had not changed much in buying power since 1945, inflation not having reached the dizzy heights of the seventies, and if you earned a thousand a year you were quite comfortably off; at the turn of the twenty-first century, prices were thirty or forty times as much. I could hardly believe it. *Each* one cost a thousand pounds? So if a submarine had a few dozen on board, and there were quite a lot of submarines, and destroyers had them too – I was gobsmacked by the thought. (Except that the word 'gobsmacked' hadn't been invented then; I was whatever the 1958 equivalent was[1].)

*

But naval memories are prompted not only in pubs on the coast. On the swinging sign outside the Royal Oak in Wantage was a painting not of the tree which hid King Charles I when he was escaping from the Roundheads but of the battleship. This was the one sunk in Scapa Flow by German submarines in a daring raid in the very early days of the Second World War. Inside was a large photograph of her in Portsmouth Harbour, with Nelson's HMS *Victory* in the background. Amongst others was one of a previous *Royal Oak*, an ironclad, a wooden ship with iron reinforcement to the hull, powered by both sail and steam. There were dozens of carved ships' badges, each with its own insignia. *Triumph. Helmsdale. Galatea.*

---

[1] Internet research in 2020 suggests that the cost of a torpedo was in fact some 10 times that – as much as a Spitfire.

Zealous. Gloucester. Nelson. Pangbourne. Forth. Coventry. Battleaxe. Kent. As far as the naval memorabilia were concerned, this pub was as good as anything on Portland.

16

The Cockleshell Heroes

Film Society. Unusually for me, I reached the Corn Exchange before the start.

'What are *you* doing here?' asked Iain, 'you're not due till half-way through the first reel.'

'Yeah, I could have had another drink.'

'What! Taken to having one beforehand, as well as afterwards? You're getting to be a bloody dipso.'

'When you're fifty, there's not much time left. Fifty-one, even worse. Got to get in as much as you can.'

Julian came up. 'Nigel! Ah. Now, are you coming on this canoe trip, down the Wye?'

'Er ... When is it, now?'

'Eighth of May. We're leaving on the Friday evening, canoeing on Saturday, staying in a ... '

'Yeah. Well ... Probably. I'll have to see. I'd just better check the date out.'

'We've got these two-man canoes, so the numbers need to be even, otherwise someone will have to go on their own.'

'Who am I going with?'

'Well, that hasn't been decided yet. I'm sure we'll all manage to work it out, in a friendly manner.'

'Why don't you do one of those sociometry things? You know, like they do at schools when they ask kids who they'd like to be in a room with, on a school trip.'

'Dangerous technique, that,' says Iain. 'Who's going to be paddling his own canoe?'

After the film Pete came up to me.

'What's all this wavering, then?'

'What?'

'About the canoeing.'

'You think I should be decisive and say yeah I'll go?'

'Yes.' He made a chopping gesture with his hand. 'You should say, "Right. Go for it".'

'Oh, okay.'

He led me back to Julian.

'He's decided. He's coming.'

'You're coming? Oh good,' said Julian.

In Tom Brown's we sat at a table at the far end, where Pete was unmercifully tormented about his boarding ladder. This is a sailing accessory, with specially-fashioned brass fittings to hang it over the side of his boat, which he co-owns with his friend Gordon. It is made of mahogany, highly varnished, and when I had last seen it, at his house to watch the rugby, it was on public view in the hall.

'You can see your face in that varnish.'

'It's a bit ecologically unsound, isn't it, making it of hardwood?'

'No, he just dismantled a valuable antique table in the dining room. Now he eats off the floor.'

'Gordon had the job of scraping the barnacles off the hull. All Pete did was make a little ladder.'

'It's right there, in full view. Anybody going into the house can't miss it.'

'Just inside the front door. You trip over it.'

'He's laid it down, so the first thing you do is stub your toe on it – "What's *that*?" '

' "That? Oh, that's just my boarding ladder." '

' "Yeah but what's it doing *there*?" '

'Lovingly created. It's a work of art.'

'The Tate had that pile of bricks[1]. Everyone who went in there said, "What the hell's that?" – "Oh, that's a pile of bricks." Go into Pete's house – well, he fancies himself as an artist, doesn't he? – "What the hell is *that*?" – "That's my boarding ladder!" '

'Fall over the sodding thing and break your neck.'

'Are you insured, in case anyone sues you?'

'He's spent so much time on it,' said Jennie, 'he hasn't got round to all those other jobs around the house that need doing. I'm having to get Iain's men in to do them instead.'

'What! What *sort* of jobs hasn't he been doing?'

'Oh, all sorts of things he can't seem to be bothered to do.'

Pete wasn't listening. 'What? What was that?'

'Jennie says you've been neglecting your duties, and that she's had to call in Iain's men to get satisfaction.'

'Well, what a relief, is all I can say,' he said.

---

[1] *Equivalent VIII*, a rectangular arrangement of firebricks by Carl Andre, bought by the Tate Gallery in 1972.

*

Later there was talk about that battle of Nelson's off Alexandria, and the French flagship that blew up. We couldn't remember its name[1].

'I must go back and look it up,' said Nick. 'It's bothering me. It's in my Ladybird Book of Nelson.'

'It was a very significant battle,' said Pete. 'Because without winning that, there wouldn't have been any Trafalgar, and we would have been invaded by the French.'

'And we'd have been here drinking lager,' said Graham.

'Those little bottles of French stuff,' said Paul.

'We'd have had a good supply of French wine as well,' said Graham.

'Yeah,' said Pete, '*and* there'd be a constant supply of good food.'

'We'd be having two-hour lunches,' I said.

'So it was not such a good idea at all, to win that battle,' said Graham. 'Look what we're missing out on.'

'We'd all have mistresses,' said Pete.

There was a pause.

'Who would they have been?' he asked.

This was too much. The subject was changed. We talked about leadership, and the people with whom we went on the last walking weekend. What would they be like in a war? Who would inspire you? Who would you follow to near-certain death? Who would inspire you and who you'd follow are different, said Graham. I said, the

---

[1] Battle of the Nile (1798).

example always quoted is that of Churchill, because although he was particularly well-suited to be a war leader, in the first election after the war he was voted out. Did people actually say to one another, 'Well, he led us very well during the war, and arguably without him we would have lost, but I don't believe he's going to make a good peacetime leader, building houses and developing the health service'?

We cycled back across Salisbury Fields, me, Pete and Nick. There was a clunk. Someone had run into a car.

'Quick!' shouted Pete. 'Go go go go!'

Nick eventually caught up with us, puffing.

'I suddenly noticed that Victorian house with a Thirties door. Green Thirties door – '

'Which they stuck there,' Pete said, 'on a house built fifty years previously.'

'So you thought, that's such an outrage – '

' – you'd wreck their car.'

'Bloody well serve them right.'

'It was only the wing mirror,' said Nick, 'it was on a spring. – And what a nice demonstration of friendship that was,' he went on. 'Nobody stopping to find out if I was all right. Just everyone scarpering as fast as they could. What friends?'

Afterwards I re-read John Keegan's recent article in the *Telegraph*, taken from a forthcoming biography of Churchill, about the great man's rhetoric, and how it helped the nation gird its loins to fight the War. It was when Keegan had heard gramophone records of Churchill's speeches that he'd come to understand just why this occurred. How could the nation be galvanised to fight, under such daunting circumstances, when the memory was still fresh of the previous devasting conflict barely twenty years earlier, and when so many voices urged compromise and accommodation? By the words he chose, by his oratory, Churchill succeeded.

Whether or not it was this that stirred Britain to find the resolve to dig in and fight, there is a parallel question concerning how Germany was similarly galvanised. Part of the answer is surely very similar. In the late sixties, not long after we'd acquired a television set (my parents held off having one for years, for fear it would distract us children from our homework), I saw a documentary containing film of some of Hitler's speeches. I knew not a word of German, but to me the power of his delivery was perfectly clear. Immediately, I had no doubt of just what a compelling speaker he was; and from that moment I understood a little of how the personality of one man could, via his voice, be a significant factor in mobilising a nation.

So why did Germany go to war? Because of Hitler's speeches. And why did Britain resist? Because of Churchill's. Germans fought because of the electrifying words of their leader; and Britons responded because of the equally commanding ones of theirs. Kipling was right: words are, indeed, the most powerful drug.

*

At Sandford Orcas in the north of Dorset is the Mitre. When I went in, it looked more like someone's house than a pub, with a large door opening on to flagstones, and a friendly golden retriever, which wanted me to rub it behind the ears. By the pleasant old brick fireplace a couple of men were chatting amiably, one of them a military-looking man of about forty puffing at a cigar of Churchillian proportions. There was an atmosphere of calm, a low murmur of unstressed conversation. I became engrossed in a book whose date of publication was not stated but which must have been just after the second world war, entitled 'Our Glorious Navy'. There were cut-away pictures of the structure of battleships, showing the anti-torpedo bulge, the tanks for the fuel oil or coal, the engine room, the ammunition stores, the living quarters. The photographs bore captions such as 'A midshipman keeps watch aboard a British destroyer', or 'Three heavy cruisers, in line astern, show the implacable strength of the Royal Navy'. Nowadays the text would be regarded as over-nationalistic, with its condescending British attitude towards Johnny Foreigner. It talked about the dastardly attitudes of the Prussians before the first world war, the wickedness of our foes, the cowardly action of the captain of the *Graf Spee* in scuttling her outside Montevideo when cornered by the British navy in 1939; and it took the side of the members of the government who resigned during the 1930s in protest against reductions in military spending.

Those jingoistic attitudes. You can understand the difficulty of people like my father who grew up between the wars, coming to terms with the idea of co-existing with our German-dominated partners in Europe after 1945. When my brother married, it was to a German girl he had met whilst travelling in the West Indies. After our parents had met hers, he told me about being warmly embraced by his future father-in-law.

'Ha! Of course he's a very nice chap, and we got on well. But if I'd run into him thirty-five years ago, I'd probably have shot him!'

He said it lightly; over the years, the substance behind the remarks had dulled, and like others he had put the events behind him. Even before that, my mother had always said earnestly to me how important she thought it was for the inhabitants of this country to travel to others and get to know people in them, because it would reduce the likelihood of future wars; and so she approved, in principle at any rate, of marriage between nationalities. 'We fought people in Europe for too long. I'm glad we're coming closer together.'

*

The canoeing weekend came round quickly and in spite of having been in the Scouts (motto: Be Prepared) I wasn't ready. This is the nearest most of us will get to being in the Marines, I reflected. We can pretend we're the Cockleshell Heroes, creeping into Bordeaux harbour to stick magnetic limpet mines to the undersides of German ships. They managed to sink several of them, but of the ten men who started off only two returned. Two of the others were drowned and the remainder were captured and shot. With a bit of luck, I thought, more of us would get home safely.

Julian arrived to collect me and waited with a cup of tea while I packed. We picked up Iain and drove up the Wye valley from Chepstow to stop at Cherry Tree at Tintern. The destination was the New Harp Inn at Hoarwithy, and a bite to eat. The others were already there. Bob told a joke we'd heard before. Then Iain told a joke, and we'd heard that before, too. After that I decided to tell one as well, in case some of the group hadn't heard it. Pete said that one day soon he'd be content with any joke provided it was a long one, because he'd always forget whether or not he'd heard it already, and therefore always enjoy it. Like his mother, with Alzheimer's poor dear, circling around the garden, remarking on flowers which she'd seen only five minutes previously.

This first night some of the party stayed in the pub and the rest of us in a bed-and-breakfast just down the road. Paul and Julian stayed downstairs for a bit, chatting up the landlady. In the morning the river was mostly flat, with a few mildly rough patches, some eddies, and breeze-induced ripples. The water was deep green, and moved at two or three miles an hour. For that reason, it was possible to stop paddling from time to time.

'Hurts your shoulders, this,' someone said.

'Did you do this for your Duke of Edinburgh's Award?' Pete asked me.

'Canoeing? No.'

'What did you do then, for the athletics?'

'Oh, I don't know ... Bit of running. Can't remember.'

'I had to do the walk,' he said. 'I had to do that for the bronze. I just couldn't get up to the standards.' (If you couldn't make the athletics levels required, there was an alternative of doing a road walk, of several miles, which was tedious but not too difficult. I suppose the administrators of the award recognised that it would need to take account of differing rates of physical development in young people.)

'Yeah, I did that for the bronze,' I said.

'But you went on to get the gold, didn't you?'

'Yes.'

'Did you get it from Prince Philip?'

'No,' I said, cleverly. 'He wasn't Prince Philip in those days. Duke of Edinburgh. Went to see him at Buckingham Palace.'

'Was your mother proud of you? Did she go with you?'

'No. She'd already been. Some relative in the war who got a medal.' (Rea Leakey.) 'But my dad hadn't been. So he came with me.'

'Was he proud?'

'Oh, I expect so.'

Pete looked up at the sky. 'You know, I thought those Duke of Edinburgh's Award things were supposed to be character-forming.'

Everyone hooted. 'Ha, ha, ha!'

'To get that far,' Pete continued, 'to the gold award, and for it to be such a resounding failure – I mean, if it had had any effect at all, then what level of character was there in the first place? Anything with less character, you'd have to go down to a worm in a compost heap.'

'Ha, ha, ha!'

We drifted on a little further, the canoes lashed together.

'An awful lot of water washing about in the bottom of this boat,' said Paul. 'Muddy stuff. Where *is* it all coming from? Give us a sponge.' A sponge came flying backwards.

Meanwhile, Martin G., in the next boat, was quietly filling his own sponge from the river and squeezing it out behind Paul's seat.

'You sprung a leak?' asked someone.

'Must be the welding on the bottom of the boat, coming apart.'

'You lot are too heavy. There's a weight limit in these canoes, you know.'

This went on for some time, until Martin squeezed a little too hard and some of the water splashed down Paul's back.

'You – you – So that's where it's coming from!'

'A low-tech solution to the problem, these sponges,' someone else said. 'Be a better idea to equip these things with a pump. Vacuum pump.'

'It would have to be a bagless one,' said Martin. 'Have to be a Dyson.'

'You bought a Dyson in the end, didn't you?' I said.

'Yes. But did I tell you about the chap who came to try to sell us this super-duper American system, gave us a demonstration?'

'What was that?' asked Iain.

'Somebody, I don't know who, supposedly friends of ours but obviously not, thought we'd like a demonstration of this other vacuum cleaner. And they were so persistent. Did I tell you about the methods they used, to get us to buy it?'

'Yes,' I said, having heard the story at least twice before. 'Do you like your Dyson?'

'Oh, excellent, yes.'

'We've got one now. But I must admit, there's one design feature – '

Pete woke up. 'I do not believe this!' he shouted. 'I can *not* believe we are having a discussion about *vacuum cleaners*! And as soon as you've finished you'll start on about bread makers! Talk about *saddoes*! Worrrgh!'

We tied up at Ross and had lunch by the water's edge at the Hope and Anchor, and then some of us took a stroll into the town to find another of the Good Beer Guide's suggestions, the Crown and Sceptre, where we drank Archer's from Swindon, 4 per cent. Did anything good ever come out of Swindon, except railway engines? Well, this beer wasn't bad.

We stopped near Goodrich Castle, a sandstone pile. There was a good view from the river; it is a fine ruin, mainly because it's not as ruined as some ruins. We tied up on the river bank, leaving Iain to sleep off the effects of lunch. I sat on a wall outside, watching a tractor ploughing the field far below. Not so long ago this would have been done by a man and a horse. An acre, a furlong by a chain, was area of land a man was reckoned to be able to plough in a day, using a horse. How much does one man plough now, using this tractor? It is a lonely job, lonelier than when acres were ploughed by horses, for there is no neighbouring tractor-driver with whom to exchange the commonplaces of the day.

In the evening we stayed at a bed-and-breakfast that was excessively clean and over-generously equipped with furniture, pictures and trinkets. It was run by two ladies assisted by a large collection of rag dolls and soft cuddly toys. When I first spoke to the one on the desk (she did the PR and the waitressing, the other did the cooking), she put her hand on my arm and called me 'darling'. This rather pleased me, but before long I noticed that everyone else's arm was being treated similarly, and she called everyone else 'darling' or 'love' as well; which somehow took the gloss off it.

Julian had arranged this trip and had given us copious notes, maps and directions, all efficiently presented in a plastic wallet. The only piece of information he had omitted was that six of us had to sleep in three double beds. Pete and I were in the bridal suite in a four-poster. Peering down from the top of the canopy were about thirty teddy bears, squirrels, dogs and pussycats.

'Now how can we avoid molesting each other in the middle of the night?' I asked.

'We'll have a row. Just before we go to bed. Then we'll spend the whole night as far away from each other as possible.'

'Right on the edge of the mattress, practically falling out.'

We watched Ben Elton's stand-up comedy programme in bed, which, as Helen pointed out when we got back, I'd never done with *her*.

Almost as soon as we started off the following morning there was an Incident. The water was slightly ripply, you could hardly call it rapids. Iain and I went through and turned round to see how the others were getting on: and there were Pete and Martin half-walking, half-floating slowly along, the canoe on its side. Pete was shouting. I didn't hear what, at first. Then I made it out.

'Get the camera!' he was saying. 'The camera!'

Good idea, I thought, and steadied myself to rummage in my belongings to find it.

'Get the camera!' he shouted again.

'All right, for chrissake,' I muttered, 'I want to be a bit careful, don't want to do what you buggers did,' but

337

finally I found it. By this time they were nearer and I took a few close-ups of the shipwreck, with both Martin and Pete grinning rather wanly.

'No!' spluttered Pete, gesticulating, 'the *camera*! Down there!'

Finally Iain and I twigged. Pete's disposable, floating camera, with other items that had been loose in their canoe, was well ahead of them, bobbing up and down on the surface. We paddled after it and managed to fish it out; and then we all stopped on the bank while Pete and Martin dried themselves off.

'Self-inflicted sinking, that,' said someone.

'Incompetence of the crew.'

'Not even any friendly fire from a Swordfish.'

'It could have been worse.'

'She could have gone down with all hands.'

'Good job we were there to pick up survivors.'

'And there were no U-boats in the area, otherwise we might have had to call off our rescue.'

But a mile downstream there *was* enemy action. We'd been warned by the canoe-hire people that the swans were sometimes aggressive. Occasionally the male of a pair would sidle up to us threateningly and we'd splash it with a paddle. After we'd passed, we said to each other, 'Well, we saw *him* off,' while the swan was able to go back to his mate and say, 'Did you see that? *Four* canoes I tackled that time. I sorted *them* out okay. They won't be back.' Thus was honour satisfied on both sides.

We had made arrangements to phone the canoe company to take us back to Hoarwithy, where of course the cars were. We'd intended to stop at Symond's Yat just above the rapids, but missed it. We went through the rapids and tied the canoes together again. In another hour we would be at our destination of Monmouth.

'Is there anywhere else we can land, so we can phone them up to tell them to come and fetch us?'

'No, Symond's Yat was the last place.'

'Want to paddle back up through the rapids?'

'We'll have to wait until we get to Monmouth, then sit in the pub and wait for them to arrive.'

'Didn't you say you had your mobile with you, Julian? Give them a ring on that.'

'Ah. Oh, all right.' He got out his mobile phone and fiddled with it, trying to get a signal.

'The trouble is, you can't get it here, we're too low down, sitting on the river. If we land, and walk up the bank, we'll be a bit higher.'

'That's not going to make any difference,' snorted Iain. 'Another six foot? Bollocks.'

'Hold on, I think I've got something.'

'What network are you on?' asked someone else.

'Cellnet. Hang on a minute, it's not working. It's not mine, you know, this phone, it's Jill's. Oh dear. I think the battery's gone.'

'That's a fat lot of good! Bringing a mobile phone with the battery wound down! Whyn'tcha charge it up before you came?'

'Well, it's Jill's.'

'Whyn'tcha get *her* to charge it up?'

'Anyone else got a phone?'

Michael, rather sheepishly, started digging through his luggage.

'You've got a phone as *well*! Go on, then, get it out.'

'I've got one,' said Bob. 'But if yours isn't working here, then I don't suppose mine will either.'

'What network is yours?'

'Orange.'

'Go on, then, give it a go.'

There was a mass fumbling with mobile phones, to no avail.

'Oh, come on,' said Pete, and he got *his* out.

'Whaat! Did that survive the capsize?'

'Yup.'

'Was it in that plastic box all the time?'

'Yup.'

'Well, that was lucky.'

'No. Not lucky. Foresight.'

On the bank, a small group of walkers had stopped. All were staring with their mouths open at the astonishing sight before them, here on a lazy stream in one of the sleepier parts of the country.

'Yes!' shouted Pete, in the intervals between beeps. 'You really are seeing what you think you're seeing! We actually are canoeing down the river using mobile phones!'

Evidently still unable to comprehend the incongruity of rural idyll juxtaposed with twenty-first-century technology, one of them called out.

'Are you in trouble?'

'Ha, ha, ha!'

'He's just phoning the coastguard!'

'The Monmouth lifeboat!'

After a lot of punching of buttons, and shushing of the rest of us, Pete, sitting up straight and holding the phone as high as he dared without overbalancing, began to get a response; and after at first speaking to an answering machine, made the arrangements, and we drifted slowly on down the river.

The banks through which it ran were green, so green; a vibrant green, never grey, never dull, never dust-laden like the trees lining roads in cities. Near our destination, where the valley sides were steep, the trees covering them seemed to be piled one on top of the other, round-headed, with not a conifer amongst them. They had recently come into leaf, and many still had that luminosity. Years ago I had five years at school in this county, but most of that time was spent within the confines of classrooms and boarding houses. Fleetingly, I saw the countryside; the undulating landscapes, the low hills, the small fields, the green that I saw now, the round-topped trees. How good it would be to return here to live, to absorb those fields and hills and be absorbed in them; for the process that was started then was never finished.

*

When all our children were growing up, on Boxing Day mornings we played family football on Salisbury Fields, just round the corner from Pete and Jennie's house. It became an institution. You'd have dads and sons playing, the occasional mum and daughter and various visiting cousins and friends, anything from ten to fifteen per side, teams decided by whether your birthday was on an even-numbered day or an odd one. Goalposts were lengths of plastic waterpipe Pete had in his garage, and the games would often be decided by the youngest player on the pitch scoring a contrived penalty with the goalkeeper letting it through his legs. There'd be oranges at half time, mince pies and mulled wine in Pete and Jennie's garden following the game, and in the afternoon a gathering of the clans at Tom Brown's.

'You wouldn't wish it any other way, would you?' Pete was saying late in the afternoon on one such occasion, as we watched our offspring, grown up now, returned for Christmas from their universities or jobs or travelling, joshing with their friends from school who'd also come down. 'Look at them. All in here. I mean, this is a *result*. What would you have wanted, years ago? All the kids in here. It's brilliant. All come back to Dorchester, Boxing Day football, now in the pub, there they are.' We agreed. It's a *result*.

Then Iain told us about this article in the *Times*. He'd had it delivered by mistake instead of the *Guardian*. It was about the destruction of the *Scharnhorst* in 1943.

'It's the 60th anniversary. The *Prince of Wales*, she had much bigger armament, she was a battleship, 14-inch guns. *Scharnhorst* had only – what? 11-inch. And the captain of the *Prince of Wales*, he turned the convoy around because he thought there was a possibility of the Germans intercepting, and, yeah, it all played into his hands. Sunk her. Needed torpedoes, though, just like the *Bismarck*. Didn't sink her by gunfire.[1]'

'*Prince of Wales*?' I said, doubtfully, 'hang on, the *Prince of Wales* was sunk with the *Repulse* – '

---

[1] For a brief account of this action, see, for instance, *The World at War*, by Mark Arnold-Foster, pp. 90-91. *Scharnhorst* was sunk on 26th December 1943, by the *Duke of York*, amongst other British naval ships.

'*Repulse* and the *Prince of Wales* in the Far East,' shouted Pete, jabbing his finger, 'that was when the Japanese came in, 1941.'

'You sure it was 1941?'

'Well, it was about the time of Pearl Harbor, that was 1941[1].'

'So she couldn't have been involved with the *Scharnhorst* in 1943.'

We looked at each other.

'*King George V*?' I suggested. 'She helped sink the *Bismarck*. What happened to her after that?[2]'

'Dunno.'

We'd had enough to drink by then. For normal circumstances. But this was Boxing Day. An hour later, there we still were.

'The old fogeys,' said Pete. 'That's what we are. Iain and you and me. I mean if you'd been able to wish for anything better – could you have thought of anything better?' His speech was slowing a bit, and he was enunciating the words carefully. 'There isn't anything, is there?'

In the loo, I looked in the mirror and thought, Am I *that* old? How is that possible? Really, I'm a little boy in Bristol, in our house there. Or I'm a teenager, older than I'd ever thought I would be, or in my twenties. I never thought I'd get that far, either. And now having *children*! – and them growing up to be *adults*! Then I remembered where I was. I hurried down the corridor for another pint.

---

[1] 7th December 1941.

[2] She survived the war and was broken up for scrap in 1958.

Pete was wobbly but Iain was unrelenting. 'Right then,' he said, peering into his empty glass. 'Ready for another?'

'No, no,' said Pete, waving his hand.

It was my turn anyway. 'Right, I'll get 'em. Iain?'

'Yes please.'

'Pete?'

'No no,' he repeated.

I started for the bar but turned back to get the empties off the table, and gave him another chance.

'Sure?'

'Well … ' and he waved his hand from side to side, as if to say, all right then, go on, get me one, I know my resistance is useless.

'You'll have another one,' Iain said to him, half cajoling and half threatening.

'Half,' said Pete.

Now normally, under these circumstances, what the person at the bar will do is buy the bloke a full pint, because he knows that when he's halfway down his half he'll wish it were a whole one. But I thought: I need to be responsible here.

'You'll thank me for it, one day,' I said, handing him his half. 'You'll realise I did you a favour.'

All Pete's children were still there but then Lucie went. Then Chris. That left only Nicky and his girlfriend, playing darts, whilst Iain and I nursed Pete through the next mouthful of his beer, and the next.

Nicky and Corinne appeared at Pete's shoulder, and they were assertive.

'You can't be corrupted by these reprobates any more,' said Nicky, taking hold of Pete's arm. Pete did not resist.

He poured the remains of his beer into my glass, grinning wanly and shrugging.

'You're in the *maison* already,' I said. 'The *maison du chien*. You're in it now, you'll continue to be in it when you get home, so you might as well stay here and enjoy it,' and I poured his beer back. But by this time Nicky had hold of him, helping him up, and Iain and I watched as he was escorted out, supported by his eldest son and future daughter-in-law, still simpering helplessly.

'Well, bloody hell!' I said to Iain. 'Did *you* ever think he'd let us down us like this?'

'He'll miss the best part of the evening.'

'Who stayed in the pub?' Helen asked when I arrived home.

'Er ... Those who didn't leave,' I said.

I looked up the information about the *Scharnhorst*. It wasn't the *Prince of Wales*. It was the *Duke of York*. An easy mistake to make. As we'd thought, the *Prince of Wales* had been sunk along with the *Repulse* in the Far East in December 1941. It had been a national tragedy, as bad as the sinking of the *Hood*. Why, I remember my father talking about it, leaning back in his chair puffing on his pipe, shaking his head in disbelief even after all those years.

So I phoned Pete. Jennie answered.

'He's much the worse for wear,' she said.

'Well just tell him something for me, could you? Can you remember this – "Not the *Prince of Wales* but the *Duke of York*".'

'What?'

'You've got to say to him, loudly and clearly, "Not the *Prince of Wales* but the *Duke of York*". You tell him and that'll do him good. He just needs that bit of information and then he'll be all right.'

'I don't think so, Nigel. He's in a bad way. He's in bed.'

'Oh. Well just tell him that, and I think it'll improve matters,' I said, not believing a word of it, and indeed wondering why I was bothering, but at the same time knowing exactly why I was bothering – namely because I, too, had had too much to drink, and it was the beer talking, not me.

'I think you guys should take better care of one another,' she said.

A parting shot. A hint of admonishment. That sobered me up. But I was quite sober already, I told myself, having had – on my own reckoning, mind you, which might not have been wholly reliable – fewer pints than Pete. And I *had* taken care of him, as a matter of fact, getting him only a half when he asked for a half, instead of a pint.

Later I phoned Iain. *He* was okay. He'd slept through the first couple of hours after getting home. 'Oh, yeah, I'm all right. Well, heh heh. We'll use this against Runeckles. We'll make sure he doesn't hear the last of it.'

17

England Expects

When you have had a shock, you wander around aimlessly.

Dazed, I begin to read the names inscribed on bricks in the wall of the new Southampton football stadium. No doubt the building was partly subsidised by fans purchasing them. Some have just a name, others include comments. 'Owen Johnson – Saints 4 Ever'. 'Dave Jones, True Saint'. 'Mr. David Hart – Eat My Goal'. 'Norman Sparkes, Lifelong Fan'. 'Eddie King – I've Suffered'. 'Baby Flynn – Born a Saint'. 'The Austins, Fans Always'. Well, it wasn't me. This may be my nearest half-decent football club but the last time I saw them play was years ago at the cramped old ground they'd been wanting to move from for years. 'Paul Turner, 76 Wot A Year'. That was when they won the FA Cup, of course. There are hundreds of names, in several panels, and then outside the main entrance are more, on hexagonal ground tiles. These are larger and the inscriptions are longer; no doubt they cost more. 'Michael Reed, Fan from 1958, Saints for Ever'. 'Clive Emerson, the not-so-perfect Saint'.

The stadium has been built in an industrial part of the city, a cement factory on one side, a gas works on another, the railway line on a third. I'm passing time in the evening, a day's driving behind me, unloading early in the morning and another full day ahead.

I'd changed jobs. My career in local government had come to an end and I was driving a lorry. I'd always wanted to do it, and here I was in a big articulated milk tanker, ferrying milk and milk products between farms and dairies and cheese factories.

I read more names, trying not to remember what Helen's just told me ... It'll be in the *Echo*. It'll be front page screaming headlines. She phoned me on my mobile as I was taking a walk, getting a bit of the exercise needed after a day sitting in a lorry. I'd parked up outside the dairy for an early-morning unloading, and the stadium was visible from close by, so I'd decided to take a look.

'I can hardly believe it,' she said. Exactly the words my mother used after my sister had been lost. She'd phoned Sarah to suggest rearranging a tennis match because it was due to take place at the same time as the England World Cup match against Denmark, which several of the team wanted to watch. The phone was answered by Sarah's parents. Rod has been lost at sea. They found no trace of the helicopter. It had sunk. They hold out no hope. Sarah had received a visit from the Commodore.

'They do,' I said. 'That's what they do. They come round, in person, to tell you.'

Helen said she'd write a letter and get Joggan to push it through the door.

This is what our armed forces are for. These are the consequences.

'Whenever Rod was away and I used to ask if she'd heard from him,' said Helen, 'she'd say, "Don't ask".' *Don't ask, because the fear of something happening is already too close to the surface.*

The King Alfred. A large-ish corner pub, a Fuller's house. Newly painted outside, and done up inside with varnished pine floor. It was in water two miles deep off the coast of America. He would have been just on exercise, I suppose, said Helen. Framed on the wall are old copies of Southampton F.C. match programmes from the late fifties and sixties. This is what happens in the armed forces. This is the price of eternal vigilance. The consequence of necessary training.

'It's what she's been dreading,' said Helen. What every Forces spouse dreads, no doubt. 'She always thought it would happen, sooner or later.'

They're trying hard, with the new paint. Banner outside, 'Under New Management'. It's nearly empty. No doubt on matchdays it's different. There is a young woman behind the bar, and a younger bloke in a peaked cap. Loud music and flashing gaming machines. Hook Norton Best Bitter. The landlady appears at my shoulder as I'm peering at one of the framed programmes.

'Yeah, they're good, these, aren't they?' she says, earnestly. 'We're trying to build up the pub. As a Southampton pub, you know, being close to the ground. This old chap came in, and he had these programmes, and he said, he'd give them to us if we'd display them. Yeah, they're good, aren't they?' I agreed, yes, they're good.

There were three of them. One was a photographer and they rescued him. In another part of the helicopter perhaps, they think. Rod was the pilot and there was an observer, a woman officer. They didn't get out. They went down with the aircraft. They're saying, if anyone knew how to get out then Rod would. If Rod couldn't then no-one could.

I return to my lorry and bed down. At four a.m. there is a banging at the window. The load is skimmed milk and mine is the only tanker waiting to be unloaded. Normally there are a couple with whole milk to be tipped, and they do those first. 'Dunno where the fuck they are,' grumbles the dairyman. I reverse the truck into the bay, climb the ladder to the top of the tank and open the lids. I step back into the cab and doze a bit while he connects up the pipes and switches on the pump.

... Here we go. The six o'clock morning news. 'The United States Navy has abandoned the search for two Royal Navy helicopter crew whose aircraft ditched in the sea in the waters off Virginia ... ' The news about the World Cup becomes hollow. Two small children. As the day wears on there are more references to the incident, but few additional details. Radio Five Live. Two Royal Navy air crew, whose Lynx helicopter crashed into the sea off Virginia. The US Navy have given up the search. Another one-liner. Jesus. This country. We owe our position, influence in the world, livelihood, identity, unity to the armed forces and any member of it who dies in the course of duty. Not only do we owe. We are responsible. We ask them to do these things. They do them. We depend on them.

I spend the day at the behest of the transport manager Dave pelting from one place to another, getting stuck in a traffic jam on the M27 for two hours on account of an accident up ahead, having to do a U-turn in the end, they'd unbolted the central reservation barriers and everyone is sent back in the direction they came. Cranes were lifting the two vans that had collided. The phone goes. Dave.

'Where are you, Nigel?'

'Had to go via Winchester.'

'*Winchester*?'

'Yeah, well … ' I tell him about the jam. The attitude that comes across is, well, that's your fault. He probably doesn't mean it. But he does mean you to do all you can to get here, to get there, on time. When the wheels are turning the company's earning.

I fill up with milk at Chard in Somerset and forget to secure all the vents on top of the tank. If you do that then as soon as you go round a corner it spills out. At the first set of traffic lights I glance in my mirror and there are gallons of the white stuff cascading down the side of the tank and into the road behind me, with other drivers too puzzled to hoot. I switch on the hazard flashers, climb up the ladder and tighten the bolts.

Up the road a few miles I listen to the radio again. A spokesman from the Navy intones, 'The pilot, Lieutenant Skidmore, was a consummate professional … '

It's on the radio today. But it won't be tomorrow. Probably some reference in the paper. Then silence.

But for those who were close to him there will never be silence. There will be the long scream, the one that lasts for ever.

This load is bound for Ashford in Kent. 'You've got to be there,' Dave had said, 'you *will* be there at six o'clock in the morning. Not five past six. Six o'clock.' His directions are rubbish and I practically run out of driving hours. I manage to get there but only after I've parked on a bus stop and walked a mile up the narrow winding road to check. Nothing worse than looking for somewhere in the dark in a lorry you can't turn round. Run back down the road to drive it back up again, and then run down again to the pub just in time for a beer. This is the Blacksmiths' Arms, just off junction 10 of the M20. It's been done out in olde-worlde style, good red Kentish brick and lots of beams, inglenook fireplace and piped music. I trudge back to my lorry and bed down in the cab, ready to unload at six a.m. sharp.

One of my friends has died. He was more than a friend, he was a protector. He was the protector of other people as well, more people than knew he was their protector. He protected me. And you. And you, and you. We trusted him with our lives. He held our lives in his hands and now he has lost his.

*

I wrote to Sarah. It cracked me up. Every time I returned to it, to get the wording right, I welled up. It was the stuff about the members of the Armed Forces, putting their lives on the line. Volunteering to die. I was not actually sure they were the right things to say. Cliché-ridden, for a start. But it was all I could write. They were meant to be fine words. And they were so fine that they broke me up as I read and re-read them.

The question was asked. *Under some circumstances, which we cannot predict, you will lose your life.*

Who is prepared to take that risk?

Rod Skidmore stood, and looked us in the eye.

I am, he said.

*

Perhaps this view ascribes imaginary noble motives which many people who join the Forces feel only fleetingly, if at all. Much of the attraction of soldiering is in the camaraderie, the excitement, seeing the world. Human beings are too frail to be sustained for long by nobility of intent alone. They need other incentives. But it can be there, underneath, underscoring everything else. A diamond amongst the lesser jewels, a nugget of gold beside the baser metals of ordinary reasons.

Do doctors work purely in order to save and enhance lives? Probably not. They wouldn't work for no pay, for example. But in common parlance, in the popular press at any rate, it is axiomatic that they are wonderful. And the nurses are wonderful. The firemen are wonderful. The policemen are sometimes wonderful. Occasionally the teachers are wonderful, especially those in special schools. The businessmen and journalists and administrators and shop assistants and garage mechanics and lawyers and accountants and gardeners and cardboard box factory workers are hardly ever wonderful. They don't have the opportunity, for one thing. And today the soldiers and the sailors and the airmen are not often thought of as wonderful, either. Unless, that is, they fought in World War Two, and especially if they were killed in it. Today they are perhaps thought of more as mercenaries. The earnings are good and so are the sporting opportunities and the travel and the early retirement on a decent pension.

But there is a case for saying that the members of the Armed Forces are more wonderful than the nurses and the firemen and all the rest. The difference is this. Some of those people are highly thought of because they save the lives of others. Others, because they risk their own lives in order to do so. But even though dying in the course of duty is sometimes an occupational hazard, it is not more than that: it is an unfortunate by-product of doing their job. That is not the case with the Forces. You could go so far as to say that, for soldiers and sailors and airmen, the contrary is the case. For them, it is a *fortunate* by-product of doing their job when they survive. Getting killed is part of the deal. If they get killed, then *they were only doing their job*. That is not to say that if they do not get killed they were *not* doing their job. But, as John Keegan said, they have settled up ahead of time. They have put up their hands, and said: I volunteer to die.

*

They do it well, this sort of thing, the Navy.

It was a glorious June day. Above the squat tower of the Fleet Air Arm Memorial Church of St. Bartholomew at Yeovilton, Somerset, the St. George's Cross was at half-mast. The tiny church seated no more than sixty. A hundred and twenty more of us stood behind the pews. Outside were perhaps another two hundred. The majority were Naval, numerous officers but also many other ranks. The gold braid around their sleeves shone: one stripe for a sub-lieutenant, two for a lieutenant, three for a commander, four for a captain ... Afterwards I asked Alastair if there is a protocol for such funerals. Is a certain number of such-and-such a rank detailed to attend, a certain number of another? No. Each person was present because he or she wished to be.

One of Rod's friends from childhood gave a homily, 'My mate Rod', barely managing to get through it. Alastair, who had not been short of naval action himself, also spoke. He ended as cheerfully as he could. 'When I was preparing these words, I thought of what Rod himself might have advised me. He'd have said, "Keep your spirits up. After all, it's a celebration, this. And keep it short. The bar's open, and you don't want to waste valuable drinking time".'

Listed for later in the service was the Last Post, expressly composed, it seems to me, for the periodic prompting of tears. In spite of Al's exhortation, I was bracing myself for it, wondering if the mental dam I had prepared against breakdown would hold. But when the moment came, the piece was omitted.

'They decided quite soon before the start of the service they weren't going to have it,' said Al afterwards. 'Sarah thought it might be too much for people.' Probably, that was just as well. There were a lot of red eyes after the service. The guys who maintained the helicopter must have been feeling it as much as anyone. Did I tighten up that nut? Did I put enough oil in the sump? Later, Joggan said, 'I was all right. But then suddenly I wasn't.' The cumulative effect of those tributes, those hymns, those prayers: perhaps that is what they too are for, designed to touch the nerves of the most robust of men, young and old.

I have been to other military memorial services. They have been for men who have spent their lives in the Forces and therefore finished all of their duty, where the emphasis has been on a life fulfilled, of service completed. Where the predominant mood has been of gratitude for that life, a closing of the book now that the final chapter has been written. As often as not, death has come as a release, a relief; the person had no longer been himself, no longer the confident and zestful character we shall all remember, and to whom the end has now arrived as scheduled – even, sometimes, a little too late. But the mood on that day was not of release and gratitude. It was of numbness and shock. Death had appeared not as the Reaper, predictable, slowly scything down in predestined order all in his path, but as one of the Horsemen of the Apocalypse, arriving on a whirlwind and blasting away to a premature death a man barely half-way through his time. Funerals are for people who have finished their lives. Not for those who have had only half of them, been cut off before they have done all their work. It is unnatural for a child to die before its parents. It was unnatural that we should have been standing there. This was not the proper order of things. At funerals you expect most of the congregation to be old, or at least middle-aged, with a sprinkling of the young. Here there were few elderly people. Most were in their twenties, thirties, forties.

'Let me die a youngman's death': the title of a Roger McGough poem. He doesn't want to die cleanly between the sheets, a 'what a nice way to go' death. He wants to be mown down by a fast car on his way back from an all-night party, or murdered by his mistress's son whilst in bed with her daughter. But here's the catch: he wants it to happen when he's seventy-three, or a hundred and four. He wants it both ways.

Between the naturalness of sunshine, green grass and birdsong on the one hand, and the unnaturalness of the death we had come to mark on the other, was a fearful contrast. Only the sound of helicopters and Harrier jets taking off reminded us that just beyond the church lay the military airfield, the machines of war and those who have mortgaged their futures to fly them.

*

There was a reception afterwards, at HMS *Heron*, the shore-based – indeed, far inland – headquarters of the Royal Naval Air Squadron. Curious how such establishments are named 'HMS': Her (or His) Majesty's Ship. Above it flew the White Ensign, the flag of the Royal Navy, at half-mast too. The mess hall was large, but on this occasion it could not have contained many more people: if you wanted to move from one group to another you had to slide sideways between them.

And at the last, there was a fly-past. Slowly, visible first at the rear of the building, clattering round in a wide sweep, came a Swordfish, flanked by two Lynx helicopters. They flew parallel to the front of the building, completed one more circuit and finally flew at right angles to it, low over our heads. From the open cockpit, in leather flying helmets of 1940s vintage, the two Swordfish crew solemnly saluted as they passed.

Melodramatic? I did not care. It was fitting. This is the Navy. This is what they do. They do it well. So they should. We expect it. England expects ... [1] In a day of lumps in the throat, here was another.

*

A few weeks later, alone, I stopped at the church. The graveyard is in three sections, separated by low walls. The oldest part of it surrounds the building, and beyond it are two extensions. The gates to the first have a pair of golden anchors built into their ironwork, and an eight-foot obelisk of yew has an anchor, too, cut proud on its surface. The graves are easy to count, because they are in rows of ten, and there were ninety-four of them, with ninety-three stones. The earth covering the last was in a convex mound, not yet having settled. I bent to place the flat of my hand on the bleached grass of its turf. It would recover, to the green of its surroundings.

I read some of the inscriptions on the gravestones, chosen by the relatives. 'At the going down of the sun, and in the morning, we will remember them'. 'Better you should forget and smile, than you should remember and be sad'. 'For ever in our thoughts'. 'Lord, lead and guide the men who ride the lonely oceans of the air'. 'In grateful remembrance of all the love and happiness you brought us'. 'Loved and remembered always'. 'Beloved husband and dear father'. 'Here for a season, then above'. 'You took the wings of the morning, and dwelt in the uttermost

---

[1] 'England expects that every man will do his duty'. Signal from Nelson to the English fleet before the Battle of Trafalgar.

parts of the sea'. And simply, but I thought most eloquently, 'R.I.P.'

A mile down the road I visited the Dolphin at Ilchester, which you don't see as you drive through the village because it is off the main road in a street of neat terraced houses fronting the pavement. Oak panelling gives the spacious bar a dark interior, but this is a good enough back-street local, selling a good enough beer ... The bar's open, and we don't want to waste valuable drinking time.

*

Later in 2002, during the deepest salvage operation ever undertaken by the Ministry of Defence, the wreck of the helicopter Lieutenant Rod Skidmore had been piloting, flying on exercise from the Royal Navy Type 23 frigate HMS *Richmond*, when both engines catastrophically failed, was recovered from the floor of the Atlantic Ocean, 200 miles off the eastern seaboard of the United States. At 4,000 metres, the water there is as deep as that in which the *Titanic* had sunk 90 years earlier. In addition to Skidmore, the observer, Lieutenant Jenny Lewis, died in the accident. Skidmore's body was recovered with the wreck but Lewis's was never found. A third member of the crew, Petty Officer Photographer Paul Hanson, managed to swim free of the helicopter as it sank, and survived.

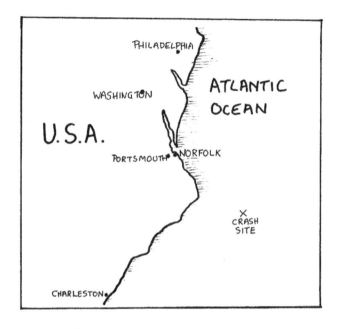

At the inquest into Skidmore's death in Dorchester, Dorset, a year after the accident, on 25 June 2003, his Commanding Officer, Tony Cramp, stated 'Rod was the consummate professional, who had been in the business a long time'. For his part, Hanson stated 'I would like to pay tribute to Rodney and Jenny for keeping the aircraft in the air for as long as they did and enabling me to get out alive'.

Both officers are now commemorated on the headstone of Rod Skidmore's grave at the Fleet Air Arm Memorial Church at Yeovilton.

18

There wasn't one

Whilst we might admire bravery when it has to be displayed, I have not intended in this book to extol the virtues of fighting itself. A year before the Second World War, Chamberlain's broadcast to the nation contained the warning 'War is a fearful thing, and we must be very clear, before we embark on it, that it is really the great issues that are at stake'. Churchill, in an attempt during a visit to Washington in 1954 to persuade Congress to seek a high-level meeting with Russia, said 'Meeting jaw to jaw is better than war.' More recently, Max Hastings, in the foreword to his *Bomber Command* (1979), states 'I am grateful that my generation has been spared the need to discover whether we could match the impossible sacrifices that they made'.

As for the great man of letters Samuel Johnson himself, the remark from which this book takes its title does not represent the whole of his view on the subject. Following the verbatim account of the discussion during which Johnson spoke those words, his biographer James Boswell reports:

> His abhorrence of the profession of a sailor was uniformly violent; but in conversation he always exalted the profession of a soldier. And yet I have, in my large and various collection of his writings, a letter to an eminent friend, in which he expresses himself thus: "My god-son called on me lately. He is weary, and rationally weary, of a military life. If you can place him in some other state, I think you may increase his happiness, and secure his virtue. A soldier's time is passed in distress and danger, or in idleness and corruption." Such was his cool reflection in his study; but whenever he was warmed and animated by the presence of company, he, like other philosophers, whose minds are impregnated with poetical fancy, caught the common enthusiasm for splendid renown.

In other words, whilst Johnson consistently expressed praise for soldiering, at the same time he did acknowledge that fighting is not, in truth, an activity to admire, nor one in which its perpetrators wish to engage for long.

*

Nowadays there are several renovated Spitfires which have been converted to two-seaters. You can arrange to take a flight. As soon as he found out, Pete booked one.

'There was a two-hour briefing beforehand,' he told us afterwards. 'They made it very clear. That you were a passenger only. That the pilot would have complete control throughout. And then, we were hardly airborne, and he said, "Put your feet on the pedals. Go on. Hold the stick. Yes! – now you're in charge".' Pete banked the aircraft gingerly from one side to the other, back again, and up and down a little. The pilot took over and did the same, needless to say much more sharply.

'And then we looped the loop, and did a victory roll. I wore his flying helmet,' he added. 'You know. My mother's brother. And I took his RAF wings.' (The fabric motif stitched to his flying jacket.) 'They told us beforehand, you weren't allowed to have anything in your pockets.'

'Oh?'

'A precaution, in case something falls out and rolls about on the cockpit floor and interferes.'

'But a small piece of cloth?'

'I took it anyway.'

*

There is a famous poster from the First World War, exhorting all able-bodied men to join up. It shows a young girl sitting on her father's knee whilst her brother is on the floor playing with toy soldiers. The girl is asking, 'Daddy, what did YOU do in the Great War?'; and the father, his hand on his chin, is looking away with a troubled expression, evidently ashamed at not having played his part.

The same question, asked of my generation.

Daddy, what did YOU do in the War?

There wasn't one.

Acknowledgements

Greatest thanks to Pete Runeckles, whose collaboration in the initial stages of compiling this book enabled the idea to take flight, and without whose more recent arm-twisting it would still be gathering dust on my computer. He also drew the maps, and made insightful comments on many aspects of various drafts.

Thanks to Chris van Schaick, who kindly put Pete and me in touch with his mother Joan, sister-in-law of Johnny van Schaick; and to Joan van Schaick herself, for sight of reports, letters and photos relating to Peter Ferris's death.

Thanks in addition to Jacqueline Tong, who made valuable comments on an early draft.

I should also like to thank my erstwhile colleague and mentor, Brian Perrett, who, many years ago at the outset of my career, impressed on me the importance of keeping detailed notes.

Many thanks too to Nick Runeckles, for the cover design (www.nickruneckles.com).

I owe a profound debt to Sarah Skidmore, for reasons that will be obvious to anyone reaching the end of this book.

And thanks to all you guys in the pub.

Finally, unlimited gratitude to my wife Helen, for steadfast support, for unfailing good humour, and for putting up with a lot.

The author

Aside from an interlude in his later years as a heavy goods vehicle driver, which put him on the steepest learning curve of his life, Nigel Austin has spent most of his working life as an educational psychologist, advising on children with special needs. He lives in Dorset, where he has been longer than anywhere else. He is married with children and grandchildren.